DANCING IDENTITY

Dancing
Identity

METAPHYSICS IN MOTION

Sondra Fraleigh

UNIVERSITY OF

PITTSBURGH PRESS

Published by the University of Pittsburgh Press,
Pittsburgh, Pa., 15260
Copyright © 2004, University of Pittsburgh Press

Manufactured in the United States of America

Printed on acid-free paper

10 9 8 7 6 5 4 3 2 1

Library of Congress Cataloging-in-Publication Data
Fraleigh, Sondra Horton, 1939–
    Dancing identity : metaphysics in motion / Sondra Fraleigh.
        p. cm.
    Includes bibliographical references and index.
    ISBN 0-8229-4239-9 (cloth : alk. paper)
    1. Dance—Philosophy. 2. Art and dance. I. Title.
    GV1588.3.F724 2004
    792.8'01—dc22

                                    2004013584

I dedicate this book,
with appreciation, to my ancestors
and to the dance of the future.

CONTENTS

Untangling the Beauty of the Not Beautiful

This book follows a puzzling course that nevertheless seeks the order and care of untangling, just as I remember in my childhood how my grandmother carefully untangled my knotted hair and how she held the threads of time together. Her death is the first scary, nonbeautiful beauty that I remember: the morning light streaming through the small bedroom, my eyes watching her delicate smile float into forever, not comprehending that she would not wake up. I began to walk in my sleep after that, searching for her. Long after that, I let her go; I began to grasp the necessity of inventing myself anew, like a sleepwalker enters the darkness on inspiration, shifting the furniture of her psyche without bumping into chairs. Through my grandmother's death, I glanced the unseen reality of my origin and perpetuity, my possible-self and perishability: the fleeting metaphysics of my being.

Eventually I became an avid sleepwalker, waking up in God knows what vacant room of the old country inn where I grew up. My parents often found me dancing. Now I devise other means to explore the dark. I dance awake, even when I close my eyes, and I write to awaken the person I want to be.

Phenomenological Fieldwork

I wish to thank the many student and professional dancers who have shared their personal descriptions of dancing with me, as well as colleagues from America and other countries whose dances and insights inform this work. I have included these throughout as intersubjective artifacts of phenomenological fieldwork. Intersubjectivity is a concept that links phenomenological research with ethnological research. It lets go of the dominant place of the author, seeking a more inclusive perspective. As Bonnie Stone Sunstein and Elizabeth Chiseri-Strater define it in *Fieldworking*, intersubjectivity is "the process of collecting and connecting many different perspectives on one piece of data. In photography, this would translate into taking many pictures of the same object from different angles" (154). I have collected many experiential descriptions of dancing and choreographic process over a period of fifteen years. They represent numerous voices converging on phenomenological data, namely the completion of the phrases "When I dance . . ." or "When I make dances. . . ." I ask dancers to finish these phrases without preparation and in less than five minutes to let their experience speak. Differing perspectives emerge, as do metaphysical links that further define the term "dance." Sometimes dancers and choreographers choose to extend this spontaneous exercise in further self-study. Through such intuitive explorations, I also tap into my own consciousness of dancing, of making dances and witnessing them.

These descriptions by novices and professional dancers are surprisingly alike in respect to the many valences of freedom and agency. Dancing is not always liberating; its practices can oppress as well as free the individual, but it does offer the possibility of experiencing freedom of movement and expression, and the opportunity to practice self-determination as well as community. Dancers' descriptions of dancing always illuminate the lived experience, what happens in the psychic, somatic life of movement in the moment of performance. Many who are not quoted in the book are nevertheless included in the spirit of the work.

. . .

I especially would like to thank feminist scholar and phenomenologist Glen Mazis for his early reading of the work, dance and cultural historian Janice Lapoint Crump for her advice and support in my efforts to produced a multivocal text, and Maxine Sheets-Johnstone, Juanita Suarez, Sara Watts, and Etta Wong for their invaluable critiques. Several photographs of June Burke and Jim Dusen greatly aid the aesthetics of the book, and I also thank Mr. Dusen for assistance in preparing other photographs. I am grateful for the advice of my daughter, Christina Fraleigh, who aided in the development of this text over the years through her expertise in philosophy, religion, and women studies. My thanks also goes to the unidentified readers selected by the University of Pittsburgh Press who contributed greatly to my understanding of my own mind through their very thorough reviews and suggestions. As always, my husband, Warren Fraleigh, practiced "active listening" through many dinner conversations as this text unfolded. I remain indebted to his encouragement and advice.

DANCING IDENTITY

Introduction

Traditionally, metaphysics searches for essences, but the post-metaphysical quest leans more toward potentials. Martin Heidegger puts it this way: "Higher than actuality lies *possibility*." Metaphysics as a branch of philosophy studies the nature of being and beings, existence, time, space, movement, and causality. It also involves underlying principles and theories that form the basis of a particular field of knowledge. Heidegger conceived the primary task of metaphysics as the clarification of *being* in his book on phenomenological metaphysics, *Being and Time*. In the analysis of being, he holds that phenomenology and ontology characterize philosophy itself, and that we can best understand phenomenology in terms of possibility.[1] The metaphysical search of *Dancing Identity* concerns soma, self, and gender in dance. My text develops dance as practice, experience, and embodied knowledge, so it is not traditional or wholly abstract in its metaphysics, but heteroglossic; its postmodern hope and descendant pathways will unfold.

Writing Self

Written over a period of about fifteen years, these essays represent my metaphysical journey toward self-definition informed by art, ritual, feminism, phenomenology, poetry, autobiographical stories, and always—dance. They are, more than anything else, meditations on memory, how we perceive and construct our unfinished lives. Aesthetic discourse is too often cut off from the lived experience of physical things. I wish to explore the inherently gendered realities of dance and to expose the political terrain of movement. Behind this is the soma—our body as we perceive it and experience our potential, not the person we believe others see when they look at us. Thus, my work as a somatic movement therapist also informs this book.

To dance is neither entertainment nor art-making per se. More, it is the struggle to find voice through one's storied self; more still, to face oneself as one faces others and the world—imaginatively. To value dance at all is to value the human, the beautiful, and the playful amid the erotic pulse of life. Dancing gives us the forms of our mind in movement, and it teaches us how to reconnect with our emotions, living them over again, sweeping clean their cellular foundations.

The word "phenomenology" comes from the Greek word *phos*. It refers to the revealing power of light—the illumination of things as they are—or what Edmund Husserl calls "things in themselves." Heidegger explains a "phenomenon" as "that which shows itself, the manifest."[2] As a phenomenologist, I want to forget what I know and slip into learning. In respect to metaphysics of dance, I want to explore beauty, not as surface but as inner guide, winding my way through a participatory landscape similar to what the Navajo call the "Beauty Way."[3] So I question, and seek illumination. What beauty do I most fear and what must die in me for it to live?

The metaphysics of this work is motivated by an integrative impulse or *thickening*, what Maurice Merleau-Ponty develops in his descriptions of incarnate language and depth in art as a semantic thickness of existence.[4] The text generates a play between dance and philosophy, weaving aesthetics and poetry with ecobiological stories. As a self-reflexive study, *Dancing Identity* extends philosophical concepts I introduced in *Dance and the Lived Body* (1987), a descriptive aesthetics written from the dancer's point of view. I hope in the present book to frame some thorny issues in dance and to unsettle taken-for-granted mastery models. In terms of contemporary cultural debates on gender and the body, I hope to bridge several adjacent discourses in dance, philosophy, developmental psychology, feminism, cultural history, and somatic practices of sensory integration. Thus, my text is multifaceted, like dancing itself.

I started this work in 1988 with an essay on feminist existentials— "Revaluing Darkness." Over time this became a mantra for the whole and lost its singular identity. In nonviolent partnership cultures, darkness was not viewed as evil and marked as female, but was symbolic of fertility and regeneration in the life/death/life cycle of nature.[5] As we move into darkness through the dance of language, we see that "regeneration" also carries forward the terms "generation" and "gender," as these also relate to "generate" (to originate, produce, hatch, make) and "engender" (to excite, to imbue form). Through these verbal links we also see how the generation/regeneration words all relate to a creative principle and ancestry.

My study of darkness and ancestry leads me to descendant postmetaphysical themes and life stories invested with dances I have experienced in theatrical, ritual, and healing performances. I begin to uncover the will and conscience of these dances and see the body politic submerged therein. Issues of perception infuse my writing as I ask questions of the reader, also placing myself into the fray. My perspectives continue to evolve as history wells up in the present, and *Miss America*, my polemical dance of 1975, morphs into *I Miss America*, a free verse response to 9/11 and patriotism at the end of chapter 3, "Thickening Ambiguity."

Descending Pathways

In a descending line of argument concerned with participation of people rather than rigid theories, the essays of *Dancing Identity* don an array of masks and voices. As self-reflexive, they explore the perspectives of dancer, scholar, mother, daughter, student, friend, therapist, and teacher. Dancing becomes a major trope for a critique of mastery. The essays focus attention on excellence as a less invasive route to bodily freedom than the linguistic of mastery and dominant goal setting. We see through them that the boundaries of the body are not static; rather, they are alive, volatile, and open to change. We can track this in terms of bodily training, dance making, and through movement styles and ideologies. As widening awareness through the revisionary gestures of feminism and anti-imperialist resistance, I have no intention of substituting one center for another, dark for light, or messiness for clarity. My project is to encourage participation in the beauty of dance, which can be clouded by competitive, dualistic models of mastery and authority.

Dancers as cultural bellwethers motivate my inclusion of chapter 7, "Messy Beauty and Butoh Invalids." This indicates beauty's ways through a descendant path, looking into the historical and political backgrounds of World War II to situate Butoh, the "dance of darkness," as it issued from postwar Japan after the American bombing of Hiroshima and Nagasaki. "Messy Beauty" juxtaposes my own exposure as a child to radiation poison from nuclear testing at Frenchman's Flat in Nevada. Behind this curiously overlooked tragedy of war I remember my child-self, the romance and melodrama of the Old West, my father's songs, and the pain of a dysfunctional family mixed with the sweet smell of sage.

In chapter 2, "First Sounds," I revisit my study in 1965 with Mary Wigman, who personified the German expressionist root of modern dance. Her influence extends to contemporary Butoh, now an international movement, and to its close relative, Pina Bausch's highly visible Tanztheater. At the end of chapter 2, I juxtapose Natsu Nakajima's Butoh work *Niwa* (The garden, 1982) with Wigman's *Witch Dance* (1926) as I reconstruct these dances in poetry. Throughout the book, I contrast expressionist forms of dance with the more objective aesthetic of American postmodern dance and examine the aesthetics of classical and eclectic ballet. I reconstruct several dance works descriptively and in poetry to demonstrate how dance grows from the times and lives of its makers, even as I investigate my own dance history.

We literally embody metaphysics when we dance; we become more present to ourselves, more alive to others and the world: everything radiates. In exegesis of the nature/culture divide, the essays in this book frame an embodied metaphysics through the voices of dancing. Chapter 4, "Anti-Essentialist Trio," a performance and critique, examines relationships of nature and culture in the lived body philosophy of three major phenomenologists who span a fifty-year history of contemporary philosophical feminism—from the emancipatory work of Simone de Beauvoir to the more radically numinous views of Judith Butler—with the prophetic body ecology of Maurice Merleau-Ponty as backdrop. Voyeurism, gender bending, and the shaking of ballet classicism surface in the critique. In this essay, I cull the values of Butler's views on the body as a cultural construction while distancing from her notion of gender as a discursive and purely cultural category fabricated through its various performances, even as I understand how she brackets, rather than dismisses, nature.

The study of this trio leads me to an explanation and critique of Martin Heidegger's existential phenomenology and his metaphysical position related to themes of mastery. I discover a temporal voice in chapter 5, "A Dance of Time Beings," moving against perfection and mastery toward the somatic dance of matching, deciphering descendant values. I am led, then, into postmetaphysical political themes that question mastery, as I mask (or masquerade) the floating metaphysics of Heidegger and political philosopher Claude Lefort in order to stage them next to dance in chapter 6, "Letting the Difference Happen."

By questioning the imperialist language and mythology of mastery I am not necessarily dismissing the large narratives that sustain dance practices around the world, for that would underestimate cultural cohesions and clashes and ignore the existence of aesthetic standards, as well as the appallingly destructive politics that often accompany high achievement. Those who might say that dancing should be limited to local games with postmodern/deconstructive disclaimers of anything universal would disregard the human potential for making connections through art and ritual or for experiencing the exercise of preference and the pleasure of enduring forms of style and performance. My critique of mastery does not disavow achievement, but it does turn toward means rather than ends, and it also implies that no one form or style of dance has absolute rights over others. It is concerned with misuse of authority, and it takes an existentially open stance in defining the intrinsic values of dancing.

At issue in dance classes and performative contexts is the use of power, and power becomes increasingly visible in the evolution of metaphysics, as though the very foundations of personal empowerment were located in the body-self. Postmetaphysical views were first articulated in the existential phenomenology of Heidegger and recast by his inheritor, Michel Foucault. Chapter 8, "Existential Haircut," looks at the implications for dance of Foucault's poststructural work, *History of Sexuality*, in which he studies the effects of power in the regulation of "docile bodies." This chapter concludes on a participatory note with "Dances to Do."

My last chapter, "The Morality of Joy," reconciles ethics and aesthetics as its title suggests. It conjoins dance form and expression with dance descriptions and poetry through contemporary choreographers Irene Hultman, Santo Giglio, and Kazuo Ohno, and concentrates on the work of Bill T. Jones. The rush of time and risky bodily sensations of falling, diving, and riding guide my choices of dances and stories. My method aims to avoid forays into social politics associated with familiar feminist stances on sex, gender, agency, repression, and empowerment. Not controlling closure, I entreat an ethic of care and joy in the body, relating these somatic qualia of aesthetic, affective experience.

Unfinished Work

I write to correct the perception that the body is second-class, a dumb thing, and that dancing is trivial. I also write in the belief that the past is not finished, but like a dance is transforming in the present. This belief rides on an existential metaphysic, the ecstasy of time articulated by Heidegger in *Being and Time,* and close to the Navajo mystique of Old John, who lived with my family when I was young and tamed horses for my father. He taught me that we are carried into time in an encompassing way. Explorations of the language and philosophy of the Navajo suggest that what most Western people call the future is experienced by the Navajo as an ever-emerging world of incompletely realized events rather than situations that persist solidly through time. The human being is a participant in a continual emergence and "becoming" rather than "being," and can, "through his thought and desire, exert an influence on these 'possibilities.'"[6]

My theoretic-somatic project is to help heal not-yet-mended splits of body and mind, nature and culture, female and male, and other dualisms that flow from these, including the more recently created (and equally false) dichotomies of biological/social in social constructivist theory. Feminism has dealt with dualism from various perspectives; thus, I narrow my scope here to produce a view from existential phenomenology and its philosophical roots, even as I allow myself the freedom to weave in other sources where they apply.

My use of poetry relates to FieldPoems developed in contemporary ethnology since they convey a portrait or reveal something significant about the culture they represent. I am also aware of a personal ethnology that arises in my process.[7] Consistent with feminist research, my crossing of contexts strives to break down boundaries that seal off knowledge in separate containers, reinforcing hierarchies. I hope this work will add something to the projects of other dancer-philosophers and writers in related fields. I do not expect that readers will have read all of the philosophers I engage here; thus, I interpret and critique my sources as succinctly as possible, providing a thumbnail sketch of the history of these in chapter 1, "Embodying Metaphysics." For those less familiar with dance history, a short discussion of modern/postmodern dance, including Butoh, is provided to foreground the dances that intersect the text.

In *Dance and the Lived Body*, I dealt at length with the history of body/mind dualism in philosophy and its implications for dance. A residue of this remains here in my few references to antiquity as the source of body/mind splits that phenomenology moved against, but in this work I juxtapose Eastern metaphysics and early Western sources that influence classical Greek philosophy. Moving forward from this history, I stage and critique existential phenomenology throughout the rest of the text, including its postmodern relative, poststructural theory. This strategy grows from ontology and metaphysics, as my critique of existentialism points toward a corporeal metaphysics, and as dancing itself is metaphysics in motion.

On Special Metaphysics

Bruce Aune's *Metaphysics* explains that special metaphysics is concerned with problems about particular aspects of being: "the distinction between the mental and the physical, the possibility of human freedom, the nature of personal identity, the possibility of survival after death, and the existence of God."[8] I concentrate on the first three concerns, dualism, freedom, and identity, and also touch upon spirituality in terms of cross-cultural mythology and dance rituals.

In part 1, "Beginning," I look at some historical sources for the theoretical mind/body split. Attendant upon this are classical and traditional metaphysics of transcendence of the body, as Western mythology and philosophy have associated body with matter (mother, *materia*). A metaphysics of bodily transcendence has consequences for our treatment of women and nature; it further signals an overcoming of the flesh in forms of dance where flesh is hated and eradicated. I question obedience to ascendant master models and consider what this costs. In practice this means master choreographers, master teachers, and mastering dance forms. Excellence in a given practice or process might well replace the ascending reflection of mastery and the language of dominance that sustains it.

We have long been aware of what we do when we dance, and of the phenomenon we call "dance," but the being that becomes the "time being" of dancing eludes us in her ever moving on. Part 2, "Becoming," is a metaphysics of dance in three sequentially linked essays. I use the tools of phenomenology and criticism in this section to explore essentialism and its alternatives—identity and gender in dance; matching the body-self instead of mastering it; and "somaesthetics," particularly the tactile-kinaesthetic basis of dance and healing.

In part 3, "Descen-dance," I study the metaphysical feature of descendance. The downward reflection of being spreads out and entwines, gathering health concerns into those of aesthetic excellence. I draw upon theoretical issues surrounding organic movement, eros, and nature to make this abstract notion concrete. Questions of aesthetic perception in our relationship to dance, particularly problems of "the primacy of optics" revolve around this. Theoretical subthemes unravel in terms of dance and metaphysics: the relationship of aesthetic master models to totalitarian hierarchies; the beginnings of a somatic kinesiology now growing in the academy that encourages a more participatory direction for dance education and aesthetics of the future (anyone can dance); intrinsic dance defined as body-for-self and, relative to this, care of the body-self. These thematics entail a shift toward means and away from end product. The values of teamwork and partnership surface. "Descendant beauty" is defined in terms of "reversibility" and introduced as an aesthetic concept. I see a study of light-reversible darkening as necessary to the vitality of art and life. My personal ethnology leads me from nuclear fallout in Utah and the invalid bodies of Japanese Butoh toward the fugitive spirit of romance and resistive melodrama.

On Dualism

This book's argument is constituted from its critique of Platonic, Aristotelian, and Cartesian dualism, in particular, how the division of body and mind in Western philosophy supports a division between culture and nature that is manifest in the violence of cultural formations: from the misogyny of theology and the optical metaphors of Western theory to the geometric abstraction of dance works that eschew the organic basis of movement and encourage the body to move against itself. I argue that tacit acceptance of the culture/nature divide underlies appropriation of the female body in an objectifying optics that goes unquestioned in much dance, and that this is the same dualism that supports nuclear testing, imperial willfulness and warfare, suppression of the ethnic other, sexism in university systems, and the atrophy of human potential.

My thesis benefits from resistance to metaphysical dualism in the phenomenology of Merleau-Ponty, the ontology of Heidegger, the existential ethics of Beauvoir, the postmodern feminism of Butler, phenomenology in Japanese philosophy, and the Goddess myths of ancient cultures, as well as the Taoism of Lao Tzu. I explore these sources to show that traditional Western metaphysics, with its "mastery" of substantive categories and naming of essences, can be transformed by an existential metaphysics (or we could call this postmetaphysics) in which there is a "matching" of the terms that Western tradition has set in opposition: body and mind, nature and culture, female and male, matter and spirit, darkness and light. As a result of this matching, the terms in each pair are elided as distinct phenomena, re-envisioned and experienced anew. Thus, while "feminine" darkness is, in Western patriarchy, associated with evil and fixed in opposition to "masculine" light, it is, as the yin principle of Taoism, in constant interchange with yang since both terms function as each other's condition of possibility.

Antidualist, anti-essentialist metaphysics thus speaks of integration and a more fluent sense of self, evidenced in, for example, the somatic education of the Feldenkrais method, the expressionist dance of Mary Wigman, the Butoh of Kazuo Ohno, the ballet of Alonzo King, the postmodern dance of Twyla Tharp, the Kumu hula dance of Hawaii, and even the existential antiheroes and outlaws of the American West. In somatics practices and in Western myths of risk and rapture, the human subject is unfixed and temporalized in a fluid state of becoming. When we dance, we have access to a supple and unpredictable self in flowing cycles of descend-dance, moving through Apollonian to Dionysian, connecting form with feeling in the ascend-dance back again. I wish through these essays presented here to describe a nondualist consciousness and also a dancing consciousness where dancing is a mode of thought, a special kind of knowledge and being-in-the-world. Theory can be refracted when it is lived in terms of the dancing body and developed further through experiential research. I hope to suggest a new way of looking at familiar dance contexts through a woman's gaze that accounts for social inscriptions of the body but does not separate from nature conceived as other.

My purpose is to take the reader on an unconventional metaphysical journey, moving past traditional metaphysics toward a postmetaphysical "sense of the world." I do not use the term "worldview" because of its optical sway. A linguistic of "world sense" substitutes a somatic interweaving of the senses, the brain as embodied ecosystem, and movement as the metaphysical starting point for our relationship to the world. The recent work of neuroscience, particularly John Raty's *A User's Guide to the Brain* supports this understanding. We are not essentially creatures of sight, but of all the senses, and of movement, as Maxine Sheets-Johnstone's *The Primacy of Movement* fully elaborates in phenomenological and metaphysical terms.[9] We are not distinct from nature in our sensitivity; nor are we superior to natural processes. Rather, we are part of what phenomenology calls "the lifeworld." According to Raty, brain research is discovering that genes and environment are also interdependent; they influence each other. Moreover, thinking and moving are not distinct processes—we think as we move, and we move as we think: "Motor function is crucial to all other brain functions." Science itself disproves body-mind dualism. Rhythm and dance, mistakenly defined in terms of body rather than mind, develop neural connections in the brain and influence positive self-image.[10] Along with new physics, relational aesthetics and phenomenology have long held that we are not passive recipients of an objective world, but participants in an ongoing mystery. Somatic practices reveal that everything we do, everything we experience leaves imprints in our nervous system, shapes our body-mind and self-understanding.

Staging Metaphysics

Dancing Identity is undertaken in the postmodern hope for diminishing boundaries between art and life, for a return to local traditions, for scrutinizing aesthetics in view of ecology, for the intersubjective inclusiveness of voice and styles, and for cross-cultural sharing. I am uncomfortable with a deconstructive dissection of the body, which is more the result of a cold semiotics than an easy postmodern idea of "anything goes." The descendance toward postmodern ease, threading back through the organicism of early modern dance in Isadora Duncan, had a reason for being in its own time. "Messy Beauty and Butoh Invalids" will discuss these reasons, which shook the sublimations of late/high modernism and classicism and toppled the aesthetic canon of disinterestedness.

Through the regenerative aesthetics of modern and postmodern dance, we glimpse the postmodern turn of metaphysics, even as we recognize that local instances do not project universal neutrality. For that seemingly impossible turn, we need to try to understand how lived experience can produce shared knowledge that is, if not universal and neutral, at least intersubjective and communal. Theory, however difficult and often tedious, leads in that direction.

As a theatrical device, I mask many of the philosophers I stage in relation to dance. More specifically, I mask them as themselves, in much the same way that Mary Wigman used a mask of her own face in *Hexentanz* (*Witch Dance*, 1926). Masks can hide, but their larger purpose is to mark character. In theater, masks change according to the wearer and imaginative view of the spectator; they double representation, making subtle and dramatic shifts. The masks I construct and discuss are my interpretations.

Many dance scholars are now choosing to stage their research in a sociopolitical sphere, conceiving the body as a cultural construction—a mask, in effect. The body as culturally constituted has also been a major theme of phenomenology, but with regard to our human situation in the life-world. Through phenomenology, I continue to stress the connection between the social, the personal, the political, and the ecological. Behind the mask of culture lies our intrinsic connection to nature that we forget at our peril. "The ecological self" is a phrase that grew both through phenomenology and developmental psychology, the latter through the work of Ulric Neisser and others.[11] My theoretical choices do not seem to me to be optional; the choice to be public or private is. I make my stories public for a reason—to witness and to warn.

Dorina Mikschy in a site-specific Butoh work in process on the Broellin Castle grounds in Germany, 2003. Mikschy calls the photograph "Zuneigung" (Inclination and affection). Photograph by Sondra Fraleigh.

PART I · Beginning

1 | Embodying Metaphysics

A basic issue in dance is how to link human agency with movement form and expression. When we dance we embody agency through bodily orientation and consciousness. The dialectic nature of these links is played out daily in our movement choices and body-mind awareness. Judith Butler asks what kind of performances will destabilize received and rehearsed categories. The possibilities of transformation may be found in a "failure to repeat, a de-formity."[1] Dance forms are repeated daily, hourly, in rehearsal rooms around the world. Thus a major question we should ask is, "What do we want to instill in this process, what do we want to repeat?" Repetition encodes movement in the body, leads toward mastery of form, and for the most part goes unquestioned. I want to understand what I need to stop repeating and what the hazards of mastery are; I want to explore how I can be more receptive to therapeutic activism toward transformation.

Mastering the Body

Entreating history and looking forward, this introductory chapter sketches the development of philosophies of the body in the West, considers body as spirit in Japanese phenomenology, and sees how philosophies of the body intersect with Western dance and Japanese Butoh.

Plato and the masculine philosophies that followed him founded the ardor of the Western mind. These Western ideologies of the body set the stage for a splitting of matter from mind, body from soul, and flesh from spirit. In some exceptional contemporary cases, that route has led to more than Greek tragedy, as it did with the Heaven's Gate cult whose leader, Marshall Herff Applewhite, taught that the body was a mere "vehicle" for a soul that could evolve to a higher level of being among exalted extraterrestrials. Thirty-eight people committed suicide with him in March 1997 in the belief that their souls would go to the "Next Level."[2] They expected to be taken up to heaven by a flying saucer trailing the Hale-Bopp comet. The group practiced celibacy and cleansing of the body through castration.

The route beyond body is not only Western, of course, but in Eastern versions the body is not alienated from the soul, from Eros and spirit. Shiva/Shakti is Lord of the Dance in India, both male and female. As Shiva performs *tapas* to transcend earthly passions, *kama,* the force that returns him to bodily and feminine embrace, troubles him.[3] The terms of dualism can be confusing, especially when translated from one period or one culture to another. Plato's dualism relates mind, soul, and spirit through psyche. And yet, at the root of Western dualism, Plato holds that the "soul is utterly superior to body. . . . What gives each one of us his being is nothing else but his soul, whereas the body is no more than a shadow which keeps us company."[4]

The *Hermetica,* a collection of writings originating in Egypt and influenced by Plato's teaching, pits mind, "O Lord, thou art Mind," against body, "the irrational torments of matter." This work passes on the belief that it is necessary to hate the body in order to fulfill a higher transcendent purpose of mind; flesh is commensurate with base sensuality. In a very Christian-sounding passage in Libellvs 13, Hermes teaches Tat that the senses must be cleansed: "Stop the working of your bodily senses, and then will deity be born in you. . . . Rejoice now my son; you are being cleansed by the Powers of God; for they have come to build up in you the body of reason. . . . Thus, my son, has the intellectual being been made up in us; and by its coming to be, we have been made gods." Hermetic views finally enter into Christian teaching as the writers themselves become Christianized.[5] The ancient world still resonates with the Father and Son of Christianity and in its obedience to a law of transcendence of the body—although, as I still remember hearing in my childhood, Jesus invites his followers to "partake" of his body in the sacrament, and the Christian church is also called "the body of Christ," notwithstanding the association of carnal evil with the feminine body through Eve's "temptation" of Adam.

What Platonic and Hermetic writers refer to as body and mind is not exactly equal to contemporary uses of the terms. In classicism, humans are related to nature and mind through perfection of form. Man is the bestower of form, and woman merely the incubator, according to Aristotle. These relations still hold in classical aesthetics of formalism and can be seen in the transcendence of ballet as it perfects an idealized bodily form in stipulated shapes conforming to plane geometry in mathematics.

In Greek classicism, body is not entirely cut off from soul/spirit/ mind and the triplicate unity this represents. Even though soul and body are empirically distinguished throughout the ancient world, the original togetherness of body and soul is, nevertheless, a fact for Plato. Therapeutically, the troubled body can be calmed in its relationship to the movements of the planets, for instance.[6] An original unity holds even more so in Aristotle, where a sense of the temporal is much stronger.[7]

Plato points heavenward,
Wearing a mask of stars.
Aristotle's feet plant firmly on the ground.
He wears the mask of a human being,
One side shaded with animals,
The other with divinity.

Modern metaphysical dualism beginning with René Descartes (1596– 1650) severs what unity we find in antiquity. Through Cartesian dualism we still assume a metaphysical gulf between material and nonmaterial phenomena. Mind is cut loose from its material physical basis, from flesh and blood bodies.

Descartes could be masked several ways,
Through his concern for education,
Or even in his velvet dressing gown
And a meditative pose.
He appears here with the soul side of his face extended into ether,
And the physical side painted as a machine.

Transcendence of the body in the airy nymphs and apparitions of ballet exemplifies metaphysical dualism, as does the objectified body mechanics of technical dance training in the West, including much of ballet and modern/postmodern dance.

> Properties are owned
> And they are metaphysical qualities
> Belonging to a painting
> Or a dance
> Colors and movements
> A sharp, shimmering sound
> Flesh

Historical Backdrop

Modern/postmodern intellectual history, in which existentialism, phenomenology, and feminism are relatively recent links, is long and complex and began in the nineteenth century with Nietzsche's questioning of religion and metaphysics. As Andreas Huyssen maps the postmodern through its modern and poststructural connections, it becomes clear that it is not easy to separate any of these intellectual movements entirely. I have elsewhere written of the modern/postmodern continuities and breaks in dance, and dance historian Sally Banes has covered the development of postmodern dance more thoroughly than anyone. The postmodern dance found many of its descendant possibilities as well as its ascendant points of departure through modern dance. As Jean-François Lyotard also points out, the postmodern "is undoubtedly a part of the modern." But it has significant differences as well, differences that intensify the modernist question put by Thierry de Duve, not "What is beautiful?" but "What can be said to be art?"[8]

Existentialism, like modern/postmodern dance, feeds on experiment, and many of its processes and products continue in that spirit. The improvisational existentialism of Foucault probes the regulatory power of knowledge and paves the way for poststructural criticism in the arts, as we see in chapter 8, "Existential Haircut." Postmodern dance, still called modern dance in the academy, continues in the experimental mode of the original modern, even as it inverts the bodily styles and practices inscribed therein. It may be obvious, but still worth saying, that revisions depend on antecedents, whether they be the highly wrought philosophy of Foucault or the neoexpressionist dance of Pina Bausch, pushing boundaries and exposing conventions. Unlike classical ballet with its codified vocabulary of movement, modern/postmodern dance improvises toward its choreographic ends and openings, maintaining an unresolved nature that stimulates radical tensions among gender, politics, and aesthetics.[9]

Ballet, on the other hand, has a long history and patriarchal tradition that often circumscribes its sexual politics, but this situation can also create tensions in valiant stances of reformation, as ballet professor Melanie Bales shows.[10] Feldenkrais teacher and ballet dancer Jocelyn Boeber researches the intersection of motor learning, somatics, and ballet, and Wallie Wolfgruber utilizes the sensitivity of Trager Mentastics in her progressive and popular ballet courses.[11] While ballet satisfies a thirst for romance, magic, and myth in airborne aesthetics, its practices need not culminate in destructive bodily practices. Dance practices can offer a chance for engagement and self-knowledge or can punish and deny the body, and the practices of ballet are no exception. It offers special challenges in this respect because of its objective, codified techniques.

As the philosophy that grows out of existentialism becomes focused through self-reflective phenomenology, it produces a fluid field for eliciting subjectivities in art, literature, psychology, and philosophy where no one size fits all. The original existentialist opening allows philosophy to darken and descend from the presumed enlightenment of the rational self and escalating positions of authority. Existentialism is not the story of the enlightened conquering hero. It articulates the limits of objectivity and tells the story of the wounded, lonely hero. It is despairing of the subject, but it can also affirm life. It has theists (Gabriel Marcel, Martin Buber, Søren Kierkegaard, and Paul Tillich) as well as atheists (Jean-Paul Sartre) and feminists (Simone de Beauvoir). It also produces a respect for nature through Paul Ricoeur, whose analyses continue to correct the field of existential phenomenology that he helped to create.

Poststructural theory through Jacques Derrida, Jacques Lacan, Michel Foucault, and Jean-François Lyotard carries existentialist improvisations further (perhaps) than Nietzsche's unleashing of the subject in *Joyful Wisdom*. Here we step beyond breath and wander into emptiness. As for Nietzsche and astronauts, "there is no above and below." I sometimes feel so unsettled—in dancing, back diving, and in meditation—but not so far from the sun: "Whither do we move? Away from all suns? Do we not dash on unceasingly? Backwards, sideways, forwards, in all directions? Is there still an above and below? Do we not stray, as through infinite nothingness? Does not empty space breathe upon us?"[12]

Recent innovations on themes of existentialism and phenomenology place me on equally precarious footing with gender and body politics. Through Judith Butler, I gather how malleable I am. Through the sensuous phenomenology of Glen Mazis, David Abrams, and Bruce Wilshire, I return the earth its due; I celebrate my senses and understand the necessity for joy in my body.

Embodying Feminism

Luce Irigaray (b. 1930), a continental feminist, participated in the radical inquiry associated with poststructural deconstruction that surfaced in the 1960s. These strategies highlighted the importance of "différance," a term coined by Jacques Derrida. A loss of common ground in Irigaray's deconstructive, divisive theory of sexual difference distinguished her from Julia Kristeva (b. 1941), the French feminist whose interdisciplinary philosophy generated the difference but also the possibility for a common genealogy of female and male sexual identity.

Irigaray as a practicing psychoanalyst provides one of the most scathing critiques of the exclusively masculine perspective of sexual identity dominated by the Oedipal complex. Irigaray and Kristeva converge on the issue of gender from different directions, but they are both critiquing Western philosophy and psychoanalysis. Kristeva's semiotic analysis never totally dismisses the subject, but explains the subject-in-process. She revives an existential position with this concept, but extends it for feminism. Kristeva also initiates a metaphysical position for feminism. For her (and for me) the maternal time of repetition and organic cycle needs to be reconciled with the linear time of history and politics. The semiotic and the symbolic are not at odds, but neither one offers permanent safety.[13]

I take a dancer's approach to metaphysics, a sometimes unpopular word in feminism, but one that draws me to it, and which I hope to provoke into whirlpools and calms. Continuing to develop the terms of embodiment, as I have elsewhere,[14] in *Dancing Identity* I expand lived body concepts beyond theatrical dance to encompass a broader conception and to press toward dance as metaphor and metaphysics. Heidegger saw an interesting connection here: "Only in metaphysics is there metaphor." We are bridging a gap or crossing an amazing synapse whenever we *leap between* and *bind up* differences in metaphors. I am interested in this gap, the space between images, and the shape it takes, for I sense that here in the gap is transformation and information dancing together.

Some feminist scholars have been critical of use of the term "embodiment" in philosophy because of its background in religion.[15] On that basis, we might well have to exclude much of our language. In India, all of Sanskrit would have to go, as would modern words like "dance" that trace back to that source.[16] I like "embodiment" as a nondualistic process descriptive. It contains material intelligence (body) and the transformative prefix "em-," which gives it motion. "To be embodied" is quite different from "to have a body," which splits subject from object and indicates "possession" as the outcome—hence, possessive materialism: self-mastery, mastery of others, owning bodies. The possibility of using the verbal infinitive form "to embody" activates the more passive word "body." I also like the metaphysics that "embodiment" implies—the ongoing mystery ruminating behind reflection. The inseparability and interactivity of all animate life, the embodiment of earth, animals, and insects, is captured in a word, and I do not wish to reject all things religious—even dance, poetry, and magic.

There is a sense in which dance and somatic process helps us to conceive of an embodied metaphysics. They open up the manner in which nature and culture are embodied in our "metaphysical artifacts." I use this term to include metaphysical products, both material and transitory, that bear a human mark. And why not some other mark? Because the manifestations of metaphysics are human inventions, tracings of human history that reflect how we came to be (and to record) who we are. I extend the linguistic of metaphysics in using the term "artifact" to include verbal and nonverbal forms. I do not privilege the metaphysical artifacts of language over those of art, architecture, ritual, and story. Dance is one of these metaphysical tracings or human artifacts. It exists through the dancer and for the time being, *an art and a fact* both material and evanescent. As embodied, particular dances become apparent as corporeal artifacts. They may be the most obvious of corporeal artifacts, but they are not the only ones. All doing and making stems from our corporeality, just as culture hangs together through the collective, invisible body of our works.

This book derives in part from the metaphysics of continental philosophy, especially as it evolves toward a more reflective feminist *poiesis*, poetry as a living process. Kristeva examines the first phase of feminism as grounded in suffrage, concerns for equality, and later in existentialism through Beauvoir. This is followed, says Kristeva, by a second phase that seeks to give language to intercorporeal experiences through a *manipulation of signs* (semiosis). The effort to articulate experiences of women as different from men, and to eliminate sex/gender difference, coincides with linguistic deconstruction in semiotics.[17] Other commentators place Beauvoir at the beginning of the second phase since she initiates its anti-essentialist stance on gender and brings existential phenomenology into the arena of feminism.

As a dancer and somatic movement therapist, I am interested in moving in tune with nonhuman nature and in the constant rediscovery of the nature of the human body. I have doubted radical anti-essentialist feminism even as I want to defend some of the liberal (original anti-essentialist) positions of Beauvoir. If biology is not destiny, as she claims (1949), our historical position now requires that we nevertheless affirm our kinship with the natural world: animals and plants, rocks and rivers, sky and water. I would rather see how we all, men and women alike, have a home in nature, our here and now obligation to take care of the nature that supports us, and how dance/movement can give us the somatic means to explore the nature-culture continuum of our human bodily being. Our body is both a natural and social phenomenon; our dances, innate movement potentials, and our natural capacity for healing provide evidence of this.

As the female founder of existential phenomenology, Beauvoir produced not only the anti-essentialist ground of feminism, but she also wrote on ethics. Her 1948 *Ethics of Ambiguity* preceded the development of standpoint theory by Sandra Harding in 1991 and the theories of situated knowledge by Donna Haraway in 1991 that inform contemporary feminist ethics and epistemology concerning women's ways of knowing.[18] Beauvoir's ethics were, however, not systematic, and she had only just begun to write her feminist standpoint in *The Second Sex*, published in 1949 after lengthy research.

As theories of relativity were being articulated in physics, existential phenomenology originated theories of relativity in philosophy. It produced "situation ethics" without naming it as such, and set forth theories of knowledge derived from partial views and particular situations, respecting how human experience also changes through time. Beauvoir noted that "An ethics of ambiguity will be one which will refuse to deny a priori that separate existants can, at the same time, be bound to each other, that their individual freedoms can forge laws valid for all."[19] No laws are valid for all, she says, yet through our bodies, the bodies of other creatures, and the body of the earth, we can see how all life is entangled. A modern imperative forges in us a new ethics and respect for nature. But Beauvoir was making her argument from another point of view: her struggle with conscience amid the onset of World War II. Beauvoir explains art as a form of transformation, not merely contemplative pleasure, but an alchemy through which we learn. As one of the original phenomenologists, she studies the positive aspects of ambiguity, mixing freedom with engagement, art with conscience, and sensitivity with the intelligent body-self.

In America, the conservative critique of Christina Hoff Sommers looks at feminism as it has grown internationally through academic discourse and politics. She calls the second phase of feminism "sex/gender feminism" and believes its male hatred and disdain for women who disagree with it to be detrimental to the advancement of women. The total overhaul of education in view of woman-centered knowledge, she says, is coming from a small but powerful elite who have "stolen" feminism and pose a danger to a society of free persons who may not wish to embrace sex/gender feminist ideology.[20] Sommers sees value in preserving and teaching important achievements of history, including "the great masters" in art. Discussion of what constitutes "great art" and what the hazards of "mastery" are do not enter into her thesis. Her aesthetic position rings hollow, but I appreciate that she exposes the dangers of discounting all male achievements, and that she traces the issues of political correctness in gender feminism.

Julia Kristeva critiques the second phase of feminism, but within its liberal quarters. She wonders what will happen through the "counter-power" of the second phase as it takes on aspects "ranging from a club of ideas to a group of terrorist commandos?" A female society as an "alter ego" of the official society would constitute a "counter-society," a place outside the law, "utopia's floodgate." Both Kristeva and Sommers believe that the problem of a counter-society is becoming massive.

In "Women's Time," Kristeva examines a third phase of feminism in a face-off with the second, where a younger generation provides another signifying space that is not exclusionary and admits the satisfactions of motherhood. In the third phase—which she envisions and advocates—"the very dichotomy man/woman as an opposition between two rival entities may be understood as belonging to *metaphysics.*" This would resolve not the difference, she holds, but the battle, and a retreat from sexism both male and female.[21]

It is in this latter sense that I hope to bring metaphysics down to earth, as I employ and critique Heidegger's metaphysics and also implicate some non-Western metaphysical concepts and corporeal artifacts.[22] To yield a cross-cultural perspective, I approach a corporeal feminism from various metaphysical backgrounds. The body itself is a site for international metaphysical convergence, as the "community body" of Akira Kasai's Butoh workshops and dances shows. Many movement and dance forms are shared across boundaries of race and culture. Whites perform African dance, all races perform Eurocentric ballet, although nonwhites like Arthur Mitchell have had to settle aesthetic quarrels in the process, and Butoh, which was originally Japanese, is now international. Somatic forms like yoga and tai chi have long since become global. Modern dance as it grew in America and Europe borrowed heavily from African and Asian aesthetics and eventually spread its creative practices and cultural fragments around the world. Modern/postmodern dance now knows no national boundaries. Indian choreographers like Chandralekha and Anita Ratnam recast Indian mythology and classical dances with postmodern techniques in a feminist guise.

The meeting of East and West is not new to philosophy, as evidenced in Nietzsche's philosophy of "eternal return," a Taoist and Hindu concept. In *Being and Time*, Heidegger's whirlwind metaphysics also cycles continuously, picking up previous arguments, setting them down in new and unfamiliar circumstances. Heidegger's mysterious nonlinearity and his critique of Western metaphysics provided one of the bases of deconstruction.[23] Time itself is Heidegger's existential deconstructive tool—as it is also Kristeva's. He uses the phenomenon of time to take apart the classical metaphysics of essence and to critique Husserl's transcendental phenomenology, even as he dedicates his work to Husserl.

If Heidegger and Kristeva were to dance together,
They would both wear masks of time:
Time is an elusive, metaphysical dancer.

Pursuing themes of gender and determinism, I take up the precarious goal of creating a corporeal metaphysics through dance aesthetics. As a branch of philosophy, phenomenology often entails ontology (theories of being) and develops existential rather than universal metaphysics. Through its concern for human agency and temporal change, existential phenomenology roots the view that humans are not biologically determined. My view rejects both biological and social determinism. I seek to valorize agency, but not a totalizing agency that is unconcerned with others and the environment. What phenomenology calls intersubjectivity, things-in-relation, steps forward from its concern for consciousness of things-in-themselves and from individual embodiment to relational embodiment, we as part of the world's body.

The mobile correlation of being with nonbeing in existential philosophy provides a critique of the traditional ontology of substances where each element of being attains its proper place and status in the universe. Like a somatically designed movement exploration, the post-metaphysical view is not unidirectional but reversible. What moves forward can just as easily retrace to its origin. Hannah Arendt represents such mobility as a gap in time between past and future when she writes of the existentialist rejection of age-old metaphysical questions to the commitments and predicaments of action in *Between Past and Future*.[24]

This gap in time is our insertion
Into the dance of time.

Being is a presence and
Absence arising in nonbeing,
Darkness in light and descent.

This seesaw way of speaking gives rise to the focus existentialism has had on ambiguity, the release of controlling impulses into an ethos of descent and not knowing. The reasons for postmetaphysical views become clear when we ponder the consequences of escalating cycles of control in politics, technology, and the arts. Beauvoir's anti-essentialist philosophy as set forth in *The Ethics of Ambiguity* provides the *cantus firmus* of my essay, "Thickening Ambiguity." Her feminist views in *The Second Sex* resound throughout the text. Beauvoir's contributions to phenomenology and existentialism, particularly her insights into corporeal metaphysics, not to mention the values of the arts, have long been hidden behind the visibility of her male counterpart, Maurice Merleau-Ponty, and her lover and lifelong companion, Jean-Paul Sartre. Her philosophy remains, nonetheless, enduring.

Beauvoir wears a mask
Of being, becoming
A woman of dissent
And immanence, thinning
 Sexual facades, and
Thickening into happiness.

Body as Spirit in Japan

Beyond the Social Body,
Ichikawa and Yuasa
Appear in masks of spirit.
Ichikawa wears the sun,
And Yuasa wears the moon
Able to integrate and dissolve
High degrees of unity,
And low degrees of unity,
Laced with *mi* and *ki*.

Japanese philosophers Ichikawa Hiroshi and Yuasa Yasuo approach the phenomenological concept of the "lived body" from another cultural perspective altogether, one that I believe more closely explains

how the body is lived and presented in Butoh dance styles, as it originated in Japan with Tatsumi Hijikata (1928–1986) and is now spreading across the globe. Yuasa's *The Body: Toward an Eastern Mind-Body
Theory*, originally published in 1977, was translated into English in
1987, the same year my *Dance and the Lived Body* was published. Ichikawa's prominent works *Seishin toshite no Shintai* (The body as spirit,
1975) and *Mi no Kozo: Shintairon wo Koete* (Structure of the body:
Overcoming the theory of the body, 1993) have not yet been translated into English, but his theories have been introduced to English
speakers in Shigenori Nagatomo's *Attunement through the Body* and
the work of Chikako Ozawa-De Silva.[25] Ichikawa counters Western
dualism in his philosophy of *the body as spirit*. He employs the phenomenology of Husserl, Sartre, and Merleau-Ponty, but carries their
work further on Eastern grounds. His thesis is that the body we live is
much closer to what we understand by the word "spirit" than it is to
matter or biology.

Ichikawa's work has implications for understanding *body as spirit* in
Butoh, as Hijikata's Butoh challenges the materiality of the body
through a nondualistic route. It is difficult to claim that Hijikata's
dance and subsequent Butoh is akin to Western notions of ethereal
spirit, even if Butoh dancers deconstruct the physical in morphing
from image to image and project the body toward *nothingness:* Theirs
is not an ethereal escape from the material body; it is a transformative
inner dance not separating the physical and spiritual. Hijikata starts
with the somaticity of the body in his writing of *Inner Material/Mate-
rial:* "There is no way to remove ignorance and misery from my
dances, but I do not want people to draw a lesson about hereditary diseases from them. . . . I have never been visited by genius and my appearance is far from that of a certified incompetent. Not a devotee of
ghost aesthetic, I am a mere virgin. My semen should bring a good
price."[26] Hijikata's surrealist writing, like his dance, is his way of getting close to his body, the closeness that is difficult to grasp through
rational means.

Medicine and science distance the body technologically. And even
dance in its highly disciplined, abstracted forms can distance us from
felt experience. Somatic amnesia, the psychic numbing of the body,
is not uncommon for dancers when the body is pushed to the brink
in punishing situations. "I knew my toenails were ready to go, and

would come right off," one of my students wrote in a recent paper, "but I put on my toe shoes and went on stage, not feeling the pain."

Dance can also bind us to the intimate contours of bodily life and bring us intuitively close to the bodies we are. If body *is spirit*, as Ichikawa holds, then we experience various degrees of spiritual connectivity through dance, even the freedom we seek through unification of body with conscious intent and intuitive life. This in turn allows us to understand the body that is beyond the skin, and connectivity as a gift of bodily being, what Ichikawa and Yuasa cite as the "immaterial body" beyond rationalization. This is the body without boundaries that so captures me in Butoh and is indeed very suspect in materialist cultures.

Ichikawa sees that studying the body "as phenomena" enables one to perceive the body as it appears on a conscious level, but not the subconscious body that supports it.[27] This is not the subconscious that Freud posits, however, nor can it be compared exactly to the collective unconscious of Jung. It is more akin to body as encompassing spirit. Hijikata projects this subconscious body in a Butoh way, not laden with Western psychoanalytic. He explores the underside or darkness that portends a telling gesture, or one half awake and forgetting itself in that difficult state to excavate that he calls "ecstasy without obstacles." "Inside this one body," Hijikata says, "there are various mythic things that are still sleeping intact. . . . The work is how to excavate them at the actual site. . . . I would like to see something where such things float up like departed spirits."[28]

Ichikawa's theory of *the body as spirit* is based on various levels of unity. He claims that our existence itself unifies the spiritual and physical levels. "Spirit" and "mind" are nothing but names given to the same reality, as I also have held.[29] The body becomes truly human when the distinction between spirit, mind, and body disappears. Thus a high degree of unity expresses our freedom, while mental disorders are characterized by a low degree of unity: "When the degree of unity is low and we are controlled by the environment and have less freedom, we feel the body. The ultimate situation is that of a corpse."[30] Hijikata's student Kayo Mikami says that he sometimes explained his Butoh in terms of a corpse: "Butoh is a dead body standing desperately upright."[31] Would this mean then in terms of Ichikawa's philosophy of the body that the Butoh dancer experiences a low level of unity, a disorder that brings the dancer closer to the body through despair and the struggle of uprightness? Clearly the Butoh dancer lacks the ballet dancer's control over gravity and uprightness. In Butoh, bodily control goes the way of imagistic morphology, the metaphysics of *becoming* through metamorphosis, not arriving, but always in process of integration and dissolution.

There is still another parallel between the Butoh body, *the body that becomes*, and Japanese phenomenology of the body. Ichikawa develops a concept of the body as unfinished "potential," unfolding the idea of the Japanese word *mi*—the body as a potential whole. He explains that *mi* is an equivalent of *body* except that *mi* has several more layers than the word "body." It expresses what phenomenology developed as "lived body dynamic" rather than the material object we generally think of as body in the West. Ichikawa examines fourteen different meanings of *mi* shifting outward from fruit to dead flesh, living flesh, a whole body, the way of the body, garments on the body (or all of the person's belongings), life, the meaning of social life, self, multiple individual selves (myself, yourself, ourselves), socialized self, social status, heart, and whole existence. Here self and heart move outward toward the whole of existence. He further draws a connection between *mi*—including the body, mind, and heart—and *ki*, the Japanese concept often translated as "spiritual energy," an organizing force field and dynamic unity. *Ki* pervades nature and connects the body to nature, whereas, in the West, the social constructivist convention sees the body as distinct from nature. As sociologist Anna Yeatman observes, sociology elaborates the category of the social inclusively, and nature is seen as a limiting and residual term in social theory.[32] Clearly the body is understood as part of nature in Japan, explicitly through the linguistic structures of *mi* and *ki*. Ichikawa explains that once we understand the embodied nature of human existence, the dichotomy of nature and culture dissolves. Nature is no longer pictured outside of culture as something to be overcome and dominated. In respect to Japanese connectivity, it is intriguing to consider how Hijikata explains that his invention of Butoh comes from his somatic associations with mud and wind.

We see Hijikata through a mask
Of Mud and Wind

As *Kaze Daruma* (Wind Daruma),
A limbless figure weighted so
It bounces back when knocked over.[33]

In February 1985, the night before the Butoh Festival '85 and one
year before his death, Tatsumi Hijikata gave a lecture titled "Kaze
Daruma" that quoted an ancient Buddhist priest, Kyogai, and then
told stories of blustery winter winds in his homeland of Akita. Darumas there come garbed in the wind. When the Wind Daruma stands
at the door and goes into the parlor, "this is already *butoh*," he said.
Then he spoke about Showa the Third (1928), the year and era of his
birth:

> In early spring the wind is something special, blowing over the sloppy,
> wet mud. Sometimes in early spring I would fall down in the mud and my
> child's body, pitiful to its core, would gently float there. I try to speak but
> it's like something has already been spoken. I have the feeling there is a
> knot of wood, somewhere in my lower abdomen stuck there in the mud,
> that is screaming something. . . . I am distinctly aware that I was born of
> mud and that my movements now have all been built on that.[34]

Yuasa investigates the inseparability of the mind and body in Eastern traditions that cultivates rather than attempts to control the body.
In the contemporary philosophy of Ichikawa and Yuasa, the body is
not an object to control and dominate by the mind, not an instrument
of art, but a part of the extensive whole of nature, at the ready for
unity or dissolution. Here art is envisioned as process and is not an
end in itself. How does art, how does dance, make meaning and engage life forms in its processes? How is the body affected at a cellular
level? Somatically? How is the body lived through movement? How is
it changed? Transformed in positive ways? These might be the guiding
questions of dance forms that issue from cultivation rather than
control.

Eastern traditions like Zen and yoga take up the question of being
through practice, seeking the basis of human nature by investigating
the body-mind as transformational. Discipline is not the master word
here; rather, cultivation is suggested. Yuasa sees in Eastern traditions
no sharp distinction between the metaphysical and physical dimensions. Rather, they are permeable as lived. Self-cultivation can free the

self from the dominance of mental forces and the experience of separation, and we can experience the bodies of others through the unlimited nature of our own body.

Yuasa articulates the difference between intrinsic mind-body connections as opposed to acquired mind-body unity. Western theories of the body typically discuss the will—whether it is free or determined, mental or somatic—but in the Eastern way the will is seldom prominent; rather, the expression of creativity is.

As Ozawa-De Silva examines Japanese contemporary thinkers, she sees how their work transcends conventional social constructivism, allowing biological, psychological, and social aspects to be understood as a unity, that they transcend cruder forms of materialism by seeing embodiment as "non-reducible to merely physical or visible phenomena."[35] Embodiment does not reduce to social categories. Thus, art in the Japanese unified view relates to life, society, and the larger body of spirit. Social constructivism, theories of the body as social/cultural constructions, enters uncritically into dance theory where the body is considered primarily as a social actor, not mitigated by concerns for the body as part of nature and the living world.

2 | First Sounds

Simone de Beauvoir was the first philosopher to look into the darkness associated with woman and nature in *The Second Sex*, which stands at the beginning of the second wave of feminism: "One is not born, but rather becomes, a woman." This most famous sentence from Beauvoir's book sums up her argument against biological determinism. Beauvoir's comprehensive and still controversial text also initiated existential feminism, as she developed her themes within the emergence of existentialist philosophy—an open-ended, anti-essentialist, and nonsystematic philosophy that studies life as an undecided project-in-the-making. She did not call herself a feminist at first, but associated with feminist causes when she officially joined the women's liberation movement in France in 1971. She said that writing the study had turned her into a feminist, as described in Toril Moi's *Simone de Beauvoir: The Making of an Intellectual Woman* (1994).

As when I first encountered Beauvoir's book in 1962, it still disturbs me to read her thoroughgoing existentialism and voluminous treatise on the "othering" of woman. As the second sex, woman receives second-class citizenship, and what is more frightening, her very personhood is stunted. I was twenty-three when I read Beauvoir's study of the consignment of woman to passivity, mystery, and darkness. It was then that I decided to earn my own money and to be vigilant. Now it is time to own the mystery.

I cut my existential/feminist teeth on Beauvoir's work. It accompanied me to Germany in 1965 when I went to study dance in Berlin with Mary Wigman (1886–1973), the principal founder, along with movement theorist Rudolph Laban, of expressionist modern dance.

Wigman's works grounded a starkly poetic aesthetic in twentieth-century dance, investigating an independent and undomesticated femininity that explored darkness, witchcraft, and hysteria. Her gestalt approach to movement influenced the development of the field of dance therapy as well as Japanese Butoh. Hers was a resistive, erotic, and grotesque feminine unheard of in traditional ballet and discouraged in the Germany of her time with its image of "the Aryan beauty" focused on scrubbed docility and sturdy blonde health. Wigman was dramatic, but she had a softer side as well, songlike, as her committed lyricism shows.

Her teaching inspired a variety of choreographic responses, some typically Wigman, and some not. One choreographic problem she gave us was on Swiss composer Honegger's music, *King David*. It involved a witch, that favorite archetype of Wigman's, still going strong. We danced around a brew that held mystery and power; even now I remember the feeling. The film I made of our dances for Wigman's seventy-ninth birthday party show several dances that are soft and inner directed, like Suzanne Linke's solo. My dance of contrasts, *Black and White*, is cast more rhythmically into space, and a duet on water and earth made by Americans Betsy Sacks and Powell Shepard is elemental and delicately detailed. Canadian Judy Jarvis performs a dance based on fencing.[1] I remember a group work where we wore gray (anything gray you could find in your closet or someone else's) and passed oranges from person to person improvisationally (quite playfully postmodern). Wigman encouraged play and experiment and spent a great deal of time reflecting with us philosophically on the importance of dance as personal development.

These two European women, Beauvoir and Wigman, influenced the unfolding of my feminist/philosophical imagination and inspired my dancing and choreography. Both of their adult lives spanned the horrors of World War II that I remember as a child. Both of them suffered and survived the darkness of Fascism, but from entirely different positions and on opposite sides. When Beauvoir's *The Blood of Others* was published after the liberation of Paris in 1945, it was acclaimed as "the great existentialist novel of the resistance."[2] Joseph Goebbels, Hitler's propaganda minister, banned Wigman's participation in the First German Arts Exhibition in Munich in 1937 because of her commitment to artists' prerogatives and decidedly "philosophical" dance.

Echoing a romantic ideal, Goebbels insisted that dance should be "buoyant and must show beautiful women's bodies."[3]

The Nazi party seized power in Germany in November 1933. Wigman's school was officially closed in 1942 after a seven-year decline during which she choreographed under restrictions. Susan Manning's history of Wigman's work now interprets it as ambiguous in its politics with proto-Fascist leanings. Manning reconstructs what she considers to be Wigman's feminism and nationalism, interpreting her work through the concept of "the male gaze," a feminist psychoanalytic polemic developed by Laura Mulvey in film studies.

Manning posits a gender division in Wigman's work during the rise of Hitler. Wigman's dances of this period, Manning theorizes, present women as passive objects, eroticized and controlled as "the other" in the male imagination. Manning believes that Wigman's choreographic strategies of "autobiography, archetype, and musical visualization" represent a shift in her work under the Third Reich to accommodate masculinist/Fascist aesthetics.[4] Wigman's inclusion of the softer female archetypes in representations of marriage and motherhood essentialize woman, in Manning's view, and open the door to Fascist aesthetics. Would feminist ideologues deny woman's positive associations with motherhood? Are dances that issue from nurturing impulses Fascist? Does she want to go that far? As she transports the theory of the male gaze from film to dance and from the present to the past, applying it globally to another cultural setting, she interprets Wigman as a supporter of the dominant Fascist order, even as she acknowledges the many resistive ploys in Wigman's aesthetic choices. Marion Kant also accuses Wigman of Fascist sympathies, more as a result of her professional choices.[5] Sally Banes critiques the reductionist tendencies of the male gaze as a critical model for dance when she charts a comprehensive feminism in *Dancing Women* (1998). In my 1991 article on phenomenology, I outline the limitations of theorizing dance through "the male gaze," tracing the broader idea of "the gaze of the other" to Sartre and the feminist root of "the objectified other" to Beauvoir.[6]

The static theory of the male gaze as a predictor of aesthetics has by now been challenged on many fronts. Wigman's nationalism and feminism, her identification with Germany and her gender, is complex in her choreography. And it is not unusual for artists to identify with their origins—Martha Graham's Americana and Jose Limon's Mexicana, for instance. Our dances say as much about national and communal identities as they do about the self, and it is not easy to sort out the difference, as Foucault's upending of egocentric anthropology reveals. We are all subject to collective powers that evade our attention, and we fool ourselves if we believe that dancing escapes national-identity. Aesthetic character marks personal style, but it is also inescapably ethnographic; as such it will convey national origins and identify the artist. Did Beethoven, Brahms, and Bach transcend nationality? No. We do recognize the Germanic source and time of their music.

Wigman's work was also ethnographic and certainly a product of her times, but it was not about obedience or mastery of accepted aesthetic rules. No movements were rejected; the ugly and the beautiful could both tell the truth so long as they were evocative. As I watch her work on film and remember my studies with her, I am aware that her choreography is formed less for the gaze than for the soul. Wigman urged her students to find motivational sources for their dances.[7] I will not forget the dance I did that she liked best. It was based on a photograph of a young boy whose hearing had suddenly been restored. I danced in silence, searching my body's memory of first sounds.

Wigman was interested in drama, sense, and mood, not so much the visualized body, but the tactile-kinaesthetic-affective body, although her group choreography was poured through a visual architecture, as we see in her book, *Die Sprache des Tanzes* (The language of dance, 1963). She taught us to use space the way a swimmer feels the water—as fluid resistance and joyful partner in facilitation of form. Her teaching sharpened powers of bodily speech and empathic connections; thus, she sometimes structured classes based on hands and touch. Concentrated in vertigo and ecstasies, her whirling classes became famous, and she described her own performances with the somatic immediacy of "a sunny day," "the beach," "the tango," or—as in the *Witch Dance*—"the forbidden."

In 1980 I choreographed *Dreh Monotony*, a solo for myself based on whirling classes that I experienced at the Wigman School in 1964 and Wigman's description of her *Dreh Monotony* in class. Dore Hoyer's *Dreh Monotony* (1965), which I saw Hoyer perform in Berlin that year also inspired me to dance on this theme. Wigman's *Dreh Monotony* developed as part of *Celebration* (*Die Feier,* 1928), an evening-long work for Wigman and her ensemble, utilizing the circular pattern of return in movement and structure. "In the Sign of Darkness" was the knotted and tragic middle section of Wigman's *Celebration.* The opening section, "The Temple," was based in part on ecstatic turning, solo and group dance. The end, "Festive Conclusion," was ceremonious. My *Dreh Monotony* is in two sections. The first, "Temple," performed to singular sounds of a large Chinese gong, gathers momentum and shows the circular line of infinity. "Sign of Darkness," with the sharp sound of woodblocks added to the music performed by percussionist Gregory Ketchum, breaks the spell of the circle, distributing the movement as in Wigman's original work—kneeling, squatting, jumping, reaching, ripping, and falling. The dance is an interpretation, not a reconstruction, of Wigman's dance.

Melodramatic Utterance

> The melodramatic utterance breaks through everything that constitutes the "reality principle," all its censorships, accommodations, tonings-down.
> PETER BROOKS, *The Melodramatic Imagination*[8]

Romance is curiously compelling. It goes in and out of fashion quite frequently, but it never goes away. On one hand it leads into fiction and on the other into relationship. There is an aura of melodrama in romance and the sweep of saga. Often it comes in disguise, but when it is unmasked, we see a life/death/life cycle underneath. Our hopes are made to face our illusions and fears. When romance reaches toward melodrama with a serious purpose, hysteria lurks there in the dark spot of consciousness.

Romance and melodrama are two doorways to the numinous, to dance experiences and dance works, per se. They provide entrance into German expressionism and the tragicomic faces of Butoh, allowing safe passage to darkness in the mythos of the senses. When we revalue the dark, we revise myth, or we make the unconscious conscious, as Carl Jung held. We also take the evil out of darkness and revision nature in the process.

New Dance in America, Neue Tanz in Germany, and Japanese Butoh are all descendant forms, rejecting the geometric purifications of classicism, and they also share a basis in the mythical feminine earth

Sondra Fraleigh in "Sign of Darkness" from her dance *Dreh Monotony* (1980), inspired by whirling classes at the Mary Wigman School in 1965, Wigman's description of her *Dreh Monotony*, and Dore Hoyer's *Dreh Monotony*, which Fraleigh saw in Berlin in 1965. Photograph by June Burke.

principle. In its rejection of idealized romance in classical ballet, the new dance of the twentieth century, which sprung from the new woman who founded it, became known as modern dance. Like modern art, it took the name of "modern dance" in America, progressing and changing into late-modern dance, evolving a postmodern rebellion, and eventually recovering expressionist roots, first in Germany through the Tanztheater of Pina Bausch and Suzanne Linke. Modern/postmodern dance still continues to bend and branch out internationally, blending with ballet at many points, as in the eclectic, passionate work of Alonzo King. It is becoming increasingly difficult to trace pure dance identities as forms continue to blend and merge, and romance wears a range of masks, from the ethereal to the darkly erotic.

The stereotypic romance of ballet is legendary and singularly attractive, Romeo and Juliet, purity and first love, the power of physical transcendence, tragedy and melodrama as youth follows love into death. Ballet has thrived on fairy tales and idealized love, honing perfected bodily forms in airborne aesthetics. The darker romance of modern dance has been more about magnetic relations and soul work, often traveling somatically inward. Martha Graham said that she wanted to dance "the heart of man."

Japanese Butoh is historically related to modern dance through German expressionism and its proliferation in Japan during roughly the first half of the twentieth century. Butoh is short for *Ankoku Butoh,* meaning "dance of utter darkness." Its mythos is primal, challenging Western notions of physical reality and embracing a wide emotional spectrum, from pathos to absurdity. It would be difficult to call it romantic in any Western sense, but it is often mysteriously erotic and melodramatic. Its chthonic romance lies in mud and wind, its identification of the human body with nature, and its radical revival of Japanese "pagan" aesthetics or "nativism," a popular movement in early 1970s Japan. Tatsumi Hijikata and Kazuo Ohno pioneered Butoh (by itself meaning "dance step") as the true form of the body. Their dance advanced bodily sensitivity as a philosophy of life. In the Butoh of *Forbidden Colors* (1959), "Hijikata threw the first stone," critic Nario Goda declared. Hijikata danced wildly and with mixed sexual metaphors. Ohno's famous solo, *My Mother* (1981), contrasted this with a gentle grace. Both of these men admitted the feminine at work in their art. They often danced as women, as is typical in Japanese Kabuki and Noh theater, and felt the spirits of their mothers and sisters move through them. The Butoh body, as in *mi*, the Japanese word for body, is not understood through physical limitations, but expansively. It includes one's personal body, the body of others, and the world's body. "Tohoku is everywhere," Hijikata says, speaking of his homeland. This vast body is a mysterious concept for Westerners, but nonetheless imaginable. Hijikata's description of dancing includes the body of his dead sister and women from Tohoku sold into prostitution when he was a child. It speaks of his empathic connections:

When I dance
my sister scratches away
the darkness inside me. . . .
I shake hands with the dead.

Tatsumi Hijikata

Butoh and German expressionist dance both acknowledge dark emotions and subconscious content. Mary Wigman, at the root of expressionist dance, used these to dramatic purpose in her dances. Below I reconstruct Wigman's *Witch Dance* from 1926 and juxtapose it with a contemporary relative, the Butoh Ghost of Natsu Nakajima in her dance *Niwa* from 1982. Having traveled full circle in the global thrust of modernity, Nakajima's dance resembles Wigman's without copying it. Both draw dangerous hysterical portraits, streaming fervent images we can inhabit corporeally. Their dances embody feminine resistance and dissatisfaction; they allow us to seize the power of hysteria, inverting its negative connotations.

Hysteria: Cooling the Witch

What was to be done? The only way out, the only possible banishment, was and became: the mask.

MARY WIGMAN

Wigman's *Hexentanz* (Witch dance) from 1926 can be seen through the poetics of hysteria, expressionist drama, and what Peter Brooks identifies above as "the melodramatic imagination." I invoke melodrama as intervention, counteracting assumptions that reality can be controlled. Through dance description and poetry, I explore Wigman's feminist resistance to ownership and mastery. Her *Witch Dance* would appear on the high end of Brooks's study of melodrama, since it bodes no happy ending. Quite the opposite: it thrives on intensity and signals to the future through its fugitive spirit. It functions as a romantic form of counterdiscourse that undermines realism and suggests a range of fears and desires that dominant social discourses simply cannot account for. The Witch cannot be contained. As Richard Murphy explains in *Theorizing the Avant-Garde* (1998), expressionist melodrama exerts an oppositional power upon repressive discourses, forcing them to reveal their limitations and sites of power.[9]

Planted and percussive gestures, untamed hair, and a polished mask with tightly distilled features render Mary Wigman's solo, *Hexentanz*, both excitingly expressionist and starkly abstract. The dance fastens our gaze on a sitting figure in silk brocade embossed with gold and black on a copper-red background. A carved mask by Noh mask maker Victor Magito covers her face and contrasts with the elaborate fabric. The simply drawn features of the mask cool the fervor of the Witch's pulsing hands and pounding feet, creating a split in the aesthetic effect of the dance. Unloosed frustrations mix with trance, ice, and silence.

The Witch is an overflow of dammed emotions: banging, stamping, and signaling powerful driving forces. Rocking on her haunches, she never goes far from her sitting place. Like an inkblot transfiguring, she turns on her spot, walks forward on her buttocks, then falls, hunched over a leg as it juts out to catch her weight. She closes her legs in front of her chin, then forces them open bluntly. Her spine curls forward as she looks down into her belly. The witch stays low on her backside and leans into one buttock as an elbow finds a knee, and her hand passes across her face, transporting a fragment of the dream-body. There is time for her breath to catch up before the Witch faces forward and looks out. Gradually both hands raise up to frame her head at a wide angle before they begin their magnetic motions.

They pulse, sucking in the witness. At moments the dance deflates its wild gesticulations. The hand calms, finds a soft direction, and Wigman, the choreographer, hedges the emotional shaping of energy in space that made her famous. This dance is not simply a wild letting go of energy in expression of the demonic. It is much more complex. The

Witch and the Demon are, after all, different creatures that represent distinct archetypes. The Witch is a hag and sorceress; she dives into feminine source and psyche. The Demon, on the other hand, is a possessor of bodies and souls. Wigman's Witch is undoubtedly woman, even as a secretive, sphinxlike smile plays on the mouth of her mask.

The repressed feminine erupts from her *Witch Dance,* and lays bare the hysteric. From Wigman's Witch, we cross over to the persecution of witches in medieval Christianity. We remember how their power was feared and how Freudian psychoanalysis later identified and treated hysteria as a madness, ignoring or turning around the hysterics' descriptions of sexual abuse. Still later, the feminism of Hélène Cixous and Catherine Clement in *The Newly Born Woman* (1975) explores linkages of hysteria and witchcraft with the repressed feminine. They critique Sigmund Freud and Jacques Lacan for their phallocentric beliefs on the hysteric. Elizabeth Grosz also examines feminine resistance to exploitation as the root of hysteria in her feminist work, *Volatile Bodies* (1994).

Wigman's *Witch Dance* may also be read as resistive. As the Witch's fingers curl in the air and scratch the space, they are full of their own power, but they are restless and unsatisfied. Wigman writes of the opposing poles of the dance and of her discovery of the split character of the Witch in which "tumultuous" and "enigmatic" actions question and answer each other. The answer is not a dissolve, however; as the hand courses the mouth it issues "a warning." Her dance is certainly aware of the complexity of the witch/hysteric. It foregrounds continental feminism, performing a response to repression and sexual ownership. With resolve, it carries us into the darkness of an expressive world: "How intensely I tried in each performance to feel myself back into the original creative condition of *Witch Dance* and to fulfill its stirring form," Wigman writes.[10]

She explains her urges in shaping *Hexentanz:* "I had the sensation of being full to the point of bursting and near desperation. I felt it ought to be possible to give shape to whatever it was that distressed me beyond measure." She worked the figures of the dance sometimes to the point of intoxication, resisting order, feeling forced into a sitting or squatting position "in possession of the ground." One night after working on the witch dance, Wigman returned to her room very agitated and caught a glimpse of the witch in the mirror: The hair unkempt, the eyes deep in their sockets, the nightgown shifted about, which made the body appear almost shapeless: there she was—the Witch—the earthbound creature with her unrestrained, naked instincts, with her insatiable lust for life, beast, and woman at one and the same time. She shuddered at this facet of her ego, she writes, even as she allowed it to emerge in recognizing the witch as a powerful aspect of woman. Wigman molds repressed and thwarted energies into an elemental gestalt. The Witch is two in one; the independent for itself commingles with the revolting. The one who shapes, stills, and breathes cuts through the ferment.[11]

Down on the ground, close to its scent, the Witch sits with her legs spread and her feet pressed into the floor. She binds her ankles with her hands, lifting and planting her feet: stronger and faster—turning—edging toward disintegration.

ON *HEXENTANZ*

Stiffly masked, the thing
cannot be shut up.
     In tipping around,
          the object circulates.

One butt sits and twists.
The next butt sits,
               back and forth, side to side
                 in the stamping.

The dance circulates as the hand
          grows a claw and reaches
            out of the embossed silk.

The witch cannot be had nor hoodwinked.
She cannot be psychoanalyzed nor hashed over by masters.
She makes the object circulate.

        Widespread with electricity,
          the circuit belongs to her.
From contact,

From refusal to conform, to be beautiful, her
pleasures and secrets break apart a paradise

Of body imaged,
gestured and sent.
Contaminating love potents and over-
turning balances.

There she sits, grown hazy and brutal,
  winding around herself,
  mixing a brew
  of precious threads and growling anima.

Turned back from behind the mask
Unholy.

Who would dare this danger,
this she-wolf reversing grace, and
bit by bit the power of dis-grace,
of strained armor grasping space.

Quick—before order gets to us—

      Open the limits.

  Death does not harm the Witch, and God shows no interest. She celebrates and vents herself. She is not exchanged or produced. *Hexentanz* is catastrophe before language got it—our dance before knowing the right answer. The feet that mock and the shoulders that hunch are their own reason and ruin. They hold a future, unleash the symbol. Astir and unashamed, the Witch passes from passion to conflict, supports the living germ man never chose for her. The scales fall from her eyes into the piece of brocade, and she dances her revolution, turning and turning on her seat.

ANOTHER WORD FOR WITCH

The dance will never be otherwise wise—
  Beldam[12] in touch with fragile contortions
  taking place in space.

Re-membering
>the pressure against her forehead
>that dis-membering broke in tears
>and sweat kept apart—far—far away—
>>in the violet fire—

Entrails pulled out
Through her mouth—
The body's extremities
Disentangling the Imaginary,
the Real, and the Eloquent.

Niwa: Goddess or Cyborg

The Ghost in Natsu Nakajima's dance *Niwa* (The garden, 1982) summons Wigman's *Witch Dance* with the same archetypal consciousness that reconnects with primal powers and bewilderment.[13] This is the receptive "yin" as cauldron, the divine well of creative energy. Ensuing from Japanese Butoh, the feminism of *Niwa* conjures a ghost and goddess symbolic of fluid change and metamorphosis. As life, the garden represents process, growth, and change—flowering and dying regeneration. It is a natural symbol, where nature meets culture, where plants are tended. Nakajima reconstructs many faces of the Goddess and explores a woman's journey in her solo dance.

Like the gripping expressionism of Wigman in the background of Butoh, Nakajima's choreography grows out of a similar search for feminine powers.[14] But the ghost in her garden of life is part of a more sweeping whole. It glances the Witch, puffs out its cheeks, and moves on. *Niwa* is Buddhist in spirit, even if it resists singular religious categories. Shinto, with its nature essence and priestesses, also motivates this dance. Its transcendence toward the Buddhist goddess takes an irrational course, and its glory is indecisive. Nakajima's Goddess imagery slides across cultures and is dialogical.

Niwa's darkness and grotesqueries, like those of Wigman's *Hexentanz* can be repulsive. But the distorted faces of *Niwa* often appear alongside a translucent beauty, requiring us to hold conflicting interpretations: Unadmitted ugliness and untapped beauty, the two sides of our original face, are held uneasily together. The body encloses an insubstantial poetry, not knowing which way to turn; a third interpretation stirs in us. Or maybe a state of breath is released, opening a space in the lower lobes of the lungs, in the belly and in the heart, as the rational mind is befuddled. Thus the healing potential of *Niwa* is revealed.

Nakajima is one of the first women in Butoh to refine works for the stage and to pioneer Butoh as therapeutic process. She crosses boundaries as a choreographer and dance therapist, so it is no surprise that *Niwa* in its spiritual essence and aesthetic structure possesses a cyclic therapy. Its elaborate theatricality is surprising. Kindling *jo-ha-kyu*,[15] Cyborg supports Goddess in *Niwa*. Single spotlights hidden in the set light the face from below as electronic music gathers to a rumble, then cuts away suddenly, or ebbs and flows in hypnotic repetitions.

Denise Fujiwara in *Sumida River,* choreographed by Natsu Nakajima. Nakajima pursues a personal and Japanese vision of intimate space known as *Ma,* or "the space between." Fujiwara's performance brings to life a mother's agonistic search for her kidnapped child. *Sumida River,* based on a popular Noh drama, *Sumidagawa,* is a dance of transformations, disclosing the metamorphic context of Butoh. Photograph by Cylla von Tiedmann.

ON *NIWA*

Unabashed, theatrical technologies

    gather the white-hot light
        as from the front row to the back
           a single slow glow inches closer,
               painting space on the diagonal.

Nakajima in her dance, *Niwa.*
    Is it so very large, this interval between us?

Seven autumn flowers
rustle with muttering lips—
lead us forward in Noh time.

Time
for changing our minds
and the rooms in the chambers of our hearts.

Cherry blossoms falling in the wind
cut the assembling *jo* of *Niwa,*
and tremble in the darkness.

In the next instant, by the hand
the dancer takes us, blown and covered,
huddled under a small tent, peeking out.

A baby sees the world from a boat,
hears the foghorn and the soldiers
shouting—smells the burning defeat.

Night falls, wobbly and walking,
Tilting her head in the fan of *ha,*
Breaking from *jo* the brilliant face
hung in space by the changing light.

Would I understand enough
of vessels that held the cooked viands,

of sleeping upright with firm footing,
to echo back the eerie steps where the ghost appears?

Sitting on the floor,
The Ghost nods her head and shakes her hands.
The head doesn't know what the hands are doing.

A muddy mask looks out at me,
Falls black in the lap of hiding,
Turns red and back to you again.

Melting appearances and costume changes—
The dancer switches with her double
Until the difference disappears.
As One—they journey from birth to birth.

   • • •

After the performance
            I returned to my room agitated
            and looked in the mirror.

Uncertain of my glance,
I saw fragments of wide loops
around the stage, and the crooked fingers
                  of Wigman's *Hexentanz,*
the image of one possessed,
               impenitent.

There she was, the earthbound creature—
            whether *Witch* or *Ogress*—
spilling out of her basket
through the murmurs of chanting
          and a high-pitched shakuhachi flute.

The lights dimmed to black as I fell asleep.
Willows are green and flowers red.
What is *MU?*[16]

   • • •

Laughter moves serenity, awash
in blazing light and shadows
of our secret gazes, complete and
relative as panels on a folding screen,
Niwa inclines away from earth.

Holding back the vigor of *kyu*
and rising up in *Kannon.*
Compassionate Bodhisattva.

Quiet over time, the ghost has
told her story. Welling up like water
her smile an afterimage,
the rapture of the burning *Kali,*
Wise and awesome *Tara,*
Madonna.

Through the vastness of such space,
Why does the glowing dancer
link the tip of her thumb
and first finger in a tender *mudra?*

Her sex is uncertain.
S(he) has been said to appear
in whatever form is needed.

3 | *Thickening Ambiguity*

Face the mirror. What you see is an image of yourself, not your body as yourself. *Turn away* and pay attention to the feelings that arise. Never mind naming or judging them. This is your Being-Body, your Soma-Self, not the object in the mirror that you believe others see, but the ongoing subject, perishing and renewing in every step. This is the "I" that radiates from your core, your starbody, your body-voice, the stirrings of your more, not less, reliable self.

If existence is indeterminate, open-ended and not predictable, then we dance as unfinished metaphysical artifacts in much the same way as phenomenology and evolutionary science explain how life is ongoing. *We are works in progress,* in other words, and like works of art we live between content and process. Our living metaphysical reality does not mount to heaven, but spreads into our everyday dances—of auspicious being and indeterminate becoming.

But not so fast. It slows down here. We further understand the created history, constrained and chosen freedom of bodily existence. We are free; we can dance and we can sing, but it is up to us to invest this open project with meaning and worth, or as Simone de Beauvoir puts it: "In order for the idea of liberation to have concrete meaning, the joy of existence must be asserted in each one, at every instant; the movement toward freedom assumes its real, flesh and blood figure in the world by thickening into pleasure, into happiness."[1]

When we dance, we throw ourselves into the eye of freedom, producing its corporeal forms. We create our body of culture and tap into our embodied nature. We explore the factual dynamic existence of our body.

> When I dance I stir, I blend, I rip and sail. I find myself—all of my selves—somewhat at the same time. I play games with my different personalities. I reach, search, push, and condense. My sensors become more active and I find myself as part of my environment, my environment as part of me. I breathe, I expand and withdraw, I turn and I test. I create lively, fun, scary imagery.
>
> **Kista Tucker, New York, 1997**

As in all our creative doings, we define ourselves in our dances, who we are, and what we can do. There is freedom in this "can do" attitude and also nature. We inherit our body through nature and celebrate this gift, yet this is the same body we create as we consciously imbue its aesthetic/cultural significance in the multifarious forms of dancing. In some sense, we are creating the body and ourselves in the artistic processes of making and doing dances, even though the nature of the body is given in each person's unique inheritance.

The child learns to sit up, and to coo, interacting with the parent. The physical rhythmic process is embroidered with movements. The parent and child adjust their shapes and efforts to coordinate shared actions. Together they create poetry, and they dance:

Patty cake, patty cake, baker man
Bake a cake as fast as you can.

As we create ourselves in our dances, we draw upon the meanings we attach to our corporeality; we stylize our body and engender its forms. *When we choreograph,* we enter into a dialogue with ourselves: conversing with our movement, probing its possibilities and what we can *make* of them, extending what comes naturally and easily, what comes with effort, and what lies waiting to be discovered, converting such potentials into shapes and flows, contrasts and relationships. We shape the self of a moving message that eventually is returned to us, but not in a mirrored reflection, for we cannot separate from the image or the message; rather, we are shaped and moved by it—swelling into all of it. We plumb our biocultural reality and focus ourselves in the message: *moving*, we are moved through it; *shaping*, we are shaped by it—*being* this person in this time with these feelings, as we thicken into the dance.

> When I dance my piece *Otherworld*, I lose the sense of being a performer. Sheep bleat, the wind blows, bagpipes filter across a distance. I become a "me" from centuries ago, weighted in drab, plain garments with a bonnet and a basket for gathering medicinals. I pass through the kissing gate to pick kindling, gathering a bouquet of bony fingers. I become a stone, a slip, a stolid oak tree with sap instead of blood, a green Wicca switch, ever malleable, a witch. . . . "So watch how you go." I fly from the stage through the blackness.
>
> *Christina Sears*, Baltimore, Maryland, 1998

Something lies under what we witness and describe of the dance, what we value, or what we might dislike. The dance is conveyed through bodily means of movement. It bears the biological and sociocultural histories already written in the body and further relays our capacities for creativity and play, ritual and art. Dance bears our body's nature and its culture on a bumpy continuum. In bodily matters of movement and meaning, dance shows how culture reflects or extends nature, how nature lives in our senses and speaks from our flesh.

> Ah but it is their illusion that I make illusion. It is merely life, scraped from the bowl and fed deliberately from my limbs to their soft mouths. A small poppet wound around a wishbone, spun into a poem and dropped in your lap.
>
> *Christina Sears*, 1998

Technology is an aspect of culture that is already extending nature, as Dorion Sagan writes in *Biosphere:* "Far from being an inert lump of matter, the Earth behaves as a giant organism . . . using people to reproduce itself."[2] Sagan postulates that the closed ecosystems of technologically produced biospheres created to explore and settle the inner solar system represent such reproductions—*baby Earths in space.* Wholes give rise to flowing dances and disseminations.

> When the universe comes unstitched,
> its seeds will scatter where?

One of physicist David Bohm's examples of the implicate order (of undivided wholeness) involves stirring ink into molasses. *Stirred one way*, the ink unwinds into a gray thread. *On reverse stirring*, the droplet is reconstituted; it becomes "explicate," just as each of us also stirs and unwinds a life in tracings and reversible threadings of the whole—inklings of a universe in process.[3]

> When we come unglued,
> the sticky universe will what?

Human dances are made. They are created forms, as Maxine Sheets-Johnstone's *The Phenomenology of Dance* (1966) demonstrates. In many ways, we "reconstruct" the natural body in dance as we envision and perform it in theatrical contexts. In addition, the adult has already become his or her particular body of habits and choices, the learned self in a cultural milieu. No one is his naked newborn body. Certainly our body of dance is not an innocent body. The paradox is that, often, dancers hope to communicate something that is not contrived, a dance that is direct and unstudied, an aesthetic distillation that is "natural." Each dance has its own particular birth in beginning and striving, its coming-into-being. And artistry in any discipline also implies effortlessness in presentation akin to nature, although artifice may sometimes be wanted or implied and the body can be reconstructed in highly dramatic forms with theatrical effects, as in Natsu Nakajima's Butoh and Pamela Wonderlich's stilt dances. Atsushi Takenouchi's Butoh moves with nature through the Japanese aesthetic of *Jinen*. Takenouchi, who learned Butoh with founder Tatsumi Hijikata, took an independent direction (explained to me at the dance festival EXIT 2003 in Broellin, Germany) that everything dances together through a cosmic wave or rhythm that is *Jinen*. He works with *Jinen* whether he is dancing on the killing fields of Cambodia, Hiroshima, or Poland, in a forest clearing under the moon, or on a site-specific work in a city. One simply needs to find the rhythms that are already there, he says: "Everything is already dancing; this is *Jinen*." The shape-shifting of Takenouchi touches the cosmic cycle of life and death, dancing in silence on the killing fields of war.

My heart starts to move when I do these dances; something changes inside me, I feel the melting of life and death. After that I don't think anymore, just offer my dance, and turn my strong sadness into peace.

Atsushi Takenouchi, Germany, 2003

Dancing Beings

What is called vitality, sensitivity, and intelligence is not a ready-made quality, but a way of casting oneself into the world and of disclosing being.

SIMONE DE BEAUVOIR, *The Ethics of Ambiguity*

The dancing body may thicken close to animal life and mesmerize as in body-voice *Dansing*, the shamanic improvisations of Christian Swenson. Or the dancer can ride closer to technology, as in contemporary computerized multimedia works or the original multimedia showstoppers of Alwin Nikolais, accomplished with armadas of equipment and body-extending cyborg costumes. Dancing gives proof of the nature-culture continuum. Even as it presses toward artifice, dance must constantly deal with the living human body, its limits and stretching of limits. Only in flights of pure imagination or in mystical experience does dance escape the perceived boundaries of what we ordinarily speak of as the natural world. The supernatural wonder that dancing may evoke contains a tacit understanding of the "natural" underlying the "super." The trance dance of the Whirling Dervishes, for instance, transcends the ordinary by means of a simple movement that most anyone can do—trans/descendant global spinning. As one is annihilated in God as a result of the whirling dance, "he sees that every tree, every plant in the garden of this world is dancing, touched by the spring breath of love."[4] In dancing the body reveals a play of natural powers and cultural strivings. Dancing contains disciplined bodily forms of culture, as basic as simple whirling and stepping patterns and as complex as lengthy memorized phrases of virtuoso movement that far extend the range of ordinary abilities. At the same time, dancing contains the given characteristics (skin color, facial features, and the like) and the endlessly varied individual forms of the dancers. And we cannot miss that dance is sexed through and through, stirring together social attractions and biological attunements. The dancer is persona (mask), masked and unmasked. The contents of any dance thicken with the biophysical and sociocultural substances of its creators and performers.

> When I dance, I feel a sense of elevation in my spirit being.
> The inner satisfaction is so soothing,
> I tend to forget I exist in a mortal world.
> Ghanaian dancer, *Eric Brew (Kwame)*, 1998

Bringing Body to Mind

When I improvise, I bring about a wonderful state of nonrational body thinking. I love to let go this way. I feel the outside of me match the inside as thoughts of color and form slide into motion. My body becomes warm and whole, sometimes happy, often sad, but fully alive in the now.

My soma and sex condition my dance, but they do not determine it. Within these and many other givens, I have choices to make daily and hourly that are more existentially constitutional than genetics. I experience myself in my choices; they create the "I" of who I am. Furthermore, this is not the changeless being of my being, but the changing person I come to know, whether I want to or not, in any small fraction of my unfinished shape. I come home to myself when I worry about wasting time, whenever I glimpse a repeated form that turns back on itself, blanks out, recovers, breathes, and moves on. I mean that I am always in a process of self-creation and recognition. Or in Butler's terms, my body is not so much material. Rather, it is matter materializing and meaning. "'To matter' means at once 'to materialize' and to 'mean.'"[5]

I create the matter and meaning of myself. Like a dance, the self I am creating is coming into being bodily, mindfully, and spiritually. I am changing daily, even as the changeless being of my being connects me to the timeless in the present. These are the times I know my body casts a shadow, and this world is the shadow of another. I create my life and my dance within my natural and culturally inscribed body. What is natural and what is acquired are in perpetual relation. In terms of human movement, nature is by no means just the passive surface on which culture plays.

Cognitive psychology is making this clear in its study of perception and the intelligent coherence of infant life. Eleanor Gibson and her husband, J. J. Gibson, conceived an ecological approach to perception in which "an animal and its environment constitute a system marked by a relation of reciprocity." Their work demonstrates a tenet of existential phenomenology that "to perceive the world is to coperceive oneself." Their scientifically grounded research shows that what we call "the self" arises perceptually as humans interface with their environment. "It is present potentially at birth and it develops as life goes forward." They called this the "ecological self" as perceived directly in relation to its environment *and through movement.*[6]

Phenomenologists had already articulated a similar view of the self relative to the "life world" and "others," a view that also distinguishes the body in its subjectivity and motility as *known through movement.* They called this self variously the "self as lived," the "lived body," and the "body of action," always in view of intersubjectivity, being-with-others, and temporality. They recognized that "self" and "other" are terms that define each other, that our subjectivity can join us to others and the living world, that with the clouds drifting overhead, we move and change through time.

We are thrown into time; like a pot on a wheel, we are in process. Unlike the pot, however, our corporeality is never finished. Rather, our body in its solidarity with the bodies of other animals and in concert with the earth's body is in every moment experiencing the mystery of time, what Heidegger sees as a dynamic intersection of three ecstasies, the past and future unfolding in the present. He holds that we are disclosed to ourselves as projected in the throws of our possibilities: "Thrownness is neither a 'fact that is finished' nor a fact that is settled . . . thrownness, as a kind of Being, belongs to an entity which in each case *is* its possibilities, and is them in such a way that it understands itself in these possibilities and in terms of them, projecting itself upon them." To underscore his thesis of temporality, Heidegger continues in movement terms: "Dasein's 'average everydayness' can be defined as 'Being-in-the-world which is falling and disclosed, thrown and projecting, and for which its own most potentiality-for-Being is an issue.'"[7] Nothing and no one is solidly caught in frozen time—except as art, literature, and dance may arrest life temporarily, lending texture, image, and meaning to movement, slicing time, sculpting space, tracing our body's memory again and again—giving us the possibility of throwing ourselves, spinning and stopping at will. In this we also differ from the pot on a wheel; our movement is of our own volition. Sucked into turbulence, we are the turning, the pot and the potter, and when we dance our angels spin with us. We explore such agency and freedom.

Movement develops in the relationship between inborn natural potential and learning, whether acquired thoughtfully as skill, or assumed uncritically as habit. Dance thrives on this assumed and therefore hidden relation, extending the innate potentials and learned behaviors of human movement.

As acquired behavior, dance is intentional, skilled, kinaesthetically intelligent action. While like any skill the actual dancing may sink to the level of habit, it can be revalued as skill in every act of awareness. At the same time, dancing is born of intuition and the ever-present dimensions of bodily affectivity from pleasure to anguish, as these can arise spontaneously, naturally (without warning and beyond our will) and manifest in movement. Such raw materials may be cultivated in dance. The innate potentialities of the body-self are purposely formulated in movement that is performed for aesthetic purposes: exemplifying geometric shapes, telling stories, poking fun, symbolizing and signaling, encoding politics and ethics, and so on.

In other words, the earth of the body, its natural intelligence and affectivity, is tilled in dancing. This is true of all dance forms. It is explicit in social dance forms where the dancing master instills discipline in the matter of acquiring social manners, as was the case in the Renaissance and Baroque courts, and again at the end of the nineteenth century when dancing masters dictated social manners.

In the theater, the body is not merely socially constituted; rather, it is aesthetically conceived and "textured," performed in verbal or nonverbal "text"—tilled to communicate human visions and personal truths, or cultivated, not necessarily in the lofty sense of the word but in the sense of making and doing. To cultivate is to till the earth, to prepare it for new growth; neither can we miss "cult" as the root of this word. To cultivate is also to instill fervor and to persuade: to advance points of view; ways of touching that are tender, violent, thrilling, or comforting; and ways of moving—head-over-heels as in the backbends of yoga, or head-flung-back in flamenco.

Dancing has taught me the inseparability of body, mind, and movement, and aroused my curiosity concerning the dialectic of nature and culture as we live it bodily through movement. Dance brings to attention what is there, though hidden, in our everyday living of our bodies in a prereflective mode. I can suddenly stop the ongoing, innocent flow of a dance to separate out some factor of bodily performance, to ask which foot steps forward on count three, for instance, or consider whether I might not like a backward step better at that particular point. This interruption is reflective and analytical, bringing body to mind. This point of analysis is a creative process in dance, one that allows a reflective experience of body (in this instance my foot and its stepping) as a point of consciousness. *Bringing body to mind* requires such shifts of consciousness, interruptions of the innocent, ongoing flow of being, as I describe:

My body is an assumed presence; though mindful (full of mind), it is not necessarily always mindful or conscious of itself. Before thought, it is myself when without question I am my dance, just as I move my choices into being in my life, unaware of the choosing until something goes wrong, or somehow reminds me of the choices I have made. I can separate out something called body when I give attention to it—to how I move, or how I will dress, or who I will allow intimacy.

My body comes to mind when I feel suddenly awkward, sick, strong, excited, weak, tired, exuberant. My body comes to mind especially when I wish to be invisible, even in a crowd. Body comes to mind in this very "wish" to disappear. When I most want to hide, there is no place to put myself. My body will be there for me, at issue, just as much as when I want to be clearly seen or heard as I teach a particular movement in a dance, or press my words to a conclusion and gesture with my hands to underscore a point.

We intentionally give body to movement when we dance. Sometimes we create contours and durations for others to perform through their own lived dynamic, or we make time/place structures that others may play and dance within. All of these are points of consciousness that pass through time and from one state to another, constantly changing. They are points in our body awareness, our living of time-space and place as these root together in experience.

The human body is not a set of definitional limits or mechanical processes, as it has been typically described in dualistic philosophy, from Aristotle's theory that the mind controls the body to Descartes's metaphysical opposition of body and soul, substance and nonsubstance. Western culture through its perpetuation of dualism has devalued body—and also woman—in her mythical and real association with the body through birth. Aristotle, the father of biology, thought woman a deformed male.[8] Descartes assigned physical matter an inferior place in his metaphysical scheme of body/soul dualism. With the notable exception of Susanne Langer's *Mind: An Essay on Human Feeling*, and the examples of existentialism and phenomenology, Western philosophy has not understood the body as sentient, conscious, and kinaesthetically intelligent.[9] After Descartes's *Meditations* was published in 1641, material reality, the body of earth and animals, was interpreted as mechanical, with laws of operation to be discerned through mathematical analysis. Foundations for the objective, "disinterested" sciences were laid, also influencing aesthetics with its theories of disinterested appreciation and aesthetic distance. Science has provided tools to create the technologies that we depend on. In this sense, dualism with its objectifying mindset has been a productive invention. But what this abstract side of materialism misses is obvious: our tangible everyday experiences in the uncertain field of everyday life. This is the central subject of phenomenology with its nondualistic understanding of body-mind unity.

Curiously enough, when we use the tools of science to study the body, they can be turned away from dualism and toward holism. Even a cursory study of the central nervous system dispels philosophical dualism. The body has a brain; or more correctly speaking, the brain manifests itself throughout the body by means of the central nervous system, and vice versa. In *Job's Body*, Deane Juhan studies the intricate relationships and intelligence of all the body's systems.[10]

The totality of the body manifests through the nervous system in the brain and all of its activities—including the mental or minded processes that Mabel Todd has called *The Thinking Body*.[11] Somatic studies, modern body therapies, and neuroscience disprove body/mind dualism. Indeed, they demonstrate, as dance also does, the inviolable unit of our body-mind integrity. Every cell thinks, as Candace Pert's biomolecular investigations now show.[12] The mere direction of awareness effects change, and as the brain absorbs the movement of change, it also changes. In this manner, the organism, the person, can dance toward composure and peace or produce anxiety and chaos.

The conscious direction of awareness, as the yogic *rishis* have always known, is ultimate empowerment. When we direct our awareness in meditation, somatic explorations, and the processes of dancing, we discover that our body is not determined. It is substance, but substance with emotional intelligence—mutable and manageable—both within and curiously beyond our control.

I can create my body in dance as I mold and carve it in space; and since I and my body are one, I am creating myself; I extend my nature and my culture through my dance. This creation is a surpassing of self as any creation is, but in dance this self-surpassing brings body to mind through the medium of movement, and I become aware of my capacity to develop my body's nature as I create its culture. My body-of-action will speak my cultural commitments louder than any words.

—STIRRING and
Striking, Thickening and Saying—

THE SHAPE OF METAPHYSICS

is not a line stretching upward,
                    a fore-having holding-closed.
Though it may hold away occurring.
            Silently, it radiates throughout our body, and into
            liquid matters—
            (Trans)descendent
            points of pointillist patterns
                        and interlacing spirals:
Capers of authentic movements that begin-stop-go:
                    forward,
                            erupt-backwards,
            burst bursting under test and into persevered mass:
Clear gels and freckled
                        dislocations—hanging loose
            and gathering-in to twist-through-and-
                            leap-over a falling-down the
            slap of winter, the gleamings that land
                        earth, and world us ever.
                        Everywhere . . . melting.

Wholes and Holiness

> The Nazis made very handsome bindings and lampshades
> out of human skin.
>
> SIMONE DE BEAUVOIR, *The Ethics of Ambiguity*

In poststructural theory, wholes are dangerous. Voices are partial and situated, discrepant and differentiated. However true this may be on one level, the discourse of difference fails to recognize that not all wholes are the same. Some lead to exclusiveness, an outside that is paraded as wholesome, an inside that is rotten; the Hitler Youth organization constituted such wholesomeness. But when all wholes are suspect, fear of wholes can also totalize: The monistic absence and darkness that has often symbolized the feminine in discourses of the body can be relegated to mystery and fear in the outlawing of wholes.

Wholes are neither full nor empty by themselves; they are simply words, except as we fill them up. If all wholes are bad, what about caves and lagoons? What about the prayer masks of the Yup'ik, a focus for ceremonial community? Would we deny any possibility of community, or affective wholeness? How about our own community body? Has it gone the way of misguided individualism? In his international Butoh workshops, Akira Kasai stresses that unless we dance the community body, we are not dancing. In Fukuoka, Japan, Nobuo Harada provides another example of community building through Butoh with his group of experienced dancers and novices—*Seriyukai*. In Harada's philosophy, Butoh begins from daily life experiences, observing self and doubting every stereotype in order to grasp new relationships between the individual and the community.[13]

I understand this to mean that our dances can and should connect us to something larger than ourselves, even as we also dance for ourselves. Mihaly Csikszentmihalyi, in his psychology of optimal experience and moral choice, discovers that *differentiation* gives us the ability to move through technical difficulties and beyond genetic and social determinism, while *integration* gives us care and community. We span these two values in expressing the fullness of our identities. His recommendations for enhancing the quality of life are outlined in a dance of life that he calls *Flow*.[14]

As Derrida suggests, we should not put closure on exteriorization. But neither should we close off interiorization. Our dances collect energies as well as they disperse them. We could say that deconstruction of the objective body begins with Sartre's "the body is lived and not known,"[15] and that Kristeva carries this still further in feminism. The body may seem accessible enough as we observe it from the outside, but when it comes to subjectivity, we escape ourselves into the unknown. Sartre feels existentially alienated in the gaze of others, as later Kristeva turns to psychoanalysis and feminist deconstruction for poetized forms of self-decentering. Postmodern theorists have powerfully called into question the notion of self as a unified subject. But if the subject is indeed unfinished in its stirrings, this does not dispel all concern for the integrity of sensory experience. Subjectivity, sense, and imagination go hand in hand. Imagination, the ability to make images come to life, rides in bodily lived aesthetics, or *aisthesis*, where sense and sensitivity collide.

I Will Walk

> Intelligence supposes good will . . . and sensitivity is nothing else but the presence which is attentive to the world and to itself.
>
> SIMONE DE BEAUVOIR, *The Ethics of Ambiguity*

Reason and intuition are often companions. In whole persons, their functioning together aids argument. I know I want reason on my side when I make points that I hope others will understand, when I write and when I structure dances, or when my messy life reaches for a calm sea. Reason, intuition, and emotion branch bodily lived tensions—dispositions dispersing, crossing and thickening into the dance.

My body brings out the order in the word around me. Sometimes I feel affectively whole, and sometimes not. Dancing can present a decentered subject, Kristeva's notion of "the subject-in-process." The process-oriented descriptions of dancers confirm this, even as they also describe a desire to converge with intentions that are whole and centered. Then the movements of the feet that feel the soft grain of the wooden floor are neither fragmented nor willful. They find their way as they go, through their contact with the floor, the flexible stage, the wet grass, and the sandy beach. The body organizes its touching and moving, its hearing and craving, its gesturing past the private thoughts that separate from the din at the cocktail party, its cognizance of the roar of the airplane as it leaves the ground, and its meditative serenity in sitting and walking. Consciousness is nothing but the awareness that unifies what might otherwise be incoherent perceptions and actions, as is made clear to me in walking:

I love to walk when the sun is high and hot, and there is
Just enough breeze to ruffle my flowered skirt, soft
Against my ankles, enough to warm my eyelids when I close them.

Walking arouses gratitude in me, for the children making faces as I pass by,

As from the air a mantra of morning sounds rise up.
I will walk til stillness overcomes me, and I am awake!

Death's rattling near, who fears we have not danced enough for love.
As ever I pause to fill the holes of doubt and open my crown to the sky.
My mind grows strong in this, and tranquil with the pink of the delicate
Hedge rose resting in the crystal candy dish, where I exhale
With ease, under the shade of my back porch roof.

If perception is subject to directives that everywhere draw us past instances of intentionality, past the figure/ground of separate things —and if perception gives us partial views, as much as ear can hear, eye can see, and hand can guide—our consciousness, sometimes, nevertheless, succeeds in finishing phrases. We can deepen trust and absorb the night in sleep. Experience is more than perception, and perception itself has varying modes—active as well as receptive, also gratefully forgetful—as when we are immersed in the meditations of walking:

I especially like to walk when I have nowhere to go.
                    Walking is simpler than most dancing,
And yet the basis for all dancing. I become more
Moral when I walk—slow down—forgive my enemies—

My heart teaches me how as my feet carry on, and the
Shift of weight from one leg to another, the easy
                    Counterbalance of arms, let dissipate the
                              tensions of

Righteousness held in my body. My neck softens; my jaw—

> My voice, and my mind shift the
> Confusions that might run
> Away with themselves.
> They settle, I settle into the creature
> Comfort of my walk, and this heals me.

The intrinsic values of walking, meditation, and dancing have a common source in our body of time and movement. These are available to us when we attune to the poetics of space and pay attention to the pleasures of movement. This is body-for-self, an intrinsic matter of consciousness, not body-for-other, the presentational body we show on stage or objectify visually when we imagine what others see. The intrinsic values of movement are by definition experiential; they indicate something of value, "the particular good" that we feel and identify, as in the following phenomenological description:

> When I dance, I trust my body and enjoy the feeling of time and space coming in a different way from ordinary life. I feel my body and spirit are often becoming so energetic and calm, which I could not imagine in the beginning. My body and mind melt into the space and time and I sometimes forget where I am, who I am. I enjoy the exchange of time and space, and the breathing of others I dance with. I find and meet another "me."
> *Takane Hirai*, University of Nara, Japan, 1994

Our First Horizon

Against butter . . . the refusal to admit to a nature. If my human form has been culturally shaped in the shoes I have worn, and freed in dancing barefoot, at least I have never mistaken myself for a table. (Well maybe once.)

Nature is more than the environment around us. It is our sleeping and waking, forgetting and remembering. *In every cell nature is moving.* In our first rolling over as a baby, nature is unfolding, as it is in the repeated lifting of the baby's head. From lying on our belly, we gradually develop the power to push up onto our hands and forearms, looking around the space close to the ground, our first independently achieved horizon. Nature is there even in the curiosity that compels

us to gain a wider access to our world, as we learn how to pull ourselves up and walk. Nature is there in all our movement. It underlies
our cultural performances in daily life as on the stage. Before we
dance in formal ways, we learn how to walk, and we also see happy
babies perform little jigs as they are learning how to stand up even before walking.

Nature prefigures society and its stylizations. It sets limits, and we
push them. If there were no such thing as nature and writing (the social inscription and cultural artifact), then bodies could only be texts.
Everything would be text—so much writing and too little dancing,
with no place to rest and nothing to trust beyond the clever computer.

If we believe biology and cognitive psychology, we come into this
world through nature and we continue to unfold a nature of core potentials. This means among other things that *we can jump*. We have in
our two legs this very natural power—even within individual compromises. As humans we can jump and we can speak, and these are not
the same things, however related they might be. JUMP IN FIRST POSI-
TION, then in second, first again, then "spraddle" (in the air), land,
and "skedaddle" (get off the stage, quickly).

Somatics and Wholeness

> **When I dance I become, I connect with others, the world, and myself.**
> **When I dance my perception of time and space is different from my**
> **everyday experiences. When I dance with each breath I reach out,**
> **become a part of a bigger whole. When I dance I feel alive.**
> *Mariel Renz*, Germany, 1997

A basic concept of somatics in both psychology and integrative movement studies is the holistic idea of human beings. "Holism" is the theory that whole entities, as fundamental components of reality, have
an existence other than as the mere sum of their parts. In terms of the
body, we are more than arms and legs, more than the circulation of
the blood, more than material, more than brain, more than movement, and more than our individual psychophysical history. We function and move as more than the sum of these parts, and all the other
myriad parts of ourselves.

The transformation of holism into somatic concept often assumes
that something called "body" and something called "mind" are being

"integrated" in therapy and in movement education. But if we speak instead of body-mind integrity, we avoid metaphysical dualism, the presumed split between bodily substance and brain processes, while acknowledging that phenomenological (lived) dualisms exist. The brain is part of the whole body. Without it, the body ceases to exist. We can feel conflicts and splits of attention, even alienation from body, but this does not mean that body and brain or body and mind are functionally different or metaphysically separate entities that need to be integrated.

Movement itself may feel integrated and whole, connected and flowing, just as it can also be experienced as halting and disjointed. And dancers do describe varying levels of bodily thinking: the problems of concentration, awareness of others watching and what they might be thinking, the training of consciousness in the movement itself, not thinking ahead or behind, gaining the ability to think in the flow of present time as the effort to remember disappears into the involuntary system of learned movement. Dancers often explain this as a matter of thinking in movement:

> When I dance time stands still and moments flash by like Polaroid snapshots. I let go if the choreography is complex, and let it be. I don't "perform"—I assimilate. I am fully involved, yet I do not count. I'm not sure where I am in the music, yet I am there with it. Everything melts into one and gels. The "ends and means" disappear. I am never lost, yet replaced. I return rested.
> *Patricia Simmons*, New York, 1994

> For me, dance is a hieroglyphics of the soul: A blueprint into another way of speaking.
> *Kitty Hawkes*, New York, 1999

How could we think or speak without our body? A more circular model of the body-self recognizes how body, self, and thought entwine, even as we now know through mind-body medicine as explored in the work of Candace Pert and others that biochemical molecules circulating in our cells link what we have historically called consciousness, mind, and body.[16] The normal body includes a brain not separated from the rest; it is already and always an inseparable integration of interwoven perceptual matters, as Maxine Sheets-Johnstone explores in

"What Is It Like to Be a Brain."[17] Mind arises throughout the whole body.

Language has gotten us into a lot of trouble concerning the supposed relationship of body and mind. Body and mind are two linguistic artifacts that may be experienced as separable, as reinforced through linguistics. Mental thought processes and even transcendental phenomena interpreted variously as soul and spirit have been attached to understandings of "mind," while emotions and perceptual sensations have typically attached to the word "body." Let us bear in *mind*, however, that "body" and "mind" are words, and as such are human constructions. Body and mind are metaphysical artifacts based on experiential facts that have an inseparable integrity in the life-world. If body disappears, so does the temporalizing mind. Live performance focuses on the integrity of hand, eye, and mind in the moment of *rasa:*

> When I dance, each time is different. When I perform (*Bharata Natyam*), it first begins with my nervousness. The first five minutes I am aware of my relationship to the audience. Then I get into it and the dance just happens. I am getting more and more into my own personal enjoyment and less concerned with the people around me all the time. This is where the true aesthetic pleasure or *rasa* arises. In India we say:
>
> Where the hand goes
> the eye goes:
>
> Where the eye goes
> the mind goes:
>
> Where the mind goes
> aesthetic pleasure is created.
>
> *Parul Shah*, Baroda, India, 1997

I use the term "body-mind" to signify the integrity and soundness of our given embodied existence. Metaphysically we are body-mind integrities, whole beings, while phenomenologically we can experience fragmentation. Pragmatically, as a writer, dancer, and somatic therapist, I have access to a fundamental soundness and integrity of bodily being in my work—as we all do. We depend on this integrity being there, as the *Dasein* of existence. This is fundamental and foundational. What we find in others and ourselves at the functional foundational level—if we go deeply enough—is a metaphysic of soundness, an integrity and wholeness that can be called upon for healing.

Curiously we seek, and what we find, woven in nerve and muscle, bone and flesh, is the flush of blood and breath throughout whole systems that work in self-adjusting, self-correcting, and self-improving ways when the body-self can become alive to new options for being and change. But the journey to this somatic metaphysic is fraught with noisy experiential overlay—much dualist tension—some sweet, some fearful, fretful, and anxious. Embodied disruptions and blockages remind us that our body-mind is fundamentally whole and sound.

In our infancy we learn how to crawl, how to pull ourselves upright and to walk, even to walk well. Beverly Stokes's *Amazing Babies* research captured on video shows that our first efforts are exploratory. We make a game out of learning, and play with falling down and getting up.[18] We also like to dance in little jigs with just the right music. No one can teach us this; it is a gift that most of us can assume at root. However, we are not born equal in this matter, as our individual rates of learning show, and body-mind systems do break down if they are not tended with care. Unconsciously assumed debilitating habits, poor habits of posture and movement can cause havoc in adult comportment—fallen arches and back pain, for instance. Social pressures and self-imposed stresses also play a part in bodily disintegration. But stress and poor habits can yield to care and inculcation of healthier, more organically whole movement patterns. We might also call organic patterns "natural," and risk this term. Organic means functional, coordinated, and organized. Natural movement is organically whole, simple, and functional for that body. In this case, everyone can be graceful, and there is no one model for grace, for we all have individualized structures and gifts. Beyond received models, that of the airborne ballet, for instance, we can at least identify a common aesthetic thread: grace is not a matter of weightlessness, nor does it rest in any particular kind of movement; it is a much broader concept predicated on *care.* Care signals attentiveness to self and is also a matter of consciousness in our relationships to others and the world.

By the mid-twentieth century, women in modern dance had articulated an ethics of care and relationship in terms of the body. Martha

Graham saw that "grace in dancers is not just a decorative thing," but exists in relational matters of consciousness, as she states:

> Grace is your relationship to the world, your attitude to the people with whom and for whom you are dancing. Grace means your relationship to the stage and the space around you—the beauty your freedom, your discipline, your concentration and your complete awareness have brought you.[19]

Beauvoir also interprets bodily expression in relation to agency and the world; the body cannot to be taken for granted in terms of vitality and care (generosity): "the body itself is not a brute fact. It expresses our relationship to the world, and that is why it is an object of sympathy or repulsion. And on the other hand, it *determines* no behavior. There is vitality only by means of free generosity."[20]

Care, as explored later in *A Dance of Time Beings*, is at the root of existential metaphysics. As a first principle, it is built upon attentiveness toward oneself, concern for shared natural resources, generosity toward others, and giving back what we take from the earth. *Form*—life forms, baby forms, and body forms—will follow function, and our functioning and structure respond to care. *Patterns* of movement and mind can also become harsh dictators, rendering forms that run amuck. Functional patterns, as opposed to nonfunctional patterns, have a "somaesthetic" structure that is not fragmented and halting, a structure that *feels good* and thus demonstrates an internal organization that *is good*. Functional movement patterns are organically whole and graceful.

In *Wild Hunger*, his work on the primal roots of addiction, Bruce Wilshire points out the price we pay for failure to realize wholeness:

> Inability to realize our deepest needs and capacities for ecstatic wholeness is a failure of responsibility to ourselves, and engenders hazy, floating guilt. But guilt is noisome and must be suppressed. So we may "pop an upper." But there is more guilt when inevitably the down follows—or threatens to follow—the artificial high. Guilt can be suppressed only through another dose of the drug or the behavior, and on and on.[21]

We have so stuffed into the background the idea that it is all right to feel good that the idea actually needs to be revived. *Natural movement feels good.* That movement might be natural and feel good is a foreign concept to many people. Here we reach toward the intrinsic value of moving well. This would be called an "internal good" in value theory, one that comes into being when we feel good in an action or activity. Functional patterns flow spontaneously; they are whole and they *feel natural*—that is, satisfying in their beneficence.

> **When I dance, I am hyper-aware of my surroundings. I am connected to the floor and to others moving about me. I feel the space differently— it is the space of possibility, space to be devoured, to be sliced, eaten, embraced, flown through.**
>
> *Marilyn Bordwell*, Iowa, 1995

Coherent Speech

Sentences are whole structures, also decrees, edicts, and judgments that are handed out. I know a lot of people who have trouble getting through a sentence, or any other coherent unit of communication, without several fragmented "umms" and "ahhhs," pauses and detours—apologies. And I find that women especially apologize often, disrupting their train of thought, derailing and undermining what they want to say. In this case, neither the thought nor the movement emerges in organic wholes. It lists into feelings of unworthiness. In *Sorties*, Hélène Cixous says:

> Every woman has known the torture of beginning to speak aloud, heart beating as if to break, occasionally falling into loss of language, ground and language slipping out from under her, because for woman speaking—even just opening her mouth—in public is something rash, a transgression.[22]

It was in an undergraduate history class. I knew the answer to the professor's question and raised my hand. As I began to form the words, they shifted—no—it would not be good enough. I dropped into context and mulled about there for a moment. Another no. No, the answer didn't matter, wouldn't make a difference. I sat there, my mind clearing of all thought as the moments stretched by and everyone waited. And my words seemed worthless—empty. But I didn't say, "Pass me by," or make any cute excuse; it wasn't in me. I was caught not mattering. The words continued to wipe away the silence, backing up. Having just taken a mental vacation, I wasn't even embarrassed. In the effort to please, my answer went down the drain. No, it evaporated, and I with it. I could fling myself into dancing, but not into words.

It was a faculty assembly, and I raised my hand to speak. The president said there would not be enough time for my remarks, that the meeting was almost over. Perhaps he feared I would disagree with his explanations of why our building should be destroyed in favor of a more modern version, since I had only the day before continued to speak over him, as he repeatedly interrupted and tried to squelch my words. In any case, I stood up and told him that my comments would be brief. In less than three minutes I summarized eight clearly reasoned points in favor of my faculty's proposal to save our building. My body was singing. Had I needed more time, I would have taken it.

We had a new president and our building was under renovation for new dance facilities. The dean had just told me that she wanted me to "step aside" as chair of the dance department as soon as possible. This was after thirty years of teaching and nine years of being chair. I had been guilty, it seems, of speaking to the president and disagreeing with her. That was a no-no. This is what happens in lockstep vertical systems where you can only speak to those below you, or on your own level, or just above you, but you can't jump over power. That's a dance you just don't do. I told her I'd think about it, and then started to work with my faculty to make it impossible for her to shove me out. I actually wanted to get out of administration altogether—enjoy writing, dancing, and lazy afternoons, but I wouldn't be forced out, or told not to speak. No way.

I am a child of the universe; I deserve to be here. This yogic remedy for the fractured self-image comes to me when I most need it (and I deserve to be heard). It is repeated with centered attentiveness and a soft outward gaze that absorbs light rather than fixing objects. It is performed with the pressed together palms of the I AM pose, like at prayer, but with the head unbowed and the eyes open. Awareness. Attention. Agency. These are key terms in drawing upon our natural abilities to move well, and to live abundantly, to dance into the everyday, and to heal. Turning inward—toward silence and breath—also relieves. In wholes, we find the holy:

> **When I dance I take in all the elements of existence in a powerful uninterrupted flow that manifests a root knowing. Yet this quintessential**

knowing precedes the mind. There is the sense of being most intimate
with myself, yet the self that I am feeling extends infinitely in space and
time. I feel my breath in my body and my body feels the wind, my feet
feel the ground yet they feel the sky too. The colors, the sounds, the pain
and the ecstasy all become one in this moment, and I know that the
only I there is, is in all of this. We must not flee from our experience of
pain, but stand in its power.
Christina Fraleigh, San Francisco, 1994

I know disabled people who dance. They do not have what we ordinarily think of as a whole body, but people prove every day that they have
access to unbroken wholeness in the midst of seeming incomplete-
ness. The man without legs and the paraplegic can dance because
they want to; without apology, they give undivided attention to the
dance they are doing.

Dancing is not getting up any time painlessly like a speck of dust
blown around in the wind. Dancing is when you rise above both worlds,
tearing your heart to pieces and giving up your soul.
Rumi, The Tavern of Rumi

Moving Off-Center

The movement of the mind, whether it be called thought or will, always
starts up in the darkness.

SIMONE DE BEAUVOIR, *The Ethics of Ambiguity*

The beauty of fractals in chaos theory is how they take us to the wavy
edges of ponds, the rough heights of mountains, the pulsing of water-
falls and cell membranes. When we dance, we also move on unpredictable edges, crossing from chaos to order and back as if by osmosis;
from one sensation to the next, we lean on the edges of movement.

Much as I love the center of quiet sitting, I love the precipice near
falling when I dance, the moment before landing when the world goes
away, and the suspense at the top of a jump. Drama is born through
these cracks in time.

I enter this crack below in the guise of Tanztheater, sifting through
gesture, song, and speech to reconstruct my *Miss America* biography
of 1975. I conceive it as an interrupted performance of popular culture and history, soma, self, and gender. The *poiesis*, or making of the

whole, is a self-study in process since 1975 that hopes to test fixed understandings of the self, even as phenomenology is an interactive method of self-reflection and transformation. I put my political body on stage and my historical body materializes; I thicken my body's national constitution, and my everyday dances experience their uncertainty. Rudolph Laban's initiation of Tanztheater sounds in the background. Should I not also see him in light of learning and transformation?

Donning my nation's mask
Of hope and competition—

              Win, I shout, Win!
              Oh Beauty Triumph!

No, cries my labor,
              But I will not fail you.

I MISS AMERICA

I, MISS AMERICA, arrange the stage
        and swing from the rope that hangs from the grid,
            holding the loop at the end.
Running and jumping into the air,
      I play, climb, and hang—
            open the trunk, musty and black with sequins,
               as the theater darkens.

Analyzing relationships of Dance, Sound, and Word (Tanz, Ton, Wort), *or what he called "the trinity of Gesture, Song, and Speech," could the brilliant and handsome Count (Rudolph von Laban, 1879–1958) ever have imagined a Miss America in his kinesphere? Miss America wondered. Then she read about Laban's advocacy of Tanztheater at the Second Dancers' Congress in Essen, Germany, in June 1928.*

I light a candle and climb the rope
Miss Arkansas, Miss Alabama
(Burt Parks wears combat boots)
Then lower myself onto the stage.

"Fight. Fight. Fight-fight-fight." Cheering for America, "Rise and shout, the Cougars are out." Sondra Fraleigh dances *Miss America* (1975). Photograph by June Burke.

Red and White Striped Pants/Bell Bottoms/Sneakers/
 Glittering stars glued to my midnight-blue torso.

Starbody Still.
Tanktop Tank.

Miss Mississippi.
Ohio in a heap on the floor,
Stars and stripes the body.

> (*In 1971 Don McLean sang*)

BYE, BYE MISS AMERICAN PIE,
drove my Chevy to the levee
but the levee was dry.

> (*As in 1975, I danced*)

Arm-over-arm,
POM-POM IN YOUR EYE,
Gold sequin pasties,
how the twirler kicked high.

> (*"No matter how scary life got," McLean wrote,*
> *"I could depend on Hopalong Cassidy."*)
> (*And he sang*)

Them good old boys
were drinkin' whisky and rye,
singin' this'll be the day that I die.
This'll be the day that I die.

> (*I pranced*)

Rise and Shout the Cougars are out
(Dig-right, Pom, Dig-right, Pom,
Dig-turn, Pom, Dig-turn, Pom)
along the trail to fame and glory.

> (*He wrote his ode to Cassidy.*)

The bad men fell, the good guys lived on.
The ladies touched your hand but never kissed . . .
I've always liked black and I loved your clothes.
My hat's off to you, Hoppy.

I skip and jump rope in time to Burt Park's song, wearing an antique starched white underslip that Sarah brought me from France and my fuzzy old pink house slippers. My jump rope is red, white, and blue.

Tie a yellow ribbon round the old oak tree . . .
Dum de dum, dum, dum, if you still love me . . .

> Long-short, Long-short, Long-short, Long.
> Step-hop, Step-hop, Hop-a-Long.

Cross-and-uncross the jump rope.
How—do—you—spell Miss-is-si-ppi?
Capital M: i‑s‑s‑i‑s‑s‑i‑p‑p‑i.
Fudge, Fudge, Tell the Judge:
(*Over-the-hands, Hop-on-one-leg*)
Mama has a newborn ba-by.

At the 1928 Congress, Laban stressed the relationship of dance and drama.
Mary Wigman (1886–1973), who had once been Laban's student and later be-
came his strongest rival, stressed "absolute dance." For her, dance was an intrin-
sic matter and space a living, breathing reality. Through Laban and Wigman the
physical culture that consumed Europe and America in the late nineteenth and
early twentieth centuries enjoyed an extraordinary success. Their work resonated
widely in early modernism. Hitler's Germany, preoccupied with a racist physical
imperative, made use of the gestural turn of the times in massive political rallies,
swastikas, and salutes. Wigman sought permission from authorities for Jews to
study at her school.[23]

COMBINE *your first cat's first name*
with your mother's maiden name,
then dance your story.
THE DRUM MAJOR'S HAT makes the still body shine,
leads the band astray with talent contests and hot tickets.
Most people she had to talk to,
she said,
then watch their solos.
BAD, *just bad.*
OBLIVIOUS to the beat: "Give us some style, folks,
and don't just play with yourself."
"Ah-hah"! through this hell-of-a-day.
Goldstar Whittaker,
white fringe on the tush—
Give us your PEP, *your* PEP, *your* PEP.
GIVE US A *"P" with step-twist, cartwheel-and-splits.*
Left foot forward and don't look down.
Lift the right arm high (as you lift the ribs),
CIRCLE the hand over the head. Watch out.
This time look to the back and around the space.

The 1930 Dancers' Congress called for government founding of a Conservatory of Dance equal to the other arts, a revitalization of the amateur practice of modern dance and its inclusion in school curricula. Goebbels answered by founding the German Master Institute for Dance in Berlin in 1930, emphasizing equal status for modern dance, ballet, and national dances—and requiring classes in National Socialist ideology. For credentials, dancers would have to prove their Aryan origins.[24] *This was not the German dance that Wigman had struggled for, but nevertheless she remained to face a difficult future, as other artists left Germany.*

FRINGE, flip-flip and flip.
Iowa I agreed.
Tom-tom created
flip-flip abortions and officers
confronted the public, longer than the ruled
floating buffer zone.

WHAT'S TAKING SO LONG in JonBenet's unsolved murder? Eleven weeks after the murder of the child beauty queen in 1997 and twenty-two years after the 1975 Miss America pageant of my Miss America *dance, I reflect back. "I think this dance is about Miss America dying," my seven-year-old daughter said after seeing my dance.*

Now the lipsticked children are dying.
The parents still aren't talking,
And the cops are taking the heat.
Experts wonder if the killer will ever be caught.
                    "Bye, bye Miss American pie . . ."
Clinic retreat, stretched in reclining.
Legs leg. Remove the fuzzy pink
Slippers to slip between the legs.
Everybody knows her name. She . . .
Does not like to feel herself confined.

From sea to shining ringlets.
More stars slide the slip contest.
Parade her talents and gowns.
Measurements 36, 24, 36.
Charming where she chooses to live
And tools made for her purpose.

"From Sea to Shining Sea." Sondra Fraleigh in *Miss America*. Photograph by June Burke.

She dances soft-shoe,
plays Mozart and "Tea for Two,"
Twirls fire baton in a white sequin bathing suit.

> *"Lights out.*
> *Now bring them up slowly."*

She wafts, she breathes and curls
her shawl around her,

sits quietly,
looks into her hands,
while the looped rope swings.

A SELF-INFLICTED WOUND—*that false generosity of the dance equipped with absolute wisdom bends over her in the mirror. How she runs with bouquets of plastic flowers and scatters her gift. And who is the fairest game? Show me. Show me your tits and ass, the fawning voices insist. Give me your tired.*

Disheartened, I Miss America.
"Downtrodden" stream our lovely voices
in vibrato, "hoed-down and haloed."

Would we rather die than see Old Glory fall?

"My own America
   (*My father sang as a patriot*)
may God preserve her liberty . . .
and help us save democracy—
   (*'Lay that pistol down babe'*)
the whole world through."

Liberty is female, I hear,
and her body is judged—Junior Miss,
Baby Miss, Miss and Mrs.—
but no Ms. AMERICA.

AS BEAUTY GRASPS FOR VICTORY,
she lifts her apple aloft.

Statued liberty—to bite this fruit and multiply—
to be alone, the one, and cherish home.

Who will love her regardless?

The apple falls from her mouth.
Miss Texas is fainting.
She lifts the golden gown around her
Wraps her head and bows it down.
She sits under the bridge.
Her arms cradle the baby
In the loving gaze of the audience.

Quite aside from Laban's efforts to keep dance integrated into theater, he at-
tempted to change society through choreographing body rhythms for amateurs
in large choral arrangements of "free dance." He also encouraged people to dance
in fresh air for the love of movement, free from the constraints of society and
clothing. I love to leaf through my books from the early modern dance—to visit
free expression cavorting in the buff. The messiness of Laban's free dance and his
communal choirs based on flux and change did not make them ideal for represen-
tation of political power.[25] *Nevertheless, Laban got along for a while within the*
rising politics of Fascism.

MISS CONGENIALITY

SHE SMILES
GETS ALONG well with others:
Everybody knows her name.

Parks pauses excitedly at the end:

"Here she comes—Miss . . ."
In the swimsuit contest, I lift my lamp
(beside the golden door . . .)
Indiana, Utah, Arizona, New York."
Her bubble is beautiful.

In September 1999, it was decided that Miss America contestants would no
longer have to swear that they had never been married, or had an abortion, or

given birth. This scandalous decision may cause some states to withdraw from the contest, the newspapers report: After all, "when they sing 'here she comes,' everyone knows this is our ideal woman."

Miss America sat on a wall
Miss America had a great fall
All the king's horses and all the king's men
Who will put her together again?

LOCKED UP IN TIME:
I Miss America . . . hanging by a thread

ON THE EVE OF 2002
How the brains of neglected children show
Neurons missing by the billions.
Squadrons of assassins,
Their children, ours and theirs who
Sing from the dust of limbic wreckage.

How the burning city
Twists into the body.
Fabled towers
Refigure rusty parts,
And smiles asunder.

What shattering falls,
       What seizure in those hours
When the pose of innocence dropped, in
              Footsteps of blossoms, and bombs.

THEN LISTEN HOW IN 1950
With waves receding down the cleft
Of time, eyes of steady quiet
See a young December sky.

> *How often at night when the heavens are bright*
> *with the light from the glittering stars*
> *have I stood there amazed and thought as I gazed*
> *that their glory exceeds that of ours.*

Her father sings this cowboy verse
HOME (*home on the range. . .*)

Locked up in time:
I miss America . . . hanging now by a string.

(He sings of home, in the distance
the purple mountains,
and the antelope, as her hand moves
slowly.)

where the graceful white swans
go gliding along
like a maid in a heavenly dream.
In slow motion, who is lifting her hand to her mouth?
Looking past the audience? Past the exit? Past the smoking towers?

After the dancers' leaving,
He sings in his crumpled Stetson
After the stars are gone;
And muddy shoes
Many a heart that is aching,
if you could read them all;
A song written by Chas Harris in 1920.
Many the hopes that have vanished,
After the ball.

LOCKED UP IN TIME:
I miss America, my great-grandmother Tennessee's black
sequin dress . . . hanging now by a thread.

Where seldom is heard . . .
and the skies are not . . .
In a covered wagon,
she had a cancerous breast removed
without anesthetic.

Tennessee. Sondra Fraleigh in *Miss America* wears her great-grandmother's dress, with the elusive metaphysics of identity, nostalgia, voice, and visible show. Photograph by June Burke.

IN 2003

It rings from the rafters in Grand Central Station:

> *Where seldom is heard such discouraging words,*

and the dancers,
                    framed in the light from the windows,
move like angels overhead.

The sequins of Tennessee's dress were sewn
in clusters on the black silk netting,
open to the waist in the back.

Oh give me a land where the bright diamond
sands flow peacefully down to the plain.
I would not exchange my home on the range
for all of your cities of gold.

Ruth Way in "Two Figures" from *Enclave,* a dance theater film codirected and produced by British dancer Ruth Way and visual/digital artist Russell Frampton. *Enclave* uses new digital technologies to consider the need to preserve personal and social identities. Photograph by Russell Frampton.

PART II · Becoming

4 | Anti-Essentialist Trio

Through Simone de Beauvoir, I understand how biology, ontology, and politics are connected, and the biological politics of domination that puts nature and indeed all forms of life in harm's way. I study Beauvoir's work here in close proximity to Maurice Merleau-Ponty, a contemporary of hers, and Judith Butler, a contemporary of mine. These three comprise a trio of related but significantly divergent phenomenological critiques of determinism. Through them we can see how the concept of determinism shifts back and forth, how it is performed. Questions of tradition and gender in ballet also shift around essentialist thinking. I provide a short sketch of ballet history to foreground the postmetaphysical reversals of balletic conventions in dances by Karol Armitage, Twyla Tharp, and Alonzo King as I also critique the inversion of classicism in the *Swan Lake* of the Motion Pictures Dance Company. I question bodily mastery involved in the mastery of nature and introduce somatic ideas of matching the body in dance rather than mastering it. My writing presents an anti-essentialist performance and critique of metaphysics.

Setting the Stage

Beauvoir advanced the original anti-essentialist view on the condition of woman, namely, that she is not determined by her biology. She set the stage for discussions to follow. Now, more than fifty years after her groundbreaking work began, we might well ask whether claims for or against biological determinist arguments in feminism are established on a false premise, namely that women have been (or now are) oppressed on the basis of their bodies. Arguments against biological determinism set the terms of the debate in assuming that women are physically weaker than men, and noting the fact that women bear children. Are women slaves to the species, then? Arguments surrounding determinism also assume that males are inherently aggressive, that this is a fact of biology through genetics, notwithstanding that aggressiveness in males and females may be a socially conditioned phenomenon, indeterminately situated in biology and contingent upon individual variation. In her analysis of this problem for feminism, Allison Jaggar points out that "arguments from animal behavior to biologically determined male dominance are equally inadequate."[1]

Social construction of the body and gender through performativity and writing is explored extensively by Judith Butler, especially in *Bodies That Matter* (1993). Susan Bordo is similarly concerned for the body as a social artifact, but with attention to context as well as text, and biological locatedness. Bordo's work on engendering the body provides a critique of Butler.[2] The cultural "reworking" of biology is taken up by Sheets-Johnstone in her feminist analysis, as she studies primate behavior throughout *The Roots of Power* (1994) and seeks to uncover prevailing conceptions of power and its uses. She calls for new conceptions of power that move from phallocentric accounts toward a more accurate understanding of "animate form and gendered bodies."[3]

Sociology lacks adequate means for entering these debates. *It brackets out nature*, as sociologist Anna Yeatman recognizes: "The central dualistic convention in sociology is that which counterpoises the terms 'social' and 'natural.'" Sociology elaborates social terms to cover "all aspects of human existence." What is "natural" (nature) is simply a residual of logic, and a limiting term.[4] If there is nothing natural about the body, it is easy enough to turn it into an artifact of social categories and of writing. Here bodies are abstract, not "lived," only "produced" or "written"—as "producing the body," the cultural body, and "writing the body" in descriptive text become linguistic conventions in poststructural feminist discourse. Debates that revolve around biological determinism continue to take on new colors, but they need to shift even further, fronting new freedoms for both sexes. Clearly some issues are still with us. Camille Paglia's blunt and layered work on art and decadence, *Sexual Personae* (1990), is a radical version of biological determinism—essentialism. This is clear throughout her work and in the following: "When I cross the George Washington Bridge or any of America's great bridges, I think: *men* have done this. Construction is a sublime male poetry. . . . If civilization had been left in female hands, we would still be living in grass huts." She believes that humans are helpless in the thrall of their sexuality and nature: "After the bomb, nature will pick up the cards we have spilled, shuffle them, and begin her game again." She writes of nature as fate, sex as the natural in man, and society as an artificial defense against nature's power. Feminism, she believes, has overstepped both nature and fate.[5]

The noted American anthropologist Helen Fisher untangles a recent perspective on woman and nature in *The First Sex—The Natural Talents of Women and How They Are Changing the World.* She asserts that girls will never be as obsessed with sports as boys because evolution wires women to be cooperators, not competitors. "For girls, peace, harmony, social stability, and noncombative, noncompetitive play are essential to having fun. . . . Boys play war." Throughout life, girls and women show more tendencies toward nurturing activities. She sees this as linked to the production of estrogen; and, as has been my concern, she also sees the problem of trying to prove that everything in human behavior is circumscribed by socialization. Her work shows that biology and culture go hand in hand. This should not discount, however, that values other than nurturance motivate women.[6]

A postmetaphysical view would assert that we should not universalize "woman." Many desire to compete, for instance, and in ways that unsettle cultural stereotypes of women as "the weaker sex," as Colette Dowling, author of *The Frailty Myth* (2000), is showing. I venture into the anti-essentialist arguments because they lead us, in their refutation of biological determinism, to an understanding of ourselves as "time beings," unfinished, indeterminate works, artifacts in progress. The question of whether anti-essentialist positions are too extendable also motivates me. If I can fly in my dreams and dances, I nevertheless do not want to fly off ten-story buildings.

As a woman, I am influenced by my biology, but as I learn from Beauvoir, the first existential feminist, "biology is not destiny." Beauvoir was the first philosopher to categorically reject any notion of natural gender hierarchy based on biology. She also traces women's role in societies throughout history, noting that the only cultures in which women were feared and revered were primitive, agrarian ones. We know now that Goddess (partnership) cultures were not based on fear and were less primitive than supposed, as Marija Gimbutas, Riane Eisler, and other cultural researchers are beginning to make clear from Neolithic records that were unavailable to Beauvoir, having only come to light after World War II.[7]

Beauvoir links the development of tools and the rise of the concept of private property to male control of work and ownership of women. The progression of male dominance examined by Eisler in her examination of metallurgy and male supremacy supports the conclusion that the first implements were not knives and clubs for killing others, as we have been taught. Gold and copper were used ornamentally and for religious purposes in Neolithic agrarian cultures that worshiped the Goddess. The use of tools and metals in developing ever more effective technologies of destruction accompany what Friedrich Engels calls "the world historical defeat of the female sex."[8]

War and other forms of social violence were essential instruments for replacing partnership with dominator models of behavior that support slavery. Beauvoir is concerned with the enslavement of woman as other, as she turns to the Hegelian master-slave dialectic, applying it to male-female relationships. Merleau-Ponty also relies on master-slave discourse in his explorations of sexuality, otherness, and shame in *The Phenomenology of Perception*. Beauvoir sums up Merleau-Ponty's work on sexuality as well Sigmund Freud's. But unlike these male authors, her discussions of sexuality give an extensive factual account of the physiology of reproduction in humans and several other species, which she sees as founded in the very "nature" of being.[9]

Woman has always been inferior because of the social conditions in which she finds herself, Beauvoir contends. Woman has been made the "Other," the absolute other, never the "fellow being" of man who might see him as the other in a partnership of reciprocity and equality. Woman is shackled to procreation and reproduction through patriarchal ownership, which inhibits her cultural creation and production: "To be situated at the margin of the world is not a position favorable for one who aims at creating anew. . . . Personal accomplishment is almost impossible in the human categories that are maintained collectively in an inferior situation."[10] Upon its French publication in 1949, *The Second Sex* was radical in a country that had granted

women suffrage just five years prior and guillotined a woman for performing abortions one year before that. The book's initial racy aura
and dangerous politics met with harsh criticism: "Unsatisfied, cold,
priapic, nymphomaniac, lesbian, a hundred times aborted, I was
everything, even an unmarried mother," Beauvoir recalls.[11] Today
Beauvoir's work still provides a basis for gender equity and main-
stream feminist rejection of biological determinism. Current feminists
have problematized Beauvoir's shaking of the assumed nature of
femininity, however—"When we are women, we are always mothers," says Lucy Irigaray. Recent feminist concerns have filled in Beauvoir's silence on race, class, and ethnicity. Bordo's arguments against
the postmodern deconstructive "retreat from female otherness"
would indicate that much of Beauvoir's work might be appropriately
resuscitated today in the aftermath of postmodern fragmented identities and a pragmatic need for political action on behalf of women.[12]

We might also trace back to Beauvoir's role in the current feminist
ambivalence toward female values of empathy and mothering. The
hostility toward women who are not politically correct (who are not
career-minded ladder climbers), which is demonstrated in the mother-
hating currents of some contemporary feminism, would hardly describe Beauvoir's position. Many of Beauvoir's analyses remain current. She exposes the hypocrisy of societies that would outlaw abortion
and make contraception difficult to obtain, then neglect unplanned
children born into poverty and broken families. She champions the importance of women's economic independence and freedom of consciousness and career. Hers is a utopian vision of a world that is gen-
der/power neutral, an ideal that is still in progress (and under debate).

Through Beauvoir I first tested the dance of existential freedom
and began to explore its limits. I learned that I am not determined by
my body, neither my particular biology nor my gender. Certainly I am
female. This is a physical fact, but there is something fundamentally
and culturally constituted beyond this fact, and it is this: I have
learned how, and continue to learn how, to be a woman in my time,
changing through time in my way, in dances that daily reinstate or
challenge my culture's norms. In other words, our socialized and gendered reality is constituted through acts of speech, of gesture and
movement, of dress and dreams, and every manner of our being in
the world. As Beauvoir first described the anti-essentialist claim of

feminism, "One is not born, but, rather, becomes a woman." She established one of feminism's enduring corporeal artifacts.

Trio

I have selected Beauvoir, Merleau-Ponty, and Butler for anti-essentialist collisions across time, principally because each has contributed pivotal positions on questions of embodiment, culture, and nature that have had consequences for feminist discourse and existential phenomenology, particularly its historical and ongoing development of an ontology of bodily being. These three philosophers comprise an anti-essentialist trio on the question of biological determinism that spans a fifty-year history of ontological feminism and phenomenology initiated by Beauvoir in 1949. Questions on determinism propel me into the present trio. How free are we to constitute the page-stage-space and body of our dancing, to socially construct the body, to construct gender?

The anti-essentialist trio would set us free from nature's boundaries and from biology in many respects. We will see how they move together and apart, and consider whether the performers substitute social for biological determinism in their positions. Butler, a prime mover in contemporary discourse on "performativity" (a word she has helped to popularize), enters the space first.

She wears a strange mask, half formed,
But malleable, so she can stretch it across
Her face to erase her features
When she wants to. Over time,
A new mask coalesces.

Butler's more recent feminist phenomenology extends Beauvoir's original anti-essentialist argument. Butler explains how we actually "perform" our gender, constituting our identity through stylized repetition of acts, and how we might think of this as a "stylization of the body." Repetitive actions are also marks of ritual. Butler marks the ritualistic in the everyday; her perspective (parallel to that of the early postmodern dance) allows us to see how the stylization of theater dance is only a further degree—or framing—of everyday rituals of which we are seldom aware. Significantly, Butler connects back to Beauvoir who first wrote of gender as a historical situation. She also draws from Merleau-Ponty's famous discussion of nature and culture when he questions the naturalness of the human species (as we soon see).

Butler stretches forward even as she
Moves backstage toward Beauvoir
To gender as historical,
Butler adds stylization, to the body as history,
Ritual repetitions in the everyday.
She draws energy for her movements
From Merleau-Ponty and questions the natural.
Flesh is matter and to matter is to mean.
Bones symbolize emptiness.
Love is content and justice is form.

Like Beauvoir and Merleau-Ponty, Butler writes of the gendered body as a historical, cultural entity in sparkling solos of appearances that separate from nature and also exit the trio at times. It is not that she dismisses nature altogether, but she brackets it in order to unsettle common notions concerning nature's inalterability. If Beauvoir is concerned to articulate gender/power relations, Butler is more specifically concerned with the cultural and legal enforcement of gender/power relations: "Gender is not scripted on the body, and neither is it determined by nature, language, the symbolic or the overwhelming history of patriarchy. Gender is what is put on, invariably, under constraint, daily and incessantly, with anxiety and pleasure."[13]

Butler's dance helps me to understand the elasticity of our material, concrete existence, as it also sets in motion a direction that desires to "unsettle" matter along with nature. Butler hopes to "free matter" from its metaphysical and political lodgings, pointing toward "new ways for bodies to matter."[14] She mirrors Beauvoir in this hope. Unlike Beauvoir, however, the body Butler's script produces bypasses history and biology; her primary concern is with forced iteration of norms.

Dodging the physical constraints of embodiment,
Butler's "unsettling" of matter transcends
Matter (material nature) altogether.
Here her dance nears a vanishing point.
If gender "is not scripted on the body,"

(As she says)
Is gender somehow disembodied?
Written in the bones of everyday dances?
Script waiting to be written?
Inborn music?

The script-body that Butler produces, having its birth and foundations in philosophy, agitates material nature but at the same time does not want women to be dematerialized. Butler effectively traces Plato's rhetorical deprivation of feminine presence. Her section, "Formless Femininity," in *Bodies That Matter*, exposes Plato's views of the feminine as "receptacle," without substance or shape. Butler ties this to Luce Irigaray's suggestion that the entire history of femininity is bound up in the problem of "receptivity."[15]

Would this be its history in philosophic and psychoanalytic script? The "entire" history of feminism has to be much larger and more pragmatic than the play of writing and philosophical script. Butler does not distinguish between receptivity and formlessness; there is an assumed linkage of receptivity, formlessness, lack, absence, and passivity, as these are often interchanged in feminist discourse and phenomenology. In its zeal to explain the active nature of perception, phenomenology rightly points out that consciousness is not passivity. But should we assume that the passive equals the receptive, or that either is necessarily negative?

Receptivity, like darkness, is aesthetically valuable, a graceful interval in consciousness that relinquishes willful control, promoting fullness and ease in action. Its quiescent or passive moments are necessary suspensions in complete actions. It would seem a mistake to get stuck in extremes of action or inaction, as Doris Humphrey (1895–1958) cautions in her metaphysics of dance: Apollo at the top of the movement, or Dionysus at the bottom, can lock into their characters. Movement is the dynamic living arc between these two deaths. Falling on the wave of a breath and not getting stuck, good dancers can recover their momentum; or they can employ "brave falling" and "trustworthy catching," as Bill T. Jones updates Humphrey's metaphysics of "fall and recovery" in explaining the qualities he looks for in dancers.[16]

Receptivity is part of a reciprocal cycle necessary to healing and to the creation of community. Most generally, receptivity defines an alert and listening space in consciousness, a quality of attention to others and one's world—even in its tendency to draw upon what is called "negative space" or open space in sculpture. This would be the formless space that Butler refers to above. Visual perspective would distinguish this from "positive space," form, or solid, filled-in space. As negative space, the feminine is *visualized* as a spacious vacancy—the "lack" that Beauvoir, Butler, and Irigaray rightly identify as problematic. The feminine is even portrayed sexually as an "obscene hole," Jean-Paul Sartre's characterization of feminine sexuality in *Being and Nothingness,* his phenomenological ontology and psychoanalytic.[17]

Emptiness without measure,
How the soft words erase her.
Deep down, her
Grace or negative space?

If she is spacious and
receptive, so is he;

If he is active substance,

        so is she; both dance

—paged and staged—

       Electrically alive and spacious.

If presence implicates absence,
By what delicate color do they meet?

So much of what is interesting in art is how absence is called forth: silence in music, space in architecture, poetry, and dance. Dance begins where words end—in movement both cognitive and precognitive, kinaesthetically alert and kinespherically intelligible.

Butler extends the original insights of Beauvoir and Merleau-Ponty concerning the influence of culture on gender, but unlike them, the limits she sees are less important than the complexities of the conditions under which sexuality is assumed (performed) culturally. She does not view "performativity" as a free theatrical device for self-presentation; it is not the same as freely assumed performance. Constraint compels performativity. In "Phantasmatic Identification and the Assumption of Sex" Butler looks at our tendency to believe that sexuality is either constructed (in some sense freely assumed), or determined (as fixed). She moves quickly past these to her identification of performativity as enforced and normative. Along the way, she produces a critique of Lacan and Freud, proposing to account for what can and cannot be constructed.[18]

She crisscrosses the stage at wide angles:
Sex is both given and assumed, her movements say,
But its performative assumption
Happens as a reiteration
Of hegemonic norms under threat of law.

At this point, Beauvoir enters the dance more actively, wearing a reversible mask, freely designed. While her existentialism objects to the "reduction" of woman to her biology, her multidisciplinary approach also studies and respects woman's biology. She specifically seeks the facts of feminine biology and reproduction. If gender is not determined by nature (biology) for Beauvoir, it nevertheless finds its condition there: "The enslavement of the female to the species and the limitations of her various powers are extremely important facts; the body of woman is one of the essential elements in her situation in the world. But that body is not enough to define her as a woman." Clearly, biology is important, but it is not everything. Feminine agency, the real process toward freedom, is more: "There is no true living reality except as manifested by the conscious individual through activities and in the bosom of a society."[19] "No true living reality except . . . society"? This construction is exaggerated—even by Beauvoir's own standards, as she makes clear throughout her book that limits are everywhere imposed on the body and living psyche of woman. But Beauvoir understandably makes the hard case against essentialist views of woman's nature: to move perception of the human situation beyond biological boundaries, to call society to task, and to urge women to employ their freedom.

Merleau-Ponty does not specifically discuss gender, although it becomes apparent in his discussion on sex in *The Phenomenology of Perception* that his perception of sexuality is incomplete. Butler's phenomenology and Elizabeth Grosz's critique of corporeal theories ascertain values in Merleau-Ponty's work for feminist discourse: Butler believes he places history, hence culture, over nature in conceiving the body, and Grosz agrees with his nondualist treatment of the body.[20] My reading draws upon Merleau-Ponty's inconsistencies regarding the nature/culture question. He does not dismiss nature, even as he contextualizes the question. David Abram in *The Spell of the Sensuous* (1996) emphasizes Merleau-Ponty's closeness to nature. As Abram sees it, Merleau-Ponty's sense of wonder at the events and powers that surround us in the natural world sent philosophy "on its way to ecology" and provided a vital foundation for current understandings of the participatory nature of perception.[21]

Metaphysics of Sex

Butler draws one side of Merleau-Ponty's
Nature-culture fusion
Into her movement.
Beauvoir skirts Merleau-Ponty's view of nature

              And incorporates it
              With a juxtaposition of woman's
                      possibilities:

              Like man's,
              Woman's nature is not a completion
              But an unfinished becoming.[22]
              Her sex enclosed
              And inside out.

Regarding nature and sexuality, there is a telling passage from Merleau-Ponty that would be difficult for Beauvoir and Butler to ignore:

> Why is our body, for us, the mirror of our being unless because it is a *natural self*, a current of given existence, with the result that we never know whether the forces which bear us on are its or ours—or with the result rather that they are never entirely either its or ours. There is no outstripping of sexuality any more than there is any sexuality enclosed within itself.[23]

Here Merleau-Ponty almost disengages from the anti-essentialist theme of the trio, defining body in terms of the natural self (his emphasis), a mirrored current of "given existence," as he uses mimesis doublethink to give texture to his phrasing.

Merleau-Ponty
Masks himself with mirrors,
With mimesis and reflection,
Doubling of vision and perceptual play.

Sexuality cannot be "outstripped," he says above. And why would we want to? Sex moves beyond controls and enclosures, he says. As part of its practice? I think not. Rather, there is the sense in which sex does close in on itself, enfold space, unfold it, embrace, spread out, and touch. Luce Irigaray's feminist psychoanalytic philosophy describes a metaphysically layered female sexuality—of depth and thickness, space and time—all touching:

> Our depth is the thickness of our body, our all touching itself. Where top and bottom, inside and outside, in front and behind, above and below are not separated, remote, out of touch. . . . Erection is no business of ours: we are at home on the flatlands. We have so much space to share . . . so many voices to invent in order to express all of us everywhere, even in our gaps, that all the time there is will not be enough.[24]

Never out of sight, Merleau-Ponty contradicts his helplessness in the face of nature, "the forces which bear us on," and dominates the trio: He sets man against nature: "Man is a historical idea and not a natural species." Merleau-Ponty's statement has been used a lot, and by both Beauvoir and Butler, but he tempers it more than they. I notice that Merleau-Ponty does not deny the facticity of nature; he just separates from it temporarily, as he also does in the following: "Indeed the natural world presents itself as existing in itself over and above its existence for me." "The birth of being" for him begins with affective life in such compelling emotions as desire and love. Is affective being beyond nature then? He sees human existence situated between nature and culture as "the transformation of contingency into necessity by the act of carrying forward." Here he dances not only toward biological evolution in what gets "carried forward," but toward one of his important existentials—"freedom."[25]

Merleau-Ponty's description of nature moves in abstractions and inconsistencies that alternately cover and discover it. He is, however, consistent with an overall nondualist thesis. He spirals inward to place consciousness clearly in the indivisible unity of body and mind. This we find in his section on "The Body as Expression, and Speech": "The body is not an object. . . . It is always something other than what it is, always sexuality and at the same time freedom, rooted in nature at the very moment when it is transformed by cultural influences." Merleau-Ponty is clear about the interchange of nature and culture within the body, and he is less a social determinist than the other two performers in this trio, as when he also calls the body "a 'natural' subject, a provisional sketch of my total being."

On the way toward architecture,
A-Being-Sketched,
Stretches toward metaphysics.
Allows for contradiction.
Leaping past the partial spectator
Through natural and social worlds.

> We have discovered, with the natural and social worlds the truly transcendental, which is not the totality of constituting operations whereby a transparent world, free from obscurity and impenetrable solidity, is spread out before an impartial spectator, but that ambiguous life in which the forms of transcendence have their *Ursprung*.[26]

Ursprung is a favorite term of existentialism, used by Heidegger to signify origin. It is also a movement, a "leap" already contained in beginnings. Merleau-Ponty sums up this passage on a cognitive and experiential level: "I know myself only in my ambiguity,"[27] a term further textured by Beauvoir in her *Ethics of Ambiguity*.

The audience follows this dance from the phenomenal to the metaphysical and is left floating in the air—in existential ambiguity at the height of the *Ursprung*. But "ambiguity" (we see in the next instant) comes dressed in dancer's clothes in the phenomenological analytic and paradox of "time": *Time*, the origin, perpetuity, and erasure of all stories and dances. Merleau-Ponty passes into "the horizon of time" as he extends the "visual sketch" of optics and material art.

Vision spans the near and the horizonal distance.
But tactile kinesthesia cannot distance;
It touches only what is near.

Over time the near and far blend:
Sight, sound, and music will merge in consciousness,
Mirroring the movements of dance.

Music and dance cannot be revisited unless they are performed again and again; nevertheless, they are realized in the concrete present, sometimes remembered and preserved as corporeal artifacts. Movement and sound cannot be sketched or painted in the singular performance that pins down the *Ursprung* once and for all. Performances come and go. Recordings (CDs, videos, and the like) capture something of the performance, but they are not the original thing. Sketches and paintings are originals headed in the direction of immortality, but even they are time beings. They will be interpreted in ever new contexts, historically. Merleau-Ponty understands that being is a fluid dance, not a solid, and that change allows for, calls for, ambiguity. The temporal dimension of existence moves beyond logos:

> We must return to the cogito in search of a more fundamental Logos than that of objective thought. . . . If we rediscover time beneath the subject, and if we relate to the paradox of time those of the body, the world, the thing, and other people, we shall understand that beyond these there is nothing to understand.[28]

At this point, the performers might walk off feeling complete and triumphant, stop dead in their tracks, giggle, move on, or fall slowly down. This section finishes with an "if" about time. If one is listening/reading/looking/ being touched by the ecorelational and metaphysical level of Merleau-Ponty's thought, one finds calm, and the lights narrow to a single spot as he and Beauvoir exit to leave the American alone on stage.

Butler dances around the notion that sex and gender can be separated from nature, that bodies materialize as products of culture in political practices. She asks, "through what regulatory norms is sex itself materialized," circling bodily materialization of sex into the behest of regulatory norms. Heterosexual imperatives enforce and materialize bodies their way, she believes, and politics decides which bodies will matter. Butler troubles the material waters with sex and gender, as the music loops to repetitive phrases in a new key. She argues that gender is mainly a product of cultural performativity within the domain of discourse, and that it might be multiplied beyond duets. The kinds of duets danced out in society have a heterosexist bias— greater aesthetic variety needs to flourish. On the margins of the stage, she strips down to "matter" in the final episode of the dance to convince us that our bodies/gender/sex might be reconstituted along new paths.[29]

I notice that she is wearing
One of my favorite masks,
That of the outlaw:

That her postmodern dance
Is exceptional and strange
In its coherent defense of incoherence.

> Hence, the strange, the incoherent, that which falls "outside," gives us a way of understanding the taken-for-granted world of sexual categorization as a constructed one, indeed, as one that might well be constructed differently.[30]

We see material reality and gender too narrowly and habitually, her final solo seems to say, as it updates the style of the dance: We need to meditate on how all things-in-themselves could be different. Her body remains in the light at the end—then, through a trickster dissolve, vaporizes.

Critique of the Trio

Gender and sex may be or become more multiple than we now know, but according to Butler's argument, what would a reconstruction of sex and gender bring? Could humans be just one gender, which would translate into no gender? We now wear unisex clothing, for instance, but does that change our sex? Or if we multiplied genders, would this profusion dilute the terms of difference altogether? Could this erase sexual differences between women and men? Would there be no difference or likeness, no heterogeneity or homogeneity? No magnetic attraction? Opposites can attract, and likes can attract, and attraction at some point extends beyond mere likeness. Perfect symmetry and harmony is never interesting or even possible for long. A broken symmetry in the binary linguistic of homo/hetero may itself constitute attractions and repulsions. Certainly power may be invested in one over the other, turning abstract asymmetry into political problems of prejudice and repression.

Attraction we commonly believe exceeds one—"it takes two to tango"—if we exclude narcissism with its limited satisfactions. What would a world of neutral subjects be like, and would neutrality lack sweet tension? With disappearance of gendered difference, would Eros and attraction disappear altogether? Would it be replaced by the robotic and mechanistic, the world of "Cyborg," "FemaleMan," and "OncoMouse" that Donna Haraway tries to code in *Modest Witness@Second Millennium: FemaleMan Meets OncoMouse?* Perhaps the instinctive dance of Eros is ending—in the "worlding" of charged microelectronic and biotechnological politics. "The cyborg," Haraway says, "is a kind of disassembled and reassembled, postmodern collective and personal self," and one feminists must code: "Communications technologies and biotechnologies are the crucial tools recrafting our bodies. These tools embody and enforce new social relations for women worldwide." *Systems designs freeze dances of time beings* and natural architectures, assembling and dissembling objects or persons. Haraway describes how cyborg and semiotic dissipate the organic through the play of writing in "frozen moments . . . as instruments for enforcing meanings."[31]

As the body is disorganized, dispersed, and reconstructed in the play of writing and systems, might we attain ternary form instead of the outward binary form and function of our present bodies?

Would we walk on three legs?
Would we grow three arms, eyes, and breasts?
Instead of two, or many arms and forms
Like the dancing Shiva/Shakti, as three arms
Become four, or more?

We seem to get along with just one nose. But it has a septum division, and we note that the paired bones of the head, the temporals and parietals, are arranged in binary fashion around the singular frontal and occipital bones, themselves symmetrically divisible.

The beautiful butterfly-shaped sphenoid
Is symmetrically winged

And separates the head through the center horizontally,
Articulating with every bone of the neurocranium in pliant attachments.
Its greater wings swing upward
Like two hands cupping the sunlight,
Held together in a core structure which is hollowed
For the passage of air.

In many ways our human structure and function display twos arranged around ones, branching into the many. Just as physical body-mind health makes use of oppositional tendencies, productive rivalry (as between osteoblasts and osteoclasts), and dynamic balances in creating beauty and strength.[32]

A strict reduction of human biology that bypasses mere palpable and observable difference still reveals an undeniable reproductive difference—sexual distinctions that allow us to fathom merging and gathering dances, scatterings, and unity with varieties. Either way, we pass through the difference. As individuals we live in a permanently fertilized state; each cell gathers together the male and female for the duration of our lives. Only the egg and sperm qualify as being distinctly sexed. All the rest of the body cells are hermaphrodites.[33]

Our binary walking on two legs does not limit the freedom of our dance, but does influence it. When we walk through space, one leg follows the other. We are in a perpetual state of falling and catching ourselves, as F. M. Alexander's work makes use of in its delicate therapeutics of poise. Consider nature's evolvement of physiological difference and admixture, that every characteristic found in one sex can be found in some members of the other sex.[34] This does not, however, erase distinction. Gender distinctions and crossings are described along a continuum that recognizes a biological male/female difference, even if the scale slides further than we know. Every argument against bipolar understandings of biology (*bios*, life) has to use male/female distinction as a backdrop. Bronwyn Davies, who has studied how children become socially identified and limited in bipolar roles that encourage the active/male and passive/female couplings, questions the place of biology in the creation of males and females. She believes that the bipolar opposition of man and woman makes no more sense than the division of the world into "stupid and intelligent people, or short and tall people, or beautiful and ugly people."[35]

Would she deny male/female difference then, or just an absolute standard? Let us not falsely parallel the beautiful and ugly, the short and tall with the biological distinctions of male and female. We do use short and tall as relative measures, and the beautiful and the ugly have a long, entwining history in aesthetic discourse. We make all of these distinctions, but not absolutely. "Everything is beautiful and everything is ugly" is the meeting of opposites expressed in the ancient holistic concept of Tao by Lao Tsu. In this way of speaking, everything is male and everything is female also, a concept that the Tao, the nameless, can also accommodate. In phenomenological aesthetics, this could mean that distinctions appear and disappear perceptually, and they transform in the eye of the beholder as labels (names) disappear. But perceptual play of *aisthesis* does not erase biological facts. Perhaps it tilts physical facts toward metaphysical artifacts. I take the point of Davies's research as the need to move beyond prejudicial absolutes.

Is it how
When we let go in mysterious actions,
Our body in a single sweep
Discovers an alchemy
Of dreams and forces
All by itself?
And how coupling,
Person to person, or vine to cottage,
Is not always of a gendered variety?

Culture plays upon and extends nature's colors and blending, and nature does not seem to play favorites. In animals, birds, rocks, and forests, we find black and brown as much as mauve. Perhaps an answer to prejudicial treatment along gender lines and the socialization that this implies lies in a fundamental change of the cultural mind about the variety of human possibilities. Would energy be put to better use in overcoming hegemonic prejudice that dictates absolute discrete categories rather than trying to prove that there is no biological basis for any bipolar distinction between males and females? Symmetry can be broken because it exists, however imperfectly.

The cracks bring the perfect pavement to life,
As suddenly the world shudders,
And I see it is not the same in all directions.

Reassembling the Trio

Life goes on, and the cosmic dance repeats itself in the merging of sperm and egg, the cycle of birth and death every day. But certainly this is not the whole story. For the story of sexuality that evolutionary science unfolds, more than any other aspect of existence, defies our rational and scientific inspections.[36] But does it defy the sweep of the robotic? I think not. The dance of attraction is deeper than sperms and eggs; it is alive with socially engendered circumstance and flows with the power of torrential waters. It is also smeared into the eye of desire through every other commercial on the airwaves, and does not escape the cybernetic systems engineers.

I appreciate Butler's attention to the role of gender performativity in the evolution of cultural norms that come to organize experience, but I see how she avoids the substantial nature of the body. There is a point where gendered culture and sexuality meet—and that point is embedded in human biology and physiology—our structural, physical, and functional nature. Is it necessary to move past the factual nature of the body to make a case against enforced heterosexuality?

As nature comes before scientific inspections in material process, it does not stand still; it dances. Growth, decay, and regeneration are the themes of its lyrical cycling. Nature sustains both organic and cataclysmic change, but it has consistency as well as delightful and baffling unpredictability, as the dramatic aesthetic search for the relationship of particles and waves in quantum theory has shown.[37] What we see and experience of nature depends on consciousness and perspective as phenomenology, feminist standpoint theory, and postmodern theories of situated knowledge hold.[38] We can observe this relativity even at the subatomic level, as physics has discovered. Nature, above culture, teaches tolerant variety in forms; it seems interested in overlaps, aesthetic contradictions, and differentiation.

Likewise, dances that move with unbroken symmetries are very boring. Our senses tell us this, and consciousness will wander away from such dances over time. The Japanese have made an art of appreciating odd asymmetry in time, with Zen incongruities in the misfitting parts of the *koan* riddle, and in the humor of erotic Ukiyo-e woodblock prints that predate the intrusion of Western morality and shame. Gauche and opaque, the uncalled-for moment is the basis for an aesthetics of "the awkward body" and "the primal body" in the dances of contemporary Japanese Butoh that seek to uncover and at the same time dramatize nature: as in Butoh's alchemy, gender is also malleable.[39]

I hold with Beauvoir and evolutionary science that the body and its sexuality has a history in nature and would mitigate Merleau-Ponty's claim, upheld by Butler, that "man" is not a natural species. This is a claim that he contradicts in his consistent theme, which does not reduce to cultural determinism but recalls us to our experienced situation *within* nature. We may have a birth in affective life that is significant for us alone, as Merleau-Ponty claims,[40] but we are born first through nature, as he and Beauvoir recognize, certainly an affective event for all humans. However we disguise it, nature never leaves us, and biological sexuality is carried forward, branching through complicated dances of contingencies and regularities as traced by evolutionary biologists as well as phenomenologists. Science and philosophy demonstrate an order in nature that influences human life and thought.[41] Are we reduced to nature, then, or by it, or have we yet to understand it in ourselves and what we will become?

Merleau-Ponty, Beauvoir, and Butler all seek a participatory aesthetics. Anti-essentialist arguments against determinist and fatalistic views of human nature are invoked against a spectator mentality. This metaphysical trio argues that we are not passive recipients of the theater of nature. They are all at odds with a perspective on nature that would soberly fix on necessity, the game that nature plays with us, as I mentioned in regard to Paglia in the beginning of this essay, but they are also in danger of devouring the tails of their anti-essentialist dragons. Only Merleau-Ponty finally escapes, but just barely. For him nature and culture have reciprocal interplay, and we are at every moment synthesizing the drama. For Butler culture is over nature; it has ominous enforcing power in our lives, and nature may just be a mirage of culture. Beauvoir finds the nature and culture of our human condition to be ambivalent, especially for woman. All of them have called for an understanding of us as actors, observant and sensitive agents in the theater of life.

SOLVING PUZZLES

When I choreograph
I make use of misfitting parts
Those I thought didn't fit at first;
They change the whole,
        And my dance becomes more interesting.

Shakable Ballet

Concerning agency and our freedom to become our own best image of ourselves, researchers like Iris Young explore how girls and women can and should break the mold of passivity into which they have been poured.[42] We know, for instance, that ballet developed in an atmosphere of titillation and sexual commercialization of the female dancer. This was the circumstance of the romantic ballet that flourished all over Europe well into the 1870s, and especially in France between the revolutions of 1830 and 1848. Writers of that time depict the fashionable man in the audience as interested not in the dance, but in the dancer's body and sexual favors. Historian Lynn Garafola observes that in the 1830s the backstage of the Paris Opera had become a privileged and sanctioned venue for sexual procurement, and Ivor Guest concludes that by the time of *Coppélia* (1870), at the end of the Second Empire of Napoleon III, the opera had become a marketplace for sex that extended even as far as the emperor.[43]

As Sally Banes looks underneath this voyeuristic climate at the ballets themselves, she sees that the issue of agency in the romantic ballet is complex. During the 1850s and 1860s, the technical development of the ballerina increased through the developments of the Italian school with the discoveries of Carlo Blasis in Milan. As the female dancer grew in status, the visibility of the male decreased, with women taking on male dress, even dancing the roles of young heroes in travesty. Banes sees the brave Swanilda in *Coppélia* as the epitome of a new ballet heroine. This dance undeniably catered to the sexual milieu of its time, but it also represented women's power, not as threatening, as in *La Sylphide* (1832) and *Giselle* (1841), but as attractive and liberating. Swanilda's articulate legs and "indomitable spirit" projected the rise of feminist activity in France in the final liberal years of the Second Empire, harbinger to the feminist dress reform movement of the nineteenth century, which attempted to liberate women's bodies: "If the female leg is a symbol of male desire on the nineteenth-century French ballet stage, it is also the sign of female mobility, outside of hearth and home, in the modern arena of public life."[44] If Isadora's free dancing broke the ballet mold, the strong legs of ballerinas were transforming the art from within, as Banes's research into women's agency in ballet allows us to see. However, ballet with its advancement through the European aristocracy, and its later subjugation to state-enforced Communism in Russia, evolved its gender rules within the circumscribed vocabulary of classicism amid romantic styles and stories. But even so, it can bend its rules and redirect its history; personal choice and agency are prerogatives in the world of ballet (in all art). Female choreographers had already begun to recognize this in the 1980s, as the quirky works of Karole Armitage and the exuberant iconoclasm of Twyla Tharp demonstrate, and which I take up below. In dances for the Ballets Russes such as *Les Biches* (*The Dinner Party*, 1924), Bronislava Nijinska (1891–1972) explored class, gender, and homosexuality, providing an early example of female authority in ballet. And in the twenty-first century, Suzanne Farrell, a Balanchine adept, formed her own school and ballet company. But such examples are too few; ballet has not generally produced a liberating climate. Rather, it has survived on the insecurity of women and their obedience to masters, although the display of the feminine often supersedes the masculine in the ballet aesthetic.

In order to subsidize their impoverished salaries, the young ballerinas of the Paris Opera took rich lovers who sustained them in a veiled system of prostitution. In late-nineteenth-century Russia, the economic system in the imperial theaters allowed women more independence. When they were accepted as children into the Imperial Theatrical School, their education was paid for, and they were guaranteed a career and a pension for life. This is the situation that Banes believes was responsible, in part, for the extraordinary agency represented by Aurora in the Russian classic, *The Sleeping Beauty* (1890). Isolated from the political struggles of its times, the dance created an illusion of order but also contradicted gender messages in the literary versions of the fairy tales that inspired it: "Beauty's world is one in which men nearly disappear and women reign supreme."[45]

History has seen shifts in the politics and economics of dancers, as also in the agency and aesthetics of their dances. Artistic production requires us to pay attention to our choices and intentions, choices to pause, to be still, recede, or rush forward. Historically, women have poked holes in glass ceilings through dance. Early modern dance was created in large measure by female choreographers. Now, "In the United States, the majority of all dance artists are women," according to Jan Van Dyke's research into gender and professional dance in America. But there is another side to this. Van Dyke also reports that since about 1961, "we have seen the emergence of male leadership in the field, as reflected in awards, recognition, and employment."[46]

In *The Elizabethan Phrasing of the Late Albert Ayler* (1986), Karole Armitage shows that ballet can stretch its attributes of movement and taste, that its plots and scenery can be free-floating and eclectic—postmodern. She casts her choreography against the characteristics of ballet, using its history and conventions as a foil for her dance. Increasing the distance between the past and the present, she dances behind and in front of painter David Salle's enormous images projected on the cyclorama, commencing with a giant eye in an orange field. The title of the dance suggests aural juxtapositions in time. Exaggerated contrasts of costumes and movement styles and the dancer's size and scale in proportion to setting all suggest both a contemporary moment and the historical past encoded in kinetics and the visual.

Salle's images frame the dance in its proportional psychology. Matthew Biro writes that Salle's work, like that of Anselm Keifer in the late sixties, is sensitive to an "overabundance and over determination of images, styles and previous works," the tendency in art for "saturation and domination." Instead of creating new images, therefore, artists like Salle select fragments of history and uncover "world views."[47] Drawing from past models or fragments seems fundamental to art and its discoveries. Artists build on or discard history and appropriate it in the process. They also cast work against ideological critiques of appropriation. "Appropriation" as a strategy has been around since at least 1917–1918 when the Berlin Dada artists began to make their photomontages.

In her "bad girl" dances, *Drastic Classicism, Paradise, Last Gone Dance,* and the *Watteau Duets,* Armitage quotes (appropriates) time frames and musical styles liberally. In *Elizabethan Phrasing,* she brings classical ballet into dialogue with spatterings of modernism. She begins the dance in a simple black costume designed by Salle. Her movement *sur la pointe* is precise, but with odd digressions from the clean lines of classical ballet—a turned-in knee more characteristic of jazz, and hands flung from the wrists. Her company dances against a large spiny creature on the backdrop of Salle's set: disparate elements coexist as dancer and dance dissolve in a filmic repetition of motorcycles jumping and falling over cliffs.

This recalls Armitage's background with Merce Cunningham rather than her start with the Geneva Ballet, but her work seems more tangible and tougher than Cunningham's, even though delicacy marks the Japanese section "Sakura, Sakura," where slow turns on point end with simple tilts of the head. In "Hypslers, Flipslers, and Fingers Poppin' Daddies," played by comedian Lord Buckley, hanging lamps blink in the background as the work gathers energy in sudden bursts of jogging and walk-offs. Hot pink umbrella tutus with silver lining amplify the movement toward the end of the first act. Dancers move with pert gestures in electric duets that finally grow mellow and sensuous in *Three Pieces for String Quartet* by Igor Stravinsky (interpreted by the Intercontemporary Quartet in the version I saw).

The second act opens with dancers in simple dresses and sunglasses that are immediately thrown off. The music sustains a drone quality through Albert Ayler's *Bells* (1966), sounding much like an orchestral rendition of bagpipes. Through rhythmic steps, hinged arm circles, and flung hand gestures repeated from the beginning, the ballet takes on a folk character. These complicated duets play against a painted backdrop of dismembered or floating arms that later give way to small, boxed-in paintings of cathedral spires. The partners weave their dance within this migrating frame, sharpening directional changes through surprising steps and facings, and then sauntering into wacky upside-down split-lifts.

Moving from "Our Prayer" by Don Ayler to "Subconscious Mind" with the sounds performed by Lord Buckley, the dance progresses from lyric to frenetic through a convulsive use of torso. Its balletic character is surprisingly precise, however, even in frantic moments; in softer ones, heads held in hands are cradled between partners. The floating eye returns to absorb the movement momentarily, then scatters into a series of lined-up lightbulbs.

Several duets bring back the dance around the eye: the first slow and delicately sustained, conscious of its epicurean style; the second more percussive with glitter added to the costuming; and at the end, three duets of partners donning black hats—fading into the eye and an iteration of the original solo by Armitage. Meanwhile, the musical collage has included fifties hep cat nightclub comedian, Lord Buckley; Anton Webern; a traditional Japanese melody performed by cellist Yo Yo Ma; Igor Stravinsky; and Albert and Don Ayler.

The program notes tell us that it was in Ayler's music and its "terrible intransigence" that Karole Armitage heard the "Elizabethan phrasing," a poetry already at work in the sensuality of the English language in the sixteenth and seventeenth centuries. Something historical and poetic in his music drives the nonverbal material of Armitage into what she calls "the delicacy of a verbal end."

The body of the late Albert Ayler was pulled out of the Hudson River in 1970. Misunderstood by the general public, he had liberated the African American musical structures as far as possible in the manner of exploration. His instrumental and rhythmic research was unbounded in scope and rigor as he mined between cultures and powers, harking back to the birth of the blues. Through its unsquare square dances and its irony, the music Armitage chose for her dance draws upon a turbulent history. The talented Ayler did not survive his thirties.

Twyla Tharp's ballet *In the Upper Room* challenges ballet classicism while retaining a classical identity in several ways. The tendency of the work, as the title indicates, is to go up. The upward ascending term *ballon* defines classical ballet—to pause midair, lift and balance, as in skillful jumping. Clarity of line and precise actions are also classical markers, as are harmony of parts and pleasing proportion. These *qualia* comprise this work, but with a glistening, athletic, postmodern twist. First performed in August 1986 at the Ravinia Festival in Highland Park, Illinois, Tharp's dance has become an American classic in its appeal and staying power.

The success of the dance depends in great measure on the dynamics of the score by Philip Glass, despite the fact that Tharp teaches her dancers the steps before they hear a note of the score, "so that they can analyze the basic movements first," she says.[48] The idea for *The Upper Room* came to Tharp after hearing a recording of an old Mahalia Jackson hymn: "It modulated eternally upwards until it hit the roof." This gave her the feeling of being in an attic that inspired the basis of her ballet and the sequential score she commissioned by Glass—a work of nine movements in his now familiar ostinato style of repetitive cycles.[49] As in Indian traditional music, Glass makes the strange familiar using rhythmic and harmonic cells as a basis while expanding the textures; the units change over time as new sounds are added and former ones extracted in subtle shifts. The result is hypnotic, evolving horizontal time, oscillating without severe breaks and upheavals. Tharp interprets the music of Glass as "a skeining: an unraveling of musical wool that is endlessly fascinating and has a life and beauty of its own."

Upper Room is costumed to present the youthful vitality of the dancers and Tharp's passionate clarity. Black-and-white-striped pants with red tank tops are the unisex dress for much of the dance. These give way to shorts sometimes and toward the end a bathing suit look. White sneakers and red shoes accent the lithe footwork of leg exchanges throughout the work. The first steps go neatly nowhere, then burst into short backward runs, silently held in-transit foot stops, and soft kicks that break from the balletically coded movement in a jazzy way. The dance cascades forward, shifting from group work to partnering, then suddenly finds itself in formal lines with dancers exacting shoulder twists that sloop into slides and tapping feet, skittering and landing florid arabesques. When the music gathers a heavy *cantus firmus*, three duets of male/female pairs coordinate shoulder-leaning parallel lines on the diagonal. Turning and waiting, the partners kick into the open spaces between body shapes, looping and connecting line-holds as they replicate the duet en masse. The doubles triple; I settle into the forms of exuberance.

A smoky atmosphere begins to permeate the dance as the air thickens from a stage effect in the lighting by Jennifer Tipton. Four dancers perform head-leading movements twisting through space. This is a ballet, but ballet askew—dragging and brushing glissades that slide into the pirouettes *à la seconde, en attitude, en arabesque.* The dancers emerge briefly from the background mist, flipping their arms like tassels, then slipping into the smoke. Sudden loosening of tightly held shapes, flashing slices of limbs, and syncopated steps against squared rhythms create a dialectic of ballet and free dance, grace and guts.

Jumps lean into back arches, and crisp leaps to the back forge front leg extensions as the dance builds an *accelerando*. Men enter in floor-skimming, breath-catching runs that fall into knee spins, and the three duets return, anew. The women are turned in the air as they are lifted with knees leading aloft, then with foot-points brushing upward. A firm gaze accents the sideward direction of the leg extensions. The men dance beneath and around their female partners, positioning them in the air momentarily, over and over. They poise: happy, serene, in a pattern that surpasses their individuality. The partners are clearly united with no need to express anything beyond the pure emblem and euphoria.

At the end, the dancers are dressed in red tank leotards, exposing their legs casually, athletically. The dance remains elegant and friendly. The music develops vocalizations, rumbling drums with flutes, then finally the blare of trumpet. The dance becomes brighter with daring duets and groups that speed through space with thrown strength. A male trio aids the shift to deeper registers in the music, even as the dynamic of the dance begins to ascend. Flight is added, and the cast begins to rock as couples in the background frame the last move of two women left in the spotlight, jumping to pull down the sky. Fire red and bright white, two dancers look into the light, reach and pull, grasp and hold the upper regions. And I see the soles of their shoes, the flash of their legs, their shining skin.

Gender-Bending Solutions

In various ways, choreographers are addressing the prejudice with which men who want to dance must contend. Homosexuality moves from subtext to main text in the works of Bill T. Jones. Lawrence Goldhuber's solos give big men a place in dance as he seizes the imagination with his 350-pound body in dances like *Love Defined*, based on King Kong. "When I dance," Goldhuber told me, "I just try to be honest. I sweat a lot, work hard, and try not to show it. Once my father said I looked like I was having a heart attack." Still developing the ground of modernism and androgyny, Garth Fagan's male dancers strive to balance poise and delicacy with strength. Since the recession of the male in romantic ballet, about 150 years ago, professional dance has not been considered an appropriate activity for men. Ramsay Burt examines the unpopularity of male dancing in *The Male Dancer*.[50]

Now male choreographers are bending the rules of ballet, and sometimes those of gender as well. Alonzo King's choreography for his contemporary ballet company Lines twists and throws the geometry of ballet off-kilter and bridges to idiomatic movement as in his work for four men, *In to Get Out* (2000). Ballet provides the springy basis of male dancing, and the clear muscle definition resulting from ballet training is unmistakable. These versatile dancers will be able to execute any typical ballet turn, jump, or leap, and land it squarely on a dime, or blend and wrap the tautly extended body of ballet creatively around functional, everyday lines. The dance has formal tendencies; the more movement is taken away, the more we see—just as the music for the dance, *Toki No Mon* (1991) by Somei Satoh brings an original flair and Western instrumentation to spare, traditional Japanese tones.

Women could undoubtedly perform this dance; its aesthetic coloration would change, however, with the shapes and expressive characteristics of the dancers. What new meaning might be derived? The dance doesn't explicitly build upon human relationships, though we might infer these through the proximity or distance of the dancers. If it were performed by two men and two women, or one plus three, we could continue to call it the same work if the movement remained intact, but each case would present new perceptual matters for the audience and performance matters for the dancers. On stage as in life, gender makes a difference. In 2003, King set *In to Get Out* for three male students and one woman at Florida State University. In photographs, this version appears as viscerally sculpted and objective as the original, even though I notice the difference the woman makes.

We are corporeal metaphysical artifacts in the gender-bending process, as various concepts in psychoanalytic feminism and current dance are testing, but the bending still appears through our understanding of pairs: hetero (the difference), homo (the same), or the two in one in varying degrees. Choreography explores sex/gender constructions with great freedom—with polarized attractions, repulsions, and deflations in every direction. Aesthetic results vary according to the quality of the choreography and dancing, and in the eye of the beholder.

For me not everything is equal. There are some dances I do not like—and with reason. The seedy misogynist production of *Swan Lake* that had a triumphant run in London's West End in the late 1990s is one of them. Mathew Bourne's unorthodox choreography for the modern dance company Adventures in Motion Pictures got rave reviews in London. This classical ballet was originally choreographed by Petipa and Ivanov, with music by Tchaikovsky, and had its premiere at the Bolshoi Theater in Moscow in 1877. I saw Bourne's production in London in January 1997, before it opened in Los Angeles and New York in 1998. I wondered if the audiences were not applauding his break from the traditional *Swan Lake* plot and the novelty of his narrative most of all. Bourne's dance mimics the *tinta*, or color, of the original music, but delineates new characters and gender roles. Gender reversals by themselves do not make a good ballet, even if they upend staid conventions. There is not a tutu—nor a decent woman—in the *Swan Lake* of Motion Pictures.

The swans are men in bare chests and feathery pants. The ballet concentrates its narrative in the life and death of its prince, and his falling in love with the male swan. The gender reversal turns unwittingly misogynist in its assignment of tensional/transformational elements to males alone. The women have singular dimensions. They are *witches* (the wicked sexually wanton queen who ignores her son and is obviously the root of his problems with alcohol abuse), *bitches* (cold, sexy seducers, a fan dancer, hostesses, barflies, princesses at the royal ball who behave like jealous, brassy . . . well, bitches), and *sluts* (the prince's slightly stupid off-and-on girlfriend, an offense to his icy, lascivious mother). There are also efficient, unremarkable female servants who take care of the prince.

The mysterious lead swan carries the dance innovations in terms of movement. Aside from William Kemp's very fine dancing of the not-too-original-but-sometimes-oblique choreography for the swan, I do not know why anyone would applaud this production, especially in its exploitation of women. It is easy enough to gender-blast the classics, but not so easy to do it well. I would rather see a well-done conventional interpretation of *Swan Lake* than to sit through a gay ballet that turns wrathfully against women. This is an unfortunate outcome that I do not think the choreographer intended.

The Odette-Odile male swan insinuates himself into the prince's life in attractive and devastating imagery. In his need to be loved, the prince is compelled and controlled by the swan. At the death of the prince, we see his child-self being lifted to heaven by the swan—now a benevolent father—while the loveless queen mother still rejects her son. The only compassion in the plot is from and between men. The women are there as foils and festering wounds. There is no kindness in them, or strength. Women are the offensive backdrop for male tenderness and transcendence. When will the gender revisionists achieve more balance as they break the mold?

A more sympathetic interpretation of the ballet might say that it spoofs the British royal family and takes pity on a prince repressed by his upbringing. The less conservative Princess Margaret might have been combined with her cool sister Elizabeth in the character of the queen, resulting in an unconvincing recklessness. Or did this dance take the issue of the male voyeur of the female body in ballet as its topic, making explicit and contemporaneous what was implicit in the decline of the romantic ballet at the Paris Opera? I don't think so. By focusing on the homoerotic, the choreographer failed to see his one-dimensional, unfriendly portrayal of women. There must be better choreographic solutions for gender troubles.

Just how far can a dance genre bend, I wonder, and still retain its identity? This question comes up for me, even though I understand the choreographer's aim as more exploratory than didactic. She or he proceeds as if there were something to be discovered rather than proven, just as Doug Elkins describes the partnering of head-first-from-behind, rapid-off-the-ground "butt dives," heads between knees, which incite dolphinlike play and lighten the gender mix-ups in his choreography. In Elkins's lecture-demonstrations, he wears a baseball cap and satirizes his process: "I don't know whether I'm deconstructing romanticism, or romanticizing postmodernism or just involved in my own form of post-Hegelian therapy." "When I dance it's like blowing soap bubbles," he told me in an interview. Below, I cast his somatic metaphor in the image of *phusis:*

Dancing against dozing skin
Precarious moments of energy
Arise and disappear:

Foreground and background
Hedging a middle—

Then the arising.

Phusis itself—

Waiting for figures on the verge—

Phusis: Performing Nature

What kind of culture will we make of our nature? We have been looking at ballet's potential for invention through iconoclastic choreography in relation to classicism. And we have examined this under the lens of anti-essentialist views of dance and the body, of culture and nature. But the anti-essentialist question for ballet goes still deeper in view of encoding the body: Can ballet retain its identity without enforcing mastery as closure through the goal of perfection? Apparently it can. This would lie in matters of training and choreography. Ballet dancers can be trained to discover the potential of the skeletal structure without force and strain. Increasingly, we see teaching that takes care of the body. Ballet dancers can be taught through an internal understanding of how individual bodies move. They can learn how to go slow to learn better, how to repeat movement combinations with awareness, not perfection, as the goal. "Perfection is a dead place," says ballet teacher and performer Wallie Wolfgruber. The movement vocabulary of ballet can be articulated with clear intentions toward fluidity, ease, grace, and power. Attention to integration of the body rather than overextension encourages expansive, cohesive, and breathtaking dance. Laura Lanphier explains her somatically inclined ballet training with John Welch and the Hartfel Ballet—where students are not looking at themselves but thinking kinaesthetically: "We use the floor as a mirror—reflecting what we give it."[51] This is an image for matching clear intentions, rather than mastering the body seen in the mirror. Dancing may be conceived in light of our ability to listen to ourselves in movement, sensing what feels good, what feels right. When King reconstructed *In to Get Out* for students at Florida State University, he taught not about perfection, but about being oneself—about "body as character." Lisa Plank, who dances in the work, says, "the challenge is to give variety and not judge 'the best' version."[52]

What kind of nature will we make of our nature? Like the natural world that supports us, the nature of the body does not respond well to rough violations. If we are free to create ourselves in our dances, and if we are not determined, neither in our bodily nature nor in society, as audience-participants in our own drama, our freedom to choose draws us into a new performance of our own. I speak of the odd, compelling performance of our *ecological body*, cycling with environmental phenomena, supportive and wounding, running through our veins and in the atmosphere, polluted or pure, imploring our feelings and testing our liberating and not-so-liberating choices. What kind of nature will we make of our nature?

However freely cast, carefully or recklessly cultivated, our dances are made of nature, the rhythms of our bodies and nights on earth, even as the dance itself is made possible through that same body rhythm, whether we decide to listen to it or not. The nonhuman forms and rhythms around us also help to root our sensibilities and movements. Children know this as they swing their linked-together arms like elephant trunks and unfold their dancer arms like the wings of a lark.

In our human structure and function, we leap from words to the world we embody—metaphysically—through our living wholeness. Much of what we say and do is learned socially, but our natural ability to speak and to dance underlies the word and the movement. Our *phusis*, our life, as arising through nature, is a gift that no one can learn or teach; yet it is the fount for all talents and teachings.[53] We can pervert and deny this gift; we can even try to photocopy it and pour it through systems designs, but its grace moves through us nevertheless. What we do with it is up to us. We can marry technology and become its passive partner, or we can critique it with aesthetic participation in the technodance. And we can teach war or love as we practiced their lessons but never learned them in the sixties. Anti-essentialist arguments against nature end where dances of time begin.

5 | *A Dance*
of Time Beings

Sociocultural processes and artifacts are human *doings*, expressions that extend from and also extend our bodily nature. Encompassing sex and gender, our performances include nature and are sown in word and deed. The body is a primal natural fact and also a sophisticated artifact, and if fact comes before "arti-fact," both dissolve in metaphysics. Artifacts reflect the nebulous material of beings-in-the-world that shaped them. Dancing brings this to us, but in a slippery way.

As a metaphysical artifact, dancing springs from our embodied state, our embodied sexuality, for instance, but overflows the body even as it contains it. This is true whether we dance for ourselves or for others (as performers). The primal and sophisticated body melds in dance and a third element arrives, ecstasis, to stand out from oneself—not a bodily overcoming but nevertheless a self-surpassing.

> Metaphysics—the coming to light of something beyond nature—is not localized at the level of knowledge: it begins with the opening out upon "another," and is to be found everywhere, and already, in the specific development of sexuality.[1]

I would accept Merleau-Ponty's above definition of metaphysics if I could change one word in the first line: "beyond" would become "within." Heidegger's phenomenology more than Merleau-Ponty's situates metaphysics in nature. Both find metaphysics in perceptual experience and the temporalizing present, a "now" that is increased in awareness and a potential already present in the world. Here I compare the two, first Merleau-Ponty:

Being established in my life, buttressed by my thinking nature, fastened down in this transcendental field which was opened for me by my first perception, and in which all absence is merely the obverse of a presence, all silence a modality of the being of sound, I enjoy a sort of ubiquity and theoretical eternity, I feel destined to move in a flow of endless life. (364)

Now Heidegger:

That *Present* which is held in authentic temporality and which thus is authentic itself, we call the "moment of vision." This term must be understood in the active sense as an ecstasis. It means the resolute rapture with which *Dasein* is carried away to whatever possibilities and circumstances are encountered.[2]

Both authors are descendant—to the degree that they locate metaphysics in this world, our being-in-the-world in present time, containing a past and opening up a future. As Heidegger explains temporality, he links it with authenticity and transcendence (401). The ecstatic unity of temporality provides the condition of "Being-there," defined as "one that has been 'cleared.'" In our "Being- there," we become both "open" and "bright" for ourselves through what Heidegger has defined as "care." *Care is the whole constitution of Dasein's Being*—a unitary basis for existential possibility (401–18). "Ecstatical temporality clears the 'there' primordially." Heidegger's dance comes full circle in defining "care" ontologically and traces back to temporality as its existential ground (401–2).

Here we see in what manner transcendental metaphysics is located in time for both Merleau-Ponty and Heidegger. In Heidegger's *Being and Time*, "authentic being" is not immobile or passive—it is, however, bodiless most of the time. Active in temporality as the past and future merge in the present, the world and our being-in-the-world is already transcendent. The issue for humans is to somehow be able to perceive (open) the transcendent nature of the world. For the oppressed and hungry, this may seem almost impossible, but even here we have examples of ecstasis amid suffering—as recorded in the diary of Anne Frank. And *Pedagogy of the Oppressed*, Paulo Freire's work first published in 1970, applies the transformative work of phenomenology to concrete situations. Education, he believes, should be "the practice of freedom." His work in dialogics develops mutual processes of

Matching History and the ecstasy of time, Susannah Newman dances in her
1969 group choreography *Chaconne in D Minor after the Solo by Jose Limon.*
With Limon's permission, she based her dance on notated themes she learned
from his experiments for group of his solo *Chaconne* (1942) to J. S. Bach's *Chaconne in D Minor* (Partita). In Newman's work the matching of body to history
and forms of otherness is doubled as she looks back through the lens of her
teacher Limon toward his Mexican-Spanish background. Photograph (1983) by
June Burke.

teacher and student interaction to replace models of teacher/student division and the rule of mastery.[3]

Ecstasis: Mastery or Matching

Heidegger wears the mask of the world. For him the world can match (I add "mask") itself. "The worlding of the world," as he writes of it in "The Thing," is a matching of the world to itself in the same curious way that somatics explorations can ask us to match our body in movement. The idea that the world worlds itself, or that the body can body itself is curious, indeed. How can we match our own body, and why would we want to? *Matching* is a somatic strategy that relieves us of our compulsions to move, think, and relate competitively.[4] When we are not self-correcting, actions stem from self-acceptance. This applies to other correcting also, as we look for and invariably find faults in others.

Matching ourselves, rather than judging, allows us to slow down and notice what we are already doing in our movements and thought processes. Subsequently, we may discover what parts of ourselves seem to be missing, personal resources we may have lost or given up. Matching opens up perception in noncompetitive, nonjudgmental processes that allow buried feelings to surface. In several ways, good therapists know how to match their clients. The work of matching utilizes *noninterference*, a first principle in the metaphysics of discovery.

In Heidegger's metaphysics, *what* we discover of the unity of temporality (ecstasis), in *what* direction, how and *how far* becomes an aspect of our freedom, even if always within the limitations of our "thrownness," as beings in process. Authenticity is found in "everydayness," or how we maintain ourselves in the everyday. But there is oppression in the everyday, or as Heidegger puts it, "*Dasein* is dominated through and through 'for life.'" In everydayness, we can "undergo dull 'suffering,' sink away in the dullness of it." But there is momentary escape: "In the moment of vision, indeed, and often just 'for that moment,' existence can even gain the *mastery* over the 'everyday'; but it can never extinguish it" (422; my emphasis). And we find out that "everydayness" is at bottom temporality for Heidegger (423).

To "master" the everyday, as I would shift away from Heidegger, would be in some manner to "match" it, dissolving its oppressiveness—opening present time rather than hanging back with nostalgia or even striving toward promise—to dance like Zorba, fearlessly from zero. As also in the simple flow of our freedom, we walk for the joy of paying attention to our feet, the symphony of breath, and the beauty around us. I substitute "matching" for "mastery." To match, rather than master, the already transcendent nature of the world would be to dance, to engage in anything for the pleasure of the doing itself and not for future rewards. Opening present time, being alive to it through matching rather than mastering, is a possibility in all our work and play.

With time as his subject, Heidegger cycles movement into stillness. This happens when he tries to state the time being of beings in their presence as "things" (phenomena). He writes a fourfold gathering dance: a ring of earth and sky, divinities and mortals. "Radiantly, the ring joins the four, everywhere open to the riddle of their presence." In their "nestling together" in the "onefold," they "world" the world.[5] This is the dance that everything already always does. *The dance is everywhere*, and we are its treasure hunters.

In *Being and Time*, Heidegger keeps circling back, dropping and picking up threads of movement, recycling them in new contexts; the metaphysical view is momentary and at the same time ubiquitous in the world. Heidegger's transcendent "moment of vision," we note, is drawn from the sense of sight. This primacy of optics is secured in the West's language of mastery, as the gaze captures the world in its *sights* and *worldviews*. Luce Irigaray, Maxine Sheets-Johnstone, and Elizabeth Grosz have all made this point in feminist contexts.[6] "Mastery" is a dangerous word in any context, for in some sense it indicates a struggle to overcome. Val Plumwood outlines the problem of mastery as belonging to dualist divisions that sustain conflict, and she also provides a philosophical framework for a way out as she mines the logic that holds oppressive networks in place, including the human/nature division that follows the convention of nature as other-than-human, a resource ripe for mastery.[7]

Heidegger's philosophy portrays mastery as an opening, a way into the mundane. He is not advocating oppression of others, but *Being and Time* does engage the linguistic of struggle. "Everydayness," the horizon closest to us, is oppressive, it "dominates" (Heidegger's word). "Mastery" is problematically cast here, as it often is, in terms of "domination." Mastery, however, might better be contrived as matching or the pursuit of excellence, where matching can lead to excellence in the acquisition of skill. Matching also can be realized in the wholeness of joy and laughter as mastery is dropped to favor care over contest. Matching promotes nonstressful, self-directed learning, and should not imply a loose or nonexistent standard of excellence. When I give my best attention to any task or activity without worry over the outcome, *this is matching.* I can learn to perfectly match my attention to a task, whether this is office work, housework, or a dance work. My quality of attention can certainly fail, as it sometimes will, but if I develop the habit of matching my tasks, I can bring myself productively back into them. This attitude has long been alive in the traditions of the East, as the Chinese Book of Changes, the *I Ching,* states in section 25, "Innocence": "We should do every task for its own sake as time and place demand and not with an eye to the result. Then each task turns out well, and anything we undertake succeeds." This *innocence* rests on a promise and on our resonance with nature, as the *I Ching* continues in the same section: "We cannot lose what really belongs to us, even if we throw it away. Therefore we need have no anxiety. All that need concern us is that we should remain true to our own natures."

Matching can be playful, therapeutic, aesthetic, or worklike, and when a contest is called forth, we can even carry matching as a quality of attention into competition. We can match our best efforts, do our best, that is, and detach from the results. Winning isn't everything; quality of attention is, and life need not be a contest nor the world a battleground. Our contests should bring pleasure as we test our abilities together and bring out the best in each other. *Mastering one another* should not be the goal. Matching is simply a quality of alertness and care. It turns toward means and not ends, away from the stressful efforts of mastery that make others into enemies in competition. The master model of competition can also be turned back on the self; then we become our own enemy. Inevitably, this enters into our dance when we dance against rather than with ourselves.

Instead of competing with ourselves, we can dance alongside, matching: as in the subtle doubling dance and slow walk of Butoh wherein the dancer multiplies herself consciously, placing a shadow self in front, another behind, and others surrounding. Her walking begins to float in the center of those self-matchings as she constitutes them over time. They walk with her. When several dancers walk to-gether as one body, many selves become multiplied from the one, and the studio begins to crackle with quiet power. Matching themselves, dancers gradually move away from each other, spreading out the space to provide more room for each person's many selves to emerge. It is sublime to feel how your own multiplied self passes by and through the selves of others in the dance. I have seen people weep silently as they walk; some say they have called an ancestor to walk with them.[8]

Heidegger's philosophy is baroque in ornate metaphors, curving and looping, returning to the fourfold threads of his gathering dances—of earth, world, divinity, and mortality—retracing these broad paths, coaxing them out of their dwelling in consciousness to their scripting in text. He creates beautiful figures in ideas. *Bella.* But where do the beautiful and the good connect? How can we know when decency and conscience are absent? What is philosophy good for if these are absent? Heidegger dedicated *Being and Time* to his teacher Husserl, the father of phenomenology and a Jew. What possessed Heidegger, then, to support Hitler? How do we recognize virtue in form? Does it emerge sometimes in the forms and figures of art? Does it appear spontaneously when we unmask a truth about our-selves? Does it develop in performance? And where does a perfor-mance begin? Is it now, here, in my writing? Or does performance break out of my dance to color my daily life? Does it only begin when the curtain rises on stage?

There is a scene from Jiri Kilian's ballet *Bella Figura* (1995) just be-fore the curtain falls that arouses these questions in me, even as I un-derstand how I am also part of the questions. The dancers are not wearing street clothes, as is favored in American postmodern dance. I sense immediately that the dance is a masque. The voluminous red bell skirts and glowing bare breasts exist somewhere between art and artificiality, between the costumed and natural body, as they marry the skin of our everyday bodies with the life of fantasy. The setting moves us into the night, and we fall into the dreaming of the dance. The stage is lit with pits of fire on either side; the flames lick the pic-ture forming in the erotic mien of the dance. Dancers kneel in the light; a glowing background appears out of which the others walk. Last images of a duet flicker in the firelight, a man and woman wheel and slice their limbs past each other. Their ballet technique aids the sharp clarity of their forms. Then the duet softens; each partner alternately squeezes an ear-to-a-shoulder as the other one observes—neutrally, profoundly. Changing places, the dancers release each other's constriction, lifting the head from the shoulder with a gentle hand, and I understand how romance in ballet opens a doorway to the numinous through touch. My body matches the divine neutrality of listening hands, witnessing and assisting.

However temporal in its metaphysics—inquisitive, visual, and kinaesthetic in movement metaphors—Heidegger's philosophy is still abstract. It lacks the tactile. That thicket is not a moment of vision but a moment of contact. Not a grasp on the world, as in the grasping of ideas so ubiquitous in philosophic discourse, but a touch that listens. Yes, we can listen with our somas when we give up grasping aggressiveness. We can hear others—the places at rest, the disturbances, where and how the next movement is forming—that we might follow and be present without judgment.

When I touch in somatic movement therapy, I follow with my hands, or just with my attention, the movement that another person is already doing; I listen to it. The movement thickens between us and becomes more of itself. Of course it changes by reason of being added to. There are two of us doing the movement now, not just one. I never know where it will go; unpredictable paths that neither one of us could have independently matched venture and progress. I match these paths of least resistance because I understand the wisdom of the body of the other that wants the best for itself. I can only follow with trust, and know that I am not the doer.

The acknowledged body doubles,
becomes more of itself, and I of it.
A dance of breath releases in its *phusis*,
and our body bodies the world's body,
nesting together in the onefold.

Nothing could be simpler than the listening touch, and nothing more vulnerable—we are not accustomed to exposing our pain. In the heat of our own hands, we match and double.

Touch and Kinesthesia

The tactile, associated with material and thus the maternal *materia*, is genderless in corporeality. It is, moreover, the perceptual ground for the kinaesthetic. Touch and movement are inextricably linked through neuromuscular proprioception informing kinesthesia, our experience of the spacio-temporal organization of movement. Kinaesthetic awareness of the dancer and the audience is the physical basis of the dance aesthetic, from frenetic to lucid, sluggish or fast, expansive, confined, broken, tilted, twisted, leaning, lunging, languid, bright, sharp, calm, confused, or contiguous. These movement properties have proprioceptive valences, and they also leave visual impressions.

Somatically, however, the visible cannot be truly contrasted to the tangible, for touch precedes and informs vision as well as movement. The *tactile* foregrounds the *visible* in the insights of Luce Irigaray: "I only see through the touching of the light." It is through the nurture of touch and the earliest movement explorations that the infant grows in relation to the mother. Touch and movement are experienced first of all through the infant's early contact with the mother, even in the darkness of the womb. Long before vision, tactile-kinaesthetic sensitivity arises in the evolution of our sexuality. The miracle of touch is expressed as love. Touch is entwined with kinaesthetic movement awareness and our aesthetic resonance with the other. Thus, we understand that the dancer is "in touch" with her body, just as we speak of "being touched" by certain performances. The dancer is not divided from her bodily consciousness. Rather, she develops it.

Contact improvisation and contact partnering in choreography explore the tactile/kinaesthetic. When dancers touch each other in their movement, they explicitly expand proprioceptive awareness in tactile terms. Contact improvisers locate kinaesthetic awareness between bodies in touch as they pursue the giving and taking of weight, mixing genders in sexually neutral terms. Touch, from the platonically impersonal to the sexually erotic, is the primary aesthetic substance in dance partnering, whether it takes place in contact improvisation or the lyricism of modern/postmodern dance or formal classical ballet. Touch is primary in dance partnering, embedded in proprioceptive space-time awareness, but it also pervades the dance aesthetic even when not explicitly given as part of the choreography. Proprioception is the perception of our body in space-time at any moment of movement, and throughout the whole of it. It is the basis for self-awareness and kinaesthetic *aisthesis*, affectivity, or the feeling of what happens in dance.

DANCING OUTSIDE IN

Keeps me in touch with my body
Self and sensibility.
The shape and line of my dance
Will never meet my eye,
Unless I dance for mirrors.

But that would not be the dance,
Only its reflection.

My dance is moved and met by me.
It touches me, even as it meets the I
Of the eye of the other and the
Lay of the land,
Changing through time and night,
Ever joyous, ever moving, in.

Soma

"Soma," we know, is the Greek word for the body as experienced by the self. If I close my eyes and pay attention to how I feel, I come into this sense of interiority. For soma is not rendered visually, but through proprioception, kinaesthetic knowledge of one's spatial and temporal condition at any moment. This kinaesthetic sense, moreover, is not static. *Rather, its most important defining element is that of movement.* The "kin-aesthetic" is literally the body's movement aesthetic, its movement "sense-ability," and its indivisible perceptual partner is touch. The tactile kinaesthetic is the foundation of the creation and aesthetic appreciation of dance.

In phenomenological terms, I sense my living of time and space through bodily movement. I can sense changes rendered through movement somaesthetically. As I turn my head, for instance, I am able through my kinaesthetic sense to feel just how far it is turning, and on which tilt or angle. I perceive the turn kinaesthetically and in relation to external referents in the environment. It makes a difference whether my feet are on the floor, touching it, or whether I am leaning on something, sitting, or lying down in the grass, floating in water, or standing on a mountaintop. I know whether my chin is lifted, bringing my eyes up to the ceiling or the sky, or whether it is lowered so that I can look down at the floor or the earth. It is most significant that I feel the exact placement of my head, even with my eyes closed.

In fact, my eyes and what they see as I turn my head do not give me information about the turning itself. The turn is the movement I sense from within through my kinaesthetic sense, and my eyes will extend this phenomenon if they are open. I take my view of the world from where I touch the environment: standing, sitting, or lying down.

My tactile connection with the environment influences all of my movement, "worlding" it, to use Heidegger's term. My turning head, through its articulation with the cervical vertebrae, involves an adjustment of the whole spine as it connects downward, articulating with the ribs, extending into the sacrum and pelvis and from there to the legs and feet. In standing, I sense the grounding of the turn through my feet in touch with the floor. If I give conscious attention to the turn of my head, I can sense it throughout my body. It takes only a little practice in standing with the eyes closed to begin to feel the bodily lived totality of the turning of the head. I might even explore this somatically, consciously allowing the sensations of the turn to unfold in my awareness, or encourage the rest of my body to follow through with a dance.

Every turn of my head will be sensed anew. My breath and heartbeat will be involved with their lived variability according to my emotional and physical condition at the time, as will my powers of concentration and relaxation. In fact, the more given I am to movement processes, trusting rather than forcing the interior journey, the more I will be aware of (able to bring my senses into) my movement. Somatic therapies and movement education based on the work of Moshe Feldenkrais and F. M. Alexander bear this out, as well as the numerous breath-work therapies of which the Middendorf and Rosen methods are good examples. Bonnie Bainbridge Cohen's Body-Mind Centering practice makes developmental use of somatic movement awareness.

Dance extends somatic (tactile/kinaesthetic) awareness, carrying the felt and moving sense of self into an imagistic and poetized field. Kinesthesia and touch, with their affective aspects, from pleasure to pain, lend this field somatic, corporeal substance. We have invented dancing to help us plumb the reality of our feelings and their corporeal source. Our ways of touching the world and relating to others are expressed and experienced concretely in dance since they are embodied in motion. And every instance of dance will give us a new experience, as surely as the moon will draw us to its ever-changing essence. When we give attention to change and regeneration—

WE ASSEMBLE

New bodies through dance,
And new eyes through moonlight.
Every day a new body.
Every day beauty.

Waiting to be known
The shapeless soma quickens
Its liquid assets.

Letting go,
The body-ego
Submerges in the crowd.

Shaped in the clay of the self,
A new body dances,
Shifting, shapelessness forms.
And we are seen.

Matching Space

Dance poetizes space-time as it shapes and gives it corporeal utterance. It will not necessarily tell a story, but it can. The impulse to dance springs from kinesthesia at a preverbal level; it comes to life when the spatio-temporal kinaesthetic sense, born in movement and founded in touch, melds with aesthetic action. In the dance-making process, every artist will give us a new body-of-action and poetics of space-time, one we will recognize because we are body.

All dances, we might notice, are originals. They are creative combinations of body/space/time in motion. Mary Wigman carved and shaped an emotional spatial body thickening time in her singular solo songs and dirges during the early expressionist period of the twenties and thirties. Also in early modern dance, Doris Humphrey unfolded a harmonious spatial body in the architectonics of interrelated group bodies, holding and breaking bilateral symmetry through a subjective formalism. Her space-time aesthetic reflected the ancient Greek meaning of symmetry—*symmetria*, the close fitting of parts together. In the beginning of the twenty-first century, Merce Cunningham still scatters space in the illogical logic of his dances and expands the parameters of technodance, just as surely as Trisha Brown slips off the air in her work, Elizabeth Streb's company propels physical stunts into high art, and Canadian dancers in the companies of La La Human Steps and O Vertigo hurl themselves impossible distances, bursting space with visceral abandon. Each and every artist, each and every dance, distills the spatial nature of movement anew and attests our body's reality of space-time and light. Space becomes real in movement and real in experience. Space is intentionally realized or made real in dance.

In making the space of the dance, we live and match it. Sometimes we even measure it as we mark it. Dancers measure or "mark" the space (and time) of a dance in practice as they trace its contours, rather than dancing them full out. The measure of space is sometimes mathematical and always sensory as a matter of marking kinaesthetic memory. When we dance, however, we do not mark the space of the dance, we match it fully. Space is matched in the doing and reception of the dance—found, uncovered or discovered in awareness, and then paid attention to—which is a somatic matching and creation. Space is incorporated in the bodies of the dance, as also in our everyday experience of bodily mass, infusing our light-dark weight and gravity: trembling and fluid, looping and braiding, coiling, winding, flailing, falling down, flying and floating, punching the air, riding it, landing on one foot, running and resting, holding a momentary shape, sinking, reaching a still point . . . quick . . . the instabilities shifting. . . .

NEVER JUST THE MOON

Missing the soft light
Of the moon on my skin,
I go back to find her.
Twice she has gone.

The next night I stop to look
At the orange-gold of the low-flying moon.
Still full, she stops to look at me.

The moon is never
Just the moon;
It is always a particular point
In experience.

September's moon drops a thin white
Whisper in the early morning sky.
Streaming clouds architect the world,
Opening a doorway to the day.

The next moment I looked,
All this had vanished.

We Limp a Little

"The world," Heidegger says, "is already 'further outside' than any Object can ever be." How is it possible to imagine the world outside of objective appearance, our local and global contact with it? The problem of transcendence does not resolve the question of how subject and object coincide where objects are identified with the idea of the world. In its dance, the world is constantly transcending the objective as well as constituting it. The world worlds in a dance, and we are not separate from it. The worlding momentum of the world is already and always "a transcendence with an ecstatico-horizonal foundation."[9] The world is not the same in all directions, as new physics explains; it dances into its worlding specter.[10]

SPIRALING

In humid torques and arabesques
                  our breath moves
            our moves away,
And returns like a wave:

We body our body
                  lose and increase our body.

                        See how we glisten,
                              Sweat, and we glisten.

Know what our body knows
                  And moves everyday:

Like the worlding of leaves,
We world in our dance.
Merge with the intentional object
The movements we perform.
The world disappears as an object
Matching our dance, as we whirl.

The ecstasis that Heidegger places at the foundation of being is not displaced romantic rapture. It is, however, a heightened sense of awareness and can be realized in dance as in any of our projects when we become one with our intentions in action. Attention is not somatically fragmented at this point. It is focused, present-centered rather than self-centered, but as is the case with attention, it is temporal and conditional, it can and does change.

When we are present-centered, we can say what we intend to without fear, and we cannot be pushed over. This is not necessarily an angry place, but it might be. We can stand up, and stand up for something, because our words and actions come from our own center of gravity and not someone else's. This is not bare theory. In my somatics practice, I have worked with people whose ability to stand without holding onto something or someone—to walk and to speak—are in various stages of disintegration, and not through any identified disease, or because of age.

Bodily lived metaphysics moves beyond theory. Dancing provides an example of this, and so does our everyday ordinary movement. The more I study walking, the more I understand how this seemingly simple action is incredibly complex. As one step replaces the next, the entire body is balancing and counterbalancing the interrelated motions that move us through space, and the pelvis spirals subtly around the hip sockets, interacting with the legs as they lift, one after the other in rhythm. No two people walk alike, and yet we all walk alike in certain fundamental ways. One of the fundamentals of a functional walk (I will avoid saying a "good" walk) is that of counterbalance through a central axis. We watch babies work this out through trial and error.

If one side of our walk does not match the other, we limp a little, or maybe a lot, or we could fall down. All of us limp to a certain degree because none of us is perfectly balanced at zero. We really are not perfectly calibrated walking machines. The interest of individual style in walking comes from human imperfection, if the measure of perfection is bilateral precision that spirals though a central axis. I once worked with a man who limped badly. Together we improved his limp over time. That is, he learned how to limp better. The limp did not go away, but he felt better about his walk: "I feel elegant" is how he put it. This is metaphysics as recourse to first principles, not as totalizing perfection.

In speculative language, metaphysics deals with "first principles" of things, concepts such as being, substance, essence, time, space, cause, and identity. In a poststructural view, metaphysics is erased and everything becomes local instance; no connections or metaconnections seem possible in a world without wholes, centers, or axial ties. On the other hand, a breaking of old ties may allow us to see new ones, especially on the local level of the human body—as singular as it is plural in human identities and affinities.

An embodied metaphysics permeates the local/personal body in its intentional movements. Tenuous, or more confident, self-surpassing phrases coalesce and come and go. They happen without our notice and beyond our conscious willing. As human beings, we are corporeal/metaphysical artifacts: We are Nature looking at Nature looking at Culture, as Susan Griffin discovered in *Woman and Nature* (1978). Or, to substitute a tactile interface for optics, I cast a metaphysical circle dance:

We are Nature

        touching Nature

touching Culture

touching Culture

        touching Nature (etc.).

We can start and end this dance with nature, but in actuality one doesn't enter and exit the loop except through words, in which case we might enter through culture. We have privileged nature with beginnings because we already do this dance at the prereflective level of "core consciousness," as defined by Antonia Damasio in his neuroscientific *The Feeling of What Happens*.[11] We make this dance conscious in our metaphysical artifacts. We match metaphysics through the desires of our becoming, and we can summon the dance of the future to unravel the past.

6 | *Letting the Difference Happen*

In ancient Greek thought, nature's naturalness is called *physis*, also translated as *phusis*, "a term that captures the appearance and disappearance of every being in its presence and absence."[1] As a phenomenologist, Heidegger carried this sense of metaphysics forward, but with a marked difference from tradition. I return to Heidegger to place him on the postmetaphysical stage that surfaced in his *Beiträge zur Philosophie* (Contributions to philosophy) written in 1936–1938, a decade later than his first undermining of traditional metaphysics in *Being and Time*, and not available in English until 1999.[2] I gather his textual dance of being still and in motion, of absence and presence, concealment and disclosure, and the space between that interests me most, especially the generative effectiveness of letting the difference happen. Heidegger's linguistics envisions this metaphysical motion as *Wesen*, or "the inmost sway of being," and uses it to bypass dualism.

Inmost Sway

In his naming of a postmetaphysical stage of philosophy, Heidegger does not herald an end of metaphysics as simple negation. Instead, he questions metaphysics as unitary ideology, perhaps in examining his own evolution through the mastery model of Fascism toward the antiheroic turn of his *Beitrage* where he spoke against "the ideal state" and idealization of art in favor of an unpossessing owning or *ereignis*, translated as "enowining," an "enabling," "bringing into condition of," or "welling up." *Ereignis* is not bent on ruling.[3] In this work concurrent with Hitler's noisy nationalism, Heidegger's descendant moods are expressed in themes of awe, reserve, reticence, premonition, and renunciation. His book joins together the ontic *qualia* of "Echo," "Playing-Forth," "Leap," "Grounding," "The Ones to Come," and "The Last God." These can all be imagined as embodied and as danced.

I mask Heidegger
In Echo
And Imago
Open to the mystery
Of letting them move in a dance.

Their various embodiments
Attune quietly to an alert and watchful silence—
Of swaying and letting go,
Of going under and abjuration.

I let the difference of his themes dance and generate new themes, more uplifting, left not to abstract manipulations of movement, however, and not to instrumental production, or to the rise of giant technologies critiqued in his work. I accept technical and technological objectifications in staging a work, but I want to go beyond them in my dance.

Despite the descendant tone of the *Beitrage*, we see once again the master mode at work, even from the first hint of *Wesen*. It surfaces in his view of "inceptual thinking" as a "masterful knowing." But it seems this is an intrinsic placement of knowing, like dancing: This is the thinking "that itself must know that it can at any time count as unrewarded" (41). Inceptual thinking is what he finally calls (in a Buddhist ruse) "mindfulness." Another mastery is needed, he says, where thinking is enacted as historical. This mastery is "sheltered" and "reserved" as preparation for those who are to come, "those who create new sites within being itself, from within which once again a stability in the strife of earth and world takes place" (43).

Heidegger sets struggle into place, but undercuts it at once: "The highest knowing is that which is strong enough to be the origin of a renunciation." But renunciation also carries a potential for mobilization.

Enactment of the "Echo," "Playing-Forth," "Leap," and "Grounding" is not conceptual but "inceptual": mobilization belongs to the joining of these qualities. They flow into and out of one another as they anticipate an ending: "The inceptual mastery of the end will show itself as the last god" (49). This end will link to pathways that signal a crossing to "the Other Beginning," a new sway, an opening and estrangement. As in postmodern discourse and dance, Heidegger's ends and beginnings are not final: in "fullness" and "gifting" lie hidden "the most sheltered essential sway of the not, as not-yet and no-longer" (288).

Imaged from Heidegger's stated project of the "still unmastered ground plan of the historicity of the crossing itself," mastery passes with the last god (5).

Or, it transforms.
Movement into the crossing and passing
Is opaque and not vertical, as ascending from below.

Facing Heidegger on the postmetaphysical stage, I place Claude Lefort, a French philosopher, political theorist, and student and close associate of Merleau-Ponty. He belongs here because of his existential, ontological critique of masterful totalitarian regimes in favor of the contingencies of democracy. Leforte's *The Political Forms of Modern Society* and *Writing the Political Test* ferret out the differences between politics and the political, the latter being more elusive and metaphysical.[4] He demonstrates how political philosophy and metaphysics come together to inquire into generative frameworks of the political, how generative space-time schemes are, particularly how they generate meaning. Thus, the generative structures of any art, as also our conceptions of the body, would be of concern. What is practiced, encoded, valued, and embodied through form? Constitutive genesis involves the assignment of meaning to events and their staging in public and sociopolitical space. Leforte shows how "staging" relates to modes of representation that acquire in some fashion a general (or universal) quality, not located on the level of particulars.

His political theory does not say how democracy is to be articulated, but its "floating representation" and "indefinability" does not prevent articulation. Democratic rule remains ambivalent, the people's identity latent, unpredictable, as in the emerging and chaotic society of post-Saddam Iraq in 2003. The microscopically small difference between the number of votes in the U.S. presidential election between Al Gore and George W. Bush in 2000, which temporarily deadlocked the decision and prompted lawsuits, is another example of such unpredictability. The opposite of this would be totalitarianism: the people as one body welded to a leader, as found in nation-states, and often replicated in cosmology and religion. The democracy Lefort posits represents a curious form of disincorporation, pure potential waiting for a body.

I mask Lefort, therefore, in democratic disarray and disincorporation. He desires an identity, but not the singular body of dictators, kings, and emperors. He moves forward a drama of historical, political, and aesthetic concern that is as wary of masters as I am. I speak of his metaphysical concern for "the dissolution of the markers of certainty" in which actors and agents (I add dancers) experience indeterminacy as the basis of their power, the basis of relation between self and other, and of staged events.[5] If I so mask Lefort, I see his striking resemblance to Merce Cunningham and the aesthetics of chance and dispersal, and to the emergence of postmodern dance—what Sally Banes has identified as its democratic bias through proliferating forms —even to the revival of fairy tales, as new tales form in resistance to fixed meanings.[6]

A tolerant multiplicity in bodily practices goes even further back historically to the beginnings of the somaesthetic movement that informed the development of modern dance. I am speaking of the European *Gymnastik* movement and its democratic basis as mapped by Don Hanlon Johnson in *Body, Spirit and Democracy*. This aesthetic and therapeutic movement began through a number of teachers who traveled back and forth between northern Europe and the Eastern seaboard of the United States during the mid- and late-nineteenth century: Emile Jacques-Dalcroze, Francois Delsarte, Genevieve Stebbins, and Bess Mensendieck, to name a few. These forerunners of the new dance of the twentieth century shared a vision of the body that did not fit the classical model found in ballet and mechanized physical education.[7] Bodies would not be judged on a normative scale; each person could manifest her potential through her own nature, as I experienced as late as 1965 in my first somatic studies with *Gymnastik* teacher Mathile Thiele at the Mary Wigman School in Berlin. Thiele later became my friend and neighbor in western New York. We often spoke of her performance in Dore Hoyer's *Tanz fur Kathe Kollwitz*, a dance based in part on a lithograph called *Nie Wieder Krieg* (Never again war) by German artist and social activist Kathe Kollwitz completed in 1924. Ten years earlier, with the beginning of World War I in 1914, Wigman created her first *Witch Dance*. Her second and most famous *Witch Dance* (1926) came two years after Kollwitz's *Nie Wieder Krieg*. In four more years, Wigman's monumental statement on war and death, *Totenmal* (1930) preceded Hitler's rise to power in 1933 and World War II beginning in 1939. Soon after the end of World War II in 1945, *Nie Wieder Krieg* became a central theme for Wigman's student Hoyer and her newly established dance group working in the one room that was left of the former Wigman Studio in Dresden after the most devastating bombing of the war.

The pacifist-feminist influence of Kollwitz on early modern dance is never so apparent as in Hoyer's dance named after her. As feminist, the dance does not have at stake the individual rights of women to pursue personal goals; the mobilization of feminine conscience in the face of what we now call "human rights" is more important. The work is morally and spiritually compelled by the perennial questions of suffering: Why do we suffer? How can we end or go beyond suffering? How shall we live?

Thiele, who survived the bombing of Dresden along with Hoyer, became the primary teacher at the Wigman School for Dance in Berlin for the nineteen years of its postwar existence. The school, very small by today's standards, occupied an old mansion that remained standing after the war, the dining room providing the main studio. Hoyer committed suicide in 1968, leaving Thiele a small bundle of her belongings and a note concerning their survival of war, "living like vagabonds and squatters."[8]

Through my study at the Wigman School, I understood that I could dance from my own place of power and need not replicate the body of another. The early modern dance as informed by exploratory and playful somaesthetics resisted biomedicine's mechanized views of the body, which separated the body as material substance from its expressive spirit.

Through the development of somatics, body and spirit were conceived as one and the same. At a time when medical doctors were engaged in crude applications of surgery and medication, the new so-

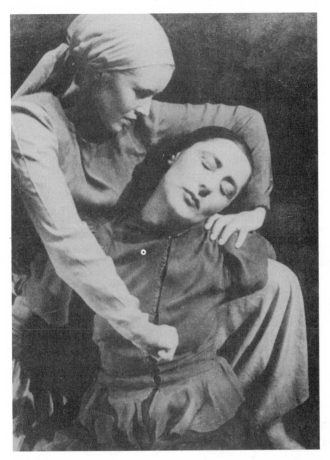

Mathilde Thiele (1907–2002) in Dore Hoyer's *Tanz fur Kathe Kollwitz* (1946), based in part on a lithograph called *Nie Wieder Krieg* (Never again war) by Kathe Kollwitz (1924). This photograph pictures a moment at the beginning of the dance where Thiele is being held and inspired with courage. Photograph courtesy Mathilde Thiele.

matics body workers were developing sophisticated healing techniques through expressive movement, sensory awareness, music, breath work, and touch. Meanwhile, two world wars shaped concerns for democracy, which also surfaced in the development of somatics and modern dance. Later, the Vietnam War would signal another descent of authoritative dance techniques in postmodern forms.

Underneath style, arising in breath and through the bones, dancing itself dissolves boundaries, moves these around in the psyche and on the stage. No artist and no particular period has a monopoly on democratic designs where exploratory aesthetics promote forms of dance available to all without privilege. Modern dance, as it entered into education, became an accessible participatory art form. If Cunningham's dances grew through contingent formulation, for all their chance arrangements they nevertheless functioned through their proximity to classical ballet with its aristocratic heritage, the certainty of their finite designs, and the sharp clarity of their motions, even where parts of the dances could be rearranged at various "events."

Uncertainty is explored every day in the consciousness of dancers, in the studio and on stage, not so much in being uncertain of their ability to perform a dance, we hope, but in the shifting thematics of their dances and in the precariousness of dancing itself.

The uncertainty that is wonder
Resides in the metaphysics of dancing.
Being wears the mask of nonbeing.
Dancing is masked in stillness and surprise.

"Disincorporation" does not point to the end of symbolism or imagery on the stages of politics and art, but to the end of singular ruling images. Disincorporation is difficult to conjure.

On this stage
We dance the empty place of power,
Or real vacuum
Amid signs of fragmentation of social space,
Relegating bodily expression to an indeterminate potency.

We remain aware, though we merely mark it, that where the social wears thin the religious appears.[9] Here we turn toward the power of difference, allowing the social and the spiritual to coexist, and we move from merely marking time to dancing, but in the curious sense of not-dancing, of not-art and no-body-in-particular.

The Dance of Equals

Since dancing has been one of my ways of being, I can consciously relate to my body-of-dance and make choices. I need not police my body, nor submit to authoritative modes and masters, but I can try to excel in whatever practice I employ. I do not mean to undermine hard work and the enjoyment this brings. I do mean to undermine hard work under duress of univocal mastery and domineering understandings of embodiment.

The original spirit of deconstruction through Jacques Derrida resulted in a metaphysics of "différance," and Derrida coined this neologism to suggest what is different and also what is deferred, a wordplay on "difference": "For us, différance remains a metaphysical name: and all the names that it receives from our language are still, so far as they are names, metaphysical." Naming, then, is a metaphysical art, and Derrida's metaphysics explains a field of equally weighted (or lifted) words akin to Schoenberg's equality of tones in music.

Derrida goes on to say: "There will be no unique name, not even the name of Being." (As in the ancient metaphysical artifact from Lao Tzu: "The name that can be named is not the name.") Like Nietzsche, Derrida turns finally toward dance. Do they hope to escape logic altogether?:

> Being must be conceived without nostalgia; that is, it must be conceived outside the myth of the purely maternal or paternal language belonging to the lost fatherland of thought. On the contrary, we must affirm it—in the sense that Nietzsche brings affirmation into play—with a certain laughter and with a certain dance. [10]

"I would not believe in a God who could not dance," is how Nietzsche put the case of metaphysics. Derrida's deconstruction would have us dance without nostalgia. But in giving equal weight to all, Derrida says, we should also dance without hope, the other side of nostalgia, which he relates to Heideggerian hope, in his hopes to deconstruct Heidegger. [11] At the same time that Derrida deconstructs "being" as a master word, he wants to affirm it. What begins in negation turns inside out; absence becomes present.

I mask Derrida
with his negations and detachments,
and stage him with the imagined presence
of his predecessors—Nietzsche and Heidegger.

I join Derrida in the dance of difference he creates. But the music of sameness bothers me. Not all tones are equal to me, and I remember that I have a difficult time listening to twelve-tone music with its carefully constructed rules of distributive counterpoint. As with democracy, differences can disappear in equalities, I see, and I do not want to push away nostalgia. I want to remember my life, even when it pains me, and I do not want to give up my body. To be a body is to remember, to be hopeful, and to be vulnerable. For the time being, I allow my dance to detach with Derrida, to laugh a little, but not to deconstruct. For joyful affirmations, I will need to turn elsewhere.

On this stage, I begin to dance the aesthetic multiplicity that the collapse of concentric authority allows me.

I root the worthy and the bright
In the spatial awareness of modern dance.
Loosen my shapes
In the fairness of the postmodern.
Get down with an African flair.
I touch my trembling Butoh chalk-face,
And float on continents of air.

Lack of Art

I observe how traditional metaphysics generates ideologies or worldviews where principles of the past are translated into cultural values and totalizing claims. In the *Beitrage*, Heidegger singles out ideals that sustain ideal states and ideal art as two such totalizing claims (perhaps in response to his own problematic history as an early exponent of Fascism). To this we could add biological elitism, as this also results in oppression. "Mindfulness" is alive in experience and larger than "lived experience" with its inevitable fall into history. Everyone can dance, and all bodies matter. In a curious way, Heidegger's philosophy helps me to envision this. One of his last projects (of undoing) was to overcome metaphysics and in so doing to also overcome aesthetics:

> Epochs which through historicism know much—and soon everything—will not grasp that a moment of history that lacks art can be more historical and more creative than times of a widespread art business. . . . Lack of art is grounded in knowing that corroboration and approval of

those who enjoy and experience "art" cannot at all decide whether the object of enjoyment stems generally from the essential sphere of art or is merely an illusionary product of historical (as discipline) dexterity, sustained by dominant goal-settings. (355–56)

Heidegger criticizes struggles that enlist worldviews, especially as they tune to production and mechanization through what he recognizes as "giant technologies." His view of struggle has changed from his earlier position in *Being and Time* as I just examined it in the previous essay, "A Dance of Time Beings." In Heidegger's *Beitrage* a linguistic play of mastery is maintained, however, even as it is constantly undercut. I substitute "matching" as a less embattled term and mode of encounter. In matching *wesen,* the sway of beings,

We unmask our lack of art,
Crossing to new beginnings,
Standing and becoming.
In this mindful space of free play,
Everyone can dance.

Marking Time

If I continue to dance the metaphysics of difference, I come to another juncture—that congruence of space and time that comes in the guise of silence. I tune to this in my dance and listen as I mark time. If I listen closely enough, I hear a new phase in process. I notice that my dance is not as elusive as I have imagined it to be, and that dance itself marks time. When I suspend my assumptions about the ephemerality of dance, I suddenly see (through this phenomenological reduction) how I can return to the contours and points of my dance when I repeat it, even in my imagination. This is also true of my dance improvisations as I polish the present moment, again and again.

My life is not so clearly iterated, only partially through memory, and through certain patterns that sediment and return. In respect to these, I can turn to somatic bodywork, accessing and working consciously with my habits to provide more options for myself. When I consider the unrepeatability of my life in relation to the near repeatability of a dance I have learned, or can improvise on the spot, I see how my dance marks time. It marks time because it leaves a mark, a momentary mark, mar, and wound. My dance marks time and signs it with my being.

She Dreamed

She lived in a peaceful village at the foot of an azure mountain. She could see that a strong wind had carved its face, scooping, curling into its belly of rock. The people there would gaze up at its sharp snags and tender slopes. Sometimes its snowcapped top would move and melt, filling the sky with a lush green overhang. The people often talked about going up the mountain and peering down at the village from the vantage of the overhang, but no one ever did. Then one day she decided to go up herself. When she looked down from the top, the village was so far away and tiny it seemed a dream in the dream she was dreaming.

Suddenly, she realized she was falling into space. Foolishly, she had leapt from the ledge before seeing how very far down and miles through space the village was. She could never survive the fall—unless—yes! She would create a great lake for her landing and swim ashore. As she fell toward the lake, she saw her daughter there in the shallow waters at the shoreline—sitting on her heels in an easy yoga pose—her long black hair blowing in the wind.

COSMIC DANCER

She strips—more naked in one fell swoop

Than death to doornails—
And patterns paths

                        of Canada geese
           a poet might say: Strewing
                glory in great flapping chevrons
        of formalist dance.

                Over New York / Creasing
Winter's sky-squawking surround / Pulling
              breaths through breasts, upward.
She covers her nakedness with armor
             and cultural makeup, with feathers

And flying fronds.
Puts on her bulky costumes—
                    spotlights and dappled lights
                                        to twirl in space—and see, how
                    her cosmic body worlds in the dance.

Molecules of Motion

PASS AND SHIFT

Uncoil and squish,
                    my sways bestumbled
Coming.

From place to pause—
                    I breathe and dissolve,
Revolve in a look,
                                        close my eyes and fumble.

Operating, performing
                                        whiskflick falling
                                        lying and feasting—by my own
seeming
                                        made singing. . . .

I can also rest—
This is a part of movement,
                    another phase of its form.

FINDING

Through my neck, head, and back,

                    Time beats,
                    Gushing like a wound—
Surrendering
Before thought unbends,
                                        Over and over,
                                                  Raining home.

ONLY PAY ATTENTION TO HOW I TOUCH

Speaking no language, she stepped
Near and touched my shoulder
Aware of some distinct aspect
Of my being.

Maybe the movement that flows freely
Drifted off to the sound, as it sometimes does
When I dance. Moments of movement
Arrive and disappear as part of that.

TWO FIGURES MERGE

One looks, as part of that,
A casual metaphysics unfolds
In fires of time unprompted.

SOFTLY HOW

Her golden form subsides,
And memory wills a flower.
All swelling streams endure
The flux of breath and
Being spoken.

SENSATION SHE SAYS

Seems stopped,
Unable to flow past
Stinging and stabbing.

PLEASURE

The pain that calls
Into being—a touch
That brings us here—

PRESSES

Now, fleet and shifting,
Running like heavy water
Coursing stones beneath.

IDLY

Through fingers the sympathy
That health has held in place,
As part of what has gone before
And uncourageous pity.

MY BACK CONSENTS TO LIE DOWN

And float in the blue, to speak
Beside you and breathe
The question I have,
Or stand where it wants to be.

Hemming its haws on all fours
The maneuvered seesaw crawls
Cross threads of time.

Still the perfect-membered scrawls,
The bits and pieces of my heart,
Set straight the stillness of my mind.

CHOOSING

A moving sound between
Myself most closely held,
And love's do-nothing stars.

THE SPINNING EARTH

The sound I hear
The color and desire
That I possess.

STEPPED BY WALKING

I run faster.

IN THE SUN OF BURNING SHAPES

I grow conscious,
Imagine my body's marvels
And cease to betray them.

SLOW DOWN

Return to the river
On scent and shade
The Soma Sea—

HISTORY FILLED WITH POSSIBILITY

Not as you would have thought
Unyielding.

The awkward future—
Not already decided,
Fatalistically.

. . .

When I dance, I hold—let go—sneeze, puncture, wound, heal.
I (me now, not me back then) engage in technique class more freely.
I (of the back then) was so engaged in discipline it forgot to be free,
but now is free—can wound yet heal, cry yet laugh, and come to a
turnout without fear.
Sarah McCormick, New York, 2003

PART III · Descen-dance

Wally Wolfgruber and Larry Goldhuber lampoon Stravinsky's *Rite of Spring* in a 2001 performance, *A Match Made in Heaven*. The photograph is from a preconcert poster by Jim Dusen.

7 | Messy Beauty and Butoh Invalids

Descen-dance, Obedience, and Resistance

Live in my shivering,
Cloud-Goddess-of-Joy.
Send down the rain.
Cast your spells once more.
Descend through the gray
Through the groans and the mutters.
We're lost if the sun bakes us all.

My experience tells me something quite different from the texts and dances of classicism and metaphysical dualism—that our transcendence is not won at the expense of flesh and body, nor is mind higher than matter: *mater,* matron, matrix, mother, the land. Rather, we pierce reality through the body, and we transcend downward as well as upward. The "descendental," a word we do not use as much as its "transcendental" opposite, is that which descends to the matter-of-fact.[1]

"Descendance," now used rarely, is a word derived from the Latin *descendentum.*[2] The sense and spelling of this word captures the downward falling moment of the radiant spiral that became a movement signature for the early modern dance as it grew throughout the first half of this century, primarily through the authorship of women. Female authors such as Isadora Duncan, Mary Wigman, and Doris Humphrey brought dance down to earth through the structure of the spiral—mirroring the structure of DNA, the shape of life. The descendance of modern dance is an earthwork, a "descen-dance" that does not transcend immediacy, but lives in the eternity of presence: reeling and "realing" in pools of experience, of learning, loving, and living. This radiant energy and its erotic reflection in word and dance also indicate ancestry and descendants. It is not a ladder to heaven with mind climbing upward overcoming matter.

With its strivings beyond the fleeting material world and its disdain of erotic origins (sacred sex), Western philosophy from the Greeks forward has had as much trouble with descendance and the flesh as ballet has. Phenomenologist Algis Mickunas traces the transcending reflection of philosophy and salvation religions through various kinds of exacting sacrifice. The transcendent being becomes "lovable, good, high" in overcoming the dissolving domain of bewitchment; but the maternal, emotional, and erotic (an entire matrix of values) has to be designated as low in the tensional overcomings.[3]

The high, good, and desirable being dances across everything to be avoided. Gravity is her enemy; she does not sink into the earth, she pulls herself up and maintains an almost impossible balance in tenuous relationship to the earth on point shoes. She learns how to breathe all over again, how to sublimate her flesh in ritual repetitions, and how to wear a smile. She starves her body, banishes its regenerative cycles, and never touches sod. Richard Tarnas sees a similar, pervasive repression:

> The evolution of the Western mind has been founded on the repression of the feminine—on the repression of undifferentiated unitary consciousness, of the *participation mystique* with nature; a progressive denial of the *anima mundi*, the soul of the world, of the community of being, of the all-pervading, of mystery and ambiguity, of imagination, emotion, instinct, body, nature, woman.[4]

In a reversal of the ascendant purifications of ballet, German choreographer Pina Bausch (b. 1940) filled the stage with sod in *The Rite of Spring* (1975), reviving a bitter beauty that fomented at the expressionist root of modern dance. (One of my undergraduate students wrote to Bausch asking if she could audition for her company. Bausch replied that she did not audition anyone under the age of thirty.) In Bausch's works, the flesh is raw and confessional, unlike the youthful ballerina's thinning rituals of anorexia nervosa and bulimia that shed the flesh and conform to an ideal. Bausch's troubling works express a comic, vulgar, and somewhat messy beauty. The beauty of ballet stems from conformity and purification in perfection of geometric movement forms. Conformity can mean unquestioning obedience, unfortunately, and even abuse.

Obedience to the Master

In a 1996 revival of *The Lesson* (1963), a ballet by Flemming Flindt based on Eugene Ionesco's absurdist play, the ballet master murders the ballerina. This dance, which Flindt choreographed for the San Francisco Ballet, is about abuse of power, manipulation, and naivete, intended as an allegory of Nazi Germany. The pianist, one of the three characters in the ballet, gives the sadistic teacher an armband (swastika). The teacher is a dictator. The pianist is like Göring or Himmler, or all those who went along with the atrocities. After the demise of the ballerina, who represents all victims, we see another hopeful coming to the door of the studio, hugging her ballet slippers. Ballet, with its toe shoes displaying the pedestaled female, has a hard time stating anything beyond its intrinsic politics: Toe shoes (like Cinderella's glass slipper) are foot binding.

George Balanchine was obsessed with his ballerinas. If other men paid attention to the current apple of his eye, he became jealous, would even peek through the keyhole during rehearsals. When Susanne Farrell finally mustered the courage to break her youthful romantic bondage to Balanchine, who was forty-one years her senior, she married Paul Mejia, and Balanchine exiled both of them. Farrell had to pack up her toe shoes and leave an impressive body of work in roles she had helped Balanchine craft for her. The dancer is a participant in the choreography, indispensable yet invisible in terms of credit. Balanchine needed his muses for more than inspiration. His work was their work also, as Farrell remembers: "The steps he asked me to do and dances I would give back to him."[5] So one can imagine vulnerability on the part of Balanchine also, but that does not change the balance of authorial power between the choreographer and the dancer, the teacher and student, employer and employee.

The curious part of *The Lesson* is how it unwittingly comments on the condition of ballet itself. Nazi Germany is a big and very easy target. The smaller, everyday compromises of the flesh in disciplines that flay the body and systematize it in exacting and sometimes punishing disciplines are harder to identify. *The Lesson* is about the tight discipline of ballet and its sadistic taskmasters, particularly in relation to their hopeful charges. Gender power relations are not far from the surface in the master's easy access to the female body. Male ballet masters have traditionally held great power over girls and women by virtue of being both teachers and masters of a stringent form of cultivation. Give body to this situation in the tens of thousands of hopeful girls and women training with masters (both male and female) and the possibilities for abuse are staggering.

As I passed by the ballet studio, I heard the teacher berate his students and call the sassy one a "bitch." What, I wondered, has this got to do with teaching ballet?

"Well, I was just kidding," the teacher said later.

My mind went back to 1962 when Louis Horst, a famous authority on modern dance composition, had called me a "constipated virgin" and told me to "read a book about love between the sexes" in his Modern Forms class. His assistant told me not to worry, since he criticized the ones he liked and tended to ignore the rest. What was I supposed to do with this? He chose all of my compositions to show onstage in the workshop gatherings at the American Dance Festival that summer, and continued to insult me sexually while I blushed. He told me I had promise as a choreographer, but needed to find my own voice. (So I could tell him to watch his mouth, maybe?)

There are some very talented and nurturing ballet masters, but also flagrant abuses of power. If one complains about an abusive style of mastery in the academy, one is apt to hear that teaching styles vary, and intimidation works (as I did). Intimidation certainly worked in the training of youths for the Chinese classical opera, where they very narrowly survived the severe punishments of the masters, as seen in *Farewell My Concubine* (1993), a film by Chen Kaige.

I am not advocating that we throw ballet out the window, merely that we examine the master model that sustains it and all dances affected by it. This includes a great deal of contemporary theater dance throughout the world and basic ballet training in gymnastics and ice skating. *Obedience* to the unquestioned authority of the master teacher was challenged in postmodern dance. As teachers, many of us started to think of ourselves more as facilitator-catalysts than models. This postmodern revolution seems to have passed by unnoticed in many ballet academies where master models rule, and there may still be some university dance departments in the United States, both ballet and modern, where students must maintain thinness to be retained in the dance major. At one time, the practice of "weighing-in" was prevalent, and it is not over yet.[6] This situation is not just in the United States; one of my graduate students from Korea in 2003 was still suffering the effects of starving her already thin body so that she could be accepted into a dance major program at a Korean university.

Violent Eroticism and Sexual Politics

Should we not also look for abuses in other directions? Pina Bausch's neoexpressionist choreography as it came to international prominence in the 1970s is no more kind than regimented ballet and modern dance. Indeed, it may sometimes be more grueling, but it is more about unmasking torments of the flesh than overcoming the flesh. Bausch continues to explore a terrible sublime that exposes (some would say exploits) victimization of women. Layered with this, she shows both sexes locked in vicious cycles of pleasure and pain. Bausch's treatment of sexuality exposes dominator sexual politics. She uncovers erotic beauty and its cultural entrapment, but whether she intends to critique dominator (shaming) models of sexual behavior is difficult to say. The association of pain with sexuality is presented for interpretation and audience engagement. Like the earlier expressionist dance of her predecessor, Mary Wigman, Bausch is emotionally engaging, her riveting works more instinctual than intellectual, sometimes comical and violently erotic despite their well-studied use of space and time. Neither Bausch nor Wigman are naively primitive in their expressionism. Entreating the shadows and revising dominant social mores, they are descendant, objective, and resistive.

Shared Powers

In *Sacred Pleasure,* Riane Eisler explores prehistoric Goddess cultures where men and women shared powers and revered nature. These cultures represent a kind of eroticism we have lost and need to recover.[7] When Christian missionaries arrived in Hawaii in the early 1800s, they deemed the sacred dance traditions of the people to be pagan. Christian fathers established a new social structure that threatened the demise of the dancer's oneness with nature, the sound of wind and surf. Today the Kumu Hula (accomplished teachers) are once again keepers of a cultural heritage and its respect for nature. By the time I saw the Kumu Hula dance in Hawaii in 1973, I was a professor of dance at the State University of New York at Brockport. I was astounded by the ancestral hula: Its performers were large women, very large, and they moved with a grace beyond description.

I saw this dance of the Goddess in performances at the international conference of the Congress on Research in Dance, where I also met Joseph Campbell and heard him speak. He spoke spontaneously of the Goddess and her generous manifestations across many cultures. When I returned to New York, I took his seminars on "Classical Mysteries of the Great Goddess" at the Theater of the Open Eye in New York City. His seminars floored me. Could God really be a woman and part of my nature as a woman? I had already left the religion of my childhood and the priesthood rule of the fathers as "head of the household." I practiced yoga and Zen meditation, but I still carried deeply embedded notions of a judgmental male God somewhere in my psyche. Campbell's revelatory teachings about the female deity changed my life and my approach to dancing. In yoga, when I chanted the Sanskrit "so ham," "I am that," "that is God," I knew I was "that," and that God did not separate me from nature nor from the land and the people I also carried within.

As Mother Earth, the female deity is tolerant and inclusive. Some of us argued with Campbell that the earth might also be represented as male. He pointed out that in some systems it is—the earth god Geb in Egypt, for instance—but that the typical association is with woman. We saw problems of relating woman to nature without inclusion of the male, and also urged him to think about woman's journey. The classical mystery as he presented it was about the heroic journey of

Odysseus, who becomes transformed through his encounters with the Goddess as mother, temptress, and partner (Penelope).

As much as I loved learning about female deities from Campbell, I also questioned his interpretation of "the classical mysteries." I felt left out. It is not enough to consider the feminine as the vehicle (the muse) for the hero's transformation. Who is she for herself? I wondered. Laka, goddess of the hula? Or Demeter/Persephone, who descends to the underworld and brings springtime in her return? And where is the reciprocity? The true partnership? Eventually I studied mythology and began to understand it as an important tool for interpretation. I learned that myths (like dances) are also subject to various readings.

Why did Persephone descend to the underworld? Because she was abducted and raped by Hades, as Homer writes? "Begging for pity and fighting him off, she was dragged into his golden chariot." Or did she go voluntarily to administer to the dead and provide safe passage for her ancestors, as was written in prepatriarchal accounts?[8] One story makes a victim of the feminine; the other gives her active spiritual power. This has consequences for how we interpret mythological structures in dance. For instance, the many choreographies on Stravinsky's *Le Sacre du printemps (The Rite of Spring)* can be read through the myths that sustain them. Early versions beginning with Nijinski's original (1913–1914) are built on virgin sacrifice, but, as later dances show, this is not a necessary interpretation of the coming of spring— or of Stravinsky's music. In the Russian folktale that inspired Stravinsky, the virgin is the Chosen One, sacrificed to consecrate the tribal community: A "Ritual of Abduction" is named by Stravinsky in the first act of his ballet score.

The *Sacre* of Maurice Bejart (1959), Martha Graham (1984), and Pina Bausch (1975) all correspond in many respects to the Persephone myth in Greek mythology through Homer, who also details a ritual of abduction. Why does the rapturous approach of spring seem to require the rape of a young girl? We need to rewrite the myths that do violence to women, or find the source myths that give women power over their own bodies, as Mara Lynn Keller has done through her participation in the Eleusinian mysteries in Greece and her study of prepatriarchal versions of the Persephone myth that do not glorify female martyrdom and rape. The work of Charlene Spretnak also rewrites the violent tendencies of Western mythology.[9]

Dancers are revising as well. Molissa Fenley's bare-breasted solo *State of Darkness* (1988) is based on Stravinsky's *Sacre,* but unlike previous dances based on his music, her interpretation does not dwell on feminine violation. She sometimes performs her dance outdoors as the day dies into darkness. In the spirit of endurance, she represents spring's renewal and cycles of darkness in the workings of nature. Marie Chouinard's *Sacre* (1993) is the most innocently animal of the version I have seen in its shuddering, quivering plastiques. The promise of Chouinard's *Sacre* seems unfulfilled against Stravinsky's mounting music, or intentionally deflated. Nothing builds toward the god's orgasm in the choreography; the erotic dancing inspired by the music remains, nevertheless.

In a surprisingly fresh subversion of the mythology behind *Sacre,* Santo Giglio choreographed an all-woman tap dance to Stravinsky's music, setting group movement to pounding rhythms in metal-sharp staccato, inflecting the whole with elastic, eccentric solos and an aura of pathos. Giglio's *Sacre* (2001) is a contrapuntal ritual of stomping rhythms and light explosions, but not of sacrificial maidens. I have begun to notice that differing versions of human nature and fate are developed in the various dances in *Sacre,* as are differing mythologies. The psychobiology of this is underscored in Carl Jung's teachings, namely that when an inner situation or myth is not brought to consciousness, it manifests in the life of the body as fate.

Organic Faults, Somatic Solutions

"He could ride, he could shoot, he could sing—and he knew the Scriptures."

One of the speakers said this of my father at his funeral. Another speaker said that dad's old dog Bo taught him how to sing: "Bo started to howl, then Bill started to howl, pretty soon it was two-part harmony." The truth, which had a hard time in the town, was that my father had studied voice with Mrs. Summerhaze at Brigham Young University. She traveled all the way to the Southern end of Utah to beseech my grandmother to let her son remain in school after the death of his father. She lost, my father was needed on the ranch, and for the rest of his life he would sing in funerals and weddings and travel with Gay Nineties Melodrama. *Many a heart that is aching, af-ter the ball.*

...

Mrs. Cannon, my high school English teacher, taught me that a sentence is a living organism. We diagrammed sentences in her class, a bit like dissecting frogs, to see what made them tick. She had two doctorates, one in botany and one in math, and was for many years the town's mayor. She was one of two Democrats in town; the other was my uncle. My father became a Democrat when my uncle, his brother with whom he enjoyed a lifetime of petty rivalry, switched to Republican. They quarreled about whose kids were smarter, and so on. People liked being around my father; he was a great storyteller. When I was small, he recited memorized poems to me by the hour. I still remember the music in his voice and the Western romance of Alfred Noyes's melodramatic "Highwayman" of 1880.

OF WIND

. . . a torrent of darkness among the gusty trees

> *(My father's tones of mellow-rose and gold)*

and the moon

. . . a ghostly galleon tossed upon cloudy seas.

> *(He sang in the meadows at twilight.)*

The road was a ribbon of moonlight

> *(Yes I could see it.)*

looping the purple moor,

> *(He said, "looping," but Noyes's word is*
>
> *"over.")*

and the highwayman came riding—
Riding—riding—
The highwayman came riding, up to the
old inn door.

Over the cobbles he clattered and clanged
into the dark inn yard,

> *(In one steady breath, and then he became*
>
> *lighter)*

And he tapped with his whip on the shutters,
but all was locked and barred.

> *(The last word stuck in his throat.)*

Then he whistled a tune to the window,
and who should be waiting there

But the landlord's black-eyed daughter,
> (*Who was this pretty girl he made sound so beloved?*)

Bess, the landlord's daughter,
Plaiting a dark red love knot into her
long black hair.

. . .

"Rhythm is the relationship of the elements,"
I wrote in a college paper when I was twenty,
"stress, quality, pitch, and pause."

Now I would add tone and weight.
Direction, position, speed, and pressure.
Intensity and density with moving transitions.
Our looping through balance to off-balance . . .

Fatigue, focus, point of contact.

My love of rhythm and organically flowing movement continues still. John Faiello, a former student of mine, is the only male dancer to take Isadora Duncan's work as his inspiration, learning most of the Duncan repertory from teachers who danced with her. When I was in San Francisco, I went to see him teach. As it turned out, I was the only one who came to class, so we danced some of the Duncan dances together, I following along behind, which is how the dances are typically learned. Duncan's dances are not teased apart and analyzed, but more organically embodied.

After years of apprenticeship, John has learned many of her dances. It was exhilarating to catch fire with him (and Isadora) as we swept through the space, dancing from the solar plexus. John works for the city to make a living, but says he really lives through the expressive essence of Duncan's dances. I particularly liked his masculine performance of Isadora's earlier dances—the lilting, swooping Chopin waltzes.

Emotionally charged dancing such as Duncan's is often associated with instinct and organicism—as well as the natural and erotic. It is therefore suspect in poststructural ideology. But what does "organicism" refer to here? Mechanically functional movement? The doctrine of adaptation in organic structure? Dualistic vitalism in nineteenth-century biology? Origins? A simplistic demand for unity? Representation? Sequential movement flow? Improvisatory path or intuitive derivation? Happy endings? Would it indicate freedom in performance? We get some idea of its meaning from Roger Copeland's critique of modern dance. At the same time, we consider what the devaluation of eros in an organically whole, free, and pleasurable movement costs— as we critique Copeland's critique.

He believes the dance aesthetics of Merce Cunningham (b. 1919) is an antidote to the organicism of early modern dance with its naturalism in Isadora Duncan (b. 1877) and Martha Graham (b. 1894). Duncan and Graham are worlds apart in their aesthetics, but Copeland links them through their organic faults.[10]

Copeland has not noticed how Cunningham refracts the feminine in his denial of organically unified motions, in his sublimating of emotion, through his employment of the purifying aesthetics of ballet, or in his use of dispersing tactics (chance methods in choreography). The latter interrupts and displaces intuitive predilections for dancing, an interesting process up to a point, like drawing straws every time you leave the house to determine which direction to walk or drive. Critic Arlene Croce admits a long apprenticeship with Cunningham's highly theoretical approach to dance before she could come to any spontaneous enjoyment of it.[11]

In classes I took with Cunningham, he explained that he used chance procedures to get away from himself, what he might ordinarily do. Throwing dice for his next move, or drawing numbers from a pile of numbered papers, for instance, extended his range and required him to make new and unusual connections. The aesthetic effect of this intellectual way of working is movement randomization in space and time, a radical abstraction, both reserved and engaging. I have enjoyed Cunningham's dances as meditations with drone flow, a sometimes unpredictable, remote steadiness. Without the offsetting stage sets of Robert Rauschenberg and the disruptive music of John Cage, the dance would space-out even more. This can be soothing, intriguing, sometimes boring, or puzzling.

I give my students chance procedure assignments in composition classes. Some like the process; some hate it. Then they ask, "What's next"? A world dictated by accidental connections (the aleatory dream-body) is not exactly where they want to remain.

Through my experiments with Cunningham's chance procedures, I have learned that true accident is hard to come by, or that (on some level) there are no accidents and that interruption can be as predictable as order in the end. In dancing through chance methods, I have discovered the unity of my body, its disposition to connect the dots, stopping and starting, transitioning and persevering. I still appreciate the clarity and neutrality of Cunningham, but I want to empower my students, so I tell them: "What's next is up to you." The future, I hope, is implied.

Copeland associates Cunningham with a "training of perception" that leads to a more authentic freedom than simply "moving freely" would involve. This training for freedom is headed in the direction of a semiotics that is "suspicious" of naturalness and plays it "cool," Copeland says. As he critiques modern dance, he believes that

> The pioneers of this form—from Isadora Duncan through Martha Graham—have always considered themselves apostles of freedom. To them, being free meant liberating oneself from the stuffy conventions of puritanical culture. But for Cunningham, Rauschenberg, and the extraordinary community of composers, painters, and dancers with whom they collaborated, *true freedom has more to do with seeing (and hearing) clearly, than with moving freely.*[12]

Here we have the transcending male reflection in a nutshell, complete with the primacy of optics—masculinist privileging of sight and mind over movement and touch (as we take up again in other contexts). Male artists Cunningham and Rauschenberg (and this would certainly involve John Cage and Jasper Johns in their collaborations with Cunningham) are to be preferred over female artists Duncan and Graham. Copeland's rejection of organicism also implies criticism of Ruth St. Denis, Mary Wigman, Hanya Holm, Doris Humphrey, Anna Sokolow, and many contemporary female choreographers such as Pina Bausch, Susanne Linke, and Irene Hultman.

Cultural training effects determine the antiorganic exacting disciplines of Cunningham: Ballet technique blended with modern dance sculpting, chance dictation of movement patterns, high-tech stage settings, and aleatory music are better training for perception (of what and for whom) than holistically articulated flowing motion. Cunningham's clean movement can be uplifting, but its abstraction is in no way superior to warmer venues organically derived, nor is it better training for the senses than narrative. And might we speak more productively of educating the senses rather than training them? Everything we do, see, smell, touch, hear, and taste is training our sense perceptions, but undertaking a conscious education of sense and perception is quite another matter, as somatic practices of embodiment reveal.

As Cunningham insists, he does not aim "to express" anything. Rather, he presents "events." It becomes apparent that regardless of its aim human movement is always expressing something. Events are corporeal artifacts also, and whether intentionally presented in Cunningham's art or just bumped into as in the 1960s' "happenings," they are human expressions.

Merce Cunningham's works are at a crossroad between modernist innovations (in dance these came through women) and postmodern innovations (which also had women at the forefront). For this and because of its abstract quality, I call Cunningham's work late/high modern. The beginnings of modern dance and postmodern dance were both descendant. Women mark this art as modern/postmodern in its progress and regression through the twentieth century. The early moderns and the early postmoderns both had an interest in organic and natural movement; in fact, one of the original names for modern dance was "natural dance."

Modern and postmodern dance began with improvisational means rather than highly technical ones. At its root, modern dance evolved into a theater that respected, even flaunted, the emotions, as shown, for example, in Agnes de Mille's description of Isadora Duncan's dancing:

> The concert I saw was during World War I. At the end of the performance, the entire audience rose and stood while the orchestra played the *Marseillaise*, the "Allies'" anthem, all six verses, and Isadora in long Greek robes and a blood red cloak danced. At the final call: "Aux armes, Citoyens, Formex vos bataillons," she threw her blood red robe over her shoulder, marched to the footlights, and confronting the audience raised her arms in heroic summons.
>
> The whole house cried out, many people wept. She gave voice to immortal anguish, to mortal endeavor. Isadora could match any monu-

ment. She could match life. And yet at the time she was an overweight woman who at frolicsome moments seemed almost inept. Anyone else doing similar things would have been downright ridiculous. Isadora was never ridiculous. Isadora raised her arms and the stars rocked.[13]

Cunningham's Platonic neutrality, however ascendant in displacements of choreographic intuition and intention, creates a contemplative field of attention and influences a gender shift marked even more clearly in the early postmodern dance. For Cunningham, dancing is about dancing, "movement in time and space," as he defines it; dancing is not about sex, or psychology, or health, or therapy. His dance seems to deflate sexual attraction of any kind because of its dispassionate neutrality, but typical male/female partnering conventions remain in his work nevertheless. In most instances, men bear the weight of their female partners. Over time women begin to assist as well as lean in Cunningham's works, but in limited ways. They will not hurl men through space as in Senta Driver's work, but so what? Every dance artist will, whether consciously or not, perform gender in his or her own way. The treatment of gender is part of dance aesthetics and preserves a history of body and culture. Through their neutrality, for instance, Cunningham's dances break with previous conventions of feminine beauty. They do not enhance female beauty as often conceived of in ballet (virginal, pure, and passive) or highly theatrical modern dance (the hot and dramatic feminine of Graham). The women in Cunningham's dances are sleek, highly concentrated in the movement, and emotionally abstract.

In the wake of Cunningham, postmodern choreography finally achieved a fully androgynous character. (Beauty is what happens to you when you're not looking for it.) Women and men lifted each other in postmodern contact choreography and in contact improvisation folk jams. The early postmodern proceeded downward in technique, away from Cunningham, assuming a pedestrian "anyone can dance" and a carefree "we all bounce off from each other" character. Cunningham continued to push modern dance closer to the exacting techniques of ballet, as also the streamlining of leotard costumes with spotted and other geometric designs, and befuddlement of chance procedures in choreography. Meanwhile, costumes were minimized in postmodern descen-dance; everyday clothes were worn, and makeup disappeared. Uncontrived beauty was prized over artifice, and dance began to examine itself in terms of nature. Postmodern dancer Simone Forti (b. 1935) explains this in somatic terms: "I recall a statement I made in exasperation one day in the Cunningham studio. I said that Merce Cunningham was a master of adult, isolated articulation. And that the thing I had to offer was still very close to the holistic and generalized response of infants."[14]

Somatic Kinesiology

Simone Forti's amazing crawling dances and her dances based on the naturalistic movement of animals and plants reject the escalation of technical dancing and Cunningham's body isolations where every dancer is a soloist, every part of the body a distinct soloist. Forti's style of dance is a descendant reaction similar to the holistic, interactive principles of responsiveness that guided somatics pioneer Gerda Alexander (b. 1908) in her development of Eutony. Eutony, which indicates "a well-balanced tension," began to develop in Alexander's pedagogy of movement around 1926 and provides a continuing influence in somatic movement education. Both Forti and Alexander respect individual exploration and reject fixed models for movement— the same concerns that inspired the discoveries of early modern dance. Alexander's Eutony is based on the setting of simple movement tasks for which students find their own solutions without interference and in accordance with their own biorhythms.[15] Like Alexander's Eutony, Forti's postmodern dance turns toward simplicity and bodily discovery in organic aesthetic process.

The latter still resonates in educational processes that listen to the body's patterns, discerning and moving with them rather than dictating choreographic outcome, a process that can extend far beyond the limited but fascinating permutations of crawling. Dance aesthetics can develop according to personal signature and can also be shared in group dances with the same respect for individuality. Bodily differences can be respected in dancers' attempts to do the same movement—if replication of movement is through resemblance and not an insisted upon ideal. Performers can then do their personal best, each according to his or her body.

Movement fundamentals that evolved in modern/postmodern dance have led to an articulation of what might be called a somatic kinesiology now growing in the academy, one that is concerned about taking care of the body. Classroom study of kinesiology, supplemented with somatic movement studies and experiential anatomy for dancers, grows out of concerns for healthy dancing as well as better training techniques with more options and less imitation of idealized bodies and movement. Somatic studies have evolved through concerns for the dancer as a whole person, not just as a tool for the choreographer. Women initiated this movement, from dance therapist Mary Whitehouse to movement analyst Irmgard Bartenieff, and men such as Eric Hawkins have also been articulating concepts of somatic kinesiology for dance. If everything is possible in dance, then crippling the body and turning to obsessive-compulsive behavior to maintain thinness does not mean that everything is desirable.

Another phenomenon that follows on the heels of somatic kinesiology can be summed up in value theory as experiential value or "intrinsic value." Intrinsic dancing and accomplishment is predicated on pleasure rather than perfection. It is attuned to the nature of the body with respect to individual differences, and its styles and ranges of difficulty are unlimited. Such an approach to choreography and performance has more to do with attitude and method than with the kind of movement performed. When performance for an audience enters the process, the possibility for sharing the pleasure of the dance is multiplied. The body to be discovered and shared with the audience through intrinsic dance is not a perfected body modeled on a single ideal; rather, it affirms natural differences and the joy of moving in tune with (matching) our own body.

I have earlier examined the original postmodern dance as a spiraling descent akin to that of Demeter/Persephone and Nammu/Inanna (the Sumerian mother/daughter goddess), an imperative for regenerating an art form.[16] The revolution of postmodern dance beginning in the 1960s with such artists as Yvonne Rainer, Simone Forti, and Deborah Hay, resulted in a return to nature in technically devolved movement. A revaluation of established techniques also motivated Isadora Duncan, Mary Wigman, and others in early modern dance as they protested artificiality in the coding systems of the ballet they experienced. They sought a freer expression through the immediacy of gesture, through locomotor variations on running, walking, skipping, turning, falling, jumping, leaping, fundamental axial movements of the torso, and the lyric properties of arms—reaching, grasping, holding, flailing, pushing, pulling, pounding, pulsing, folding, fisting, and much more.

In its beginnings, modern/postmodern dance was motivated by a search for an intrinsic dance and a more naturally expressive body. For the early moderns this produced a somatic focus on purpose and feeling—dancing from the inside out. For the postmoderns the search championed everyday movement and devolution of style, a deconstructive somatic emphasis. Both aimed to reinvent dance and the trope of the natural body.

But the natural carries cultural baggage, as poststructural and somatic studies draw forward. What feels natural is laced with habit. "Uninhabiting" or letting go of the body is part of somatic strategies that lower kinaesthetic thresholds to release a habit's hold on movement, "to allow" rather than "to make" the movement happen. This has both aesthetic and therapeutic implications. Consciousness makes a difference in how movement is conceived and experienced, in other words, and in what we consider to be natural. Duncan, for instance, used "the natural" as "an artistic invention as well as a rhetorical strategy," as Ann Daly shows.[17]

Attuned to the possible and the natural (inescapable) expressiveness of the human body, the work of women was the genesis of modern dance. Its regeneration on postmodern descendant grounds was also accomplished in great measure through the work of women. If women founded and regenerated the modernist impulse in dance, over the twentieth century men aided its development. The early work of Jose Limon, with his heft and lyrical drop of body weight—and later the contact improvisation of Steve Paxton, spontaneously giving and taking weight, rolling into the floor—helped to cultivate the "earthbodies" of modernist dance.

Modernist beginnings were motivated as much by political concerns as by aesthetics. A concern for women's health and empowerment fueled the emergence of modern dance. The female body was freed from Victorian corsets, and liberated women began to dance barefoot. In its own way the early postmodern dance also cared for the body. Its workaday playful forms evoked the "everydaybodies," and championed a kind of urban folk dance in pedestrian, nontechnical movements of walking, running, sitting, crawling, climbing buildings, walking on walls with the help of harnesses, and so on. Finely tuned skill in virtuoso performance began to evolve again, but with a significant difference. Intrinsic dance and somatic kinesiology became more important than extrinsic appearance—or at least *as* important for the new dance. "Beauty is as beauty does" might well define the postmodern shift toward means and away from end product. Presence, play, teamwork, descendant beauty, physicality, and partnership become highly valued in the growth of American postmodern dance. The alchemy of dreams, messy beauty, and agonies of the soul were left to Japanese Butoh and German Tanztheater.

Nuclear Fallout and Butoh Invalids

LIVING BEYOND THE SHADOWLANDS

The shadowlands, they loom
and they howl. The shadowlands,
they bring fear and make small
the middle of my name.

All may be in form,
but I am not my own.
The shadows have consumed me
all but my heart.

I only know from the Love
where there is no other,
that my heart is my best soul,
and that when it is but a teardrop
more full, it will empty itself
like a stream, and I will flow
out of the shadowlands.

I will arrive into a new universe
able to live my best life again,
feeling the beauty, the love,
and the gentleness that abound.

I will have come full circle
and my heart will become full again,
but not heavy.

It will be radiant,
It will be strong,
It will be giving,
It will be wild, it will be free,
and it will no longer feel the pain
but the joy of my sorrow.

The shadowlands, everyone
will someday have to go there.

I have done my time
in this prison of shadows.
When I leave the only shadow
that will be cast
is my own shadow,
on my own wall.

Christina Fraleigh, 2000

I was twelve and living in a sleepy valley in southern Utah. Our solution to World War II had already been dropped on Hiroshima and Nagasaki, and subsequent testing of nuclear bombs was just beginning in Nevada—timed with the wind to blow toward Utah. I remember standing on my back porch with my whole family to see the first flash, and how the government assured us there was no danger. We were to be part of a grand experiment, so they said in their leaflets. As it turned out, we were the fifty thousand expendables of the southern Utah towns, and as we later learned, the atomic fallout had traveled on the wind at least as far north as Salt Lake City. In Utah's legal grievance, history would also recount that the dangers of radiation were not unknown to the government.

They said the white ash that fell on us could be "inconvenient." The Mormons were expendable, as before in their mid-nineteenth-century expulsion from New York, Ohio, and Illinois, where their prophet Joseph Smith was apprehended and murdered in his jail cell. After their westward migration with covered wagons and hand carts, the government continued to persecute the Mormons in their new home in Utah. *(To this day, the government is still testing in Nevada, now underground with jet fuel, and barely a cockroach alive. To add to the insult, they want to bury nuclear waste in Nevada's Yucca Mountain!)*[18]

My sister was also born when I was twelve. About two years before this, the doctors attending my mother administered shock treatments for her depression. She had not recovered by the time my sister was born. I had a lot of responsibility for the family after that. Mother's health was poor, and her memory sometimes failed. I would coax her out of bed, and I thought if I could make things pleasant enough she would want to. She died in her mid-fifties of a cancer at the top of the list of diseases attributed to the atomic and nuclear testing in Nevada.

Earlier, my brother's first child had died from another disease associated with the bomb and rare in the United States, more money for another life. Heather became ill very suddenly at age eight and suffered progressive deterioration as her body rejected its skin and organs. At twelve, she begged her parents to let her go. Her body was transparent by then, tiny, and her eyes big and liquid. After death, the glow of Heather's aura was so strong, even people who do not ordinarily see the natural light emanating from the body could see hers. Doctors and nurses came from around the hospital to see the glowing child. Now my sister's grown children suffer the effects of radiation fallout, as also does my daughter, Christina, and the wastelands of my dreams are full of strangely silent, charred, and burning bodies. The unborn were at greatest risk.

Eventually the government escalated its tests from atomic to nuclear weapons. Utah's two beautiful small cities in the south, St. George and Cedar City, were hit hard. Priscilla, a thirty-seven-kiloton nuclear bomb, was dropped from a helium balloon suspended seven hundred feet above the ground on June 24, 1957, the year I graduated from high school. I was in Piute County, about a hundred miles from the blast, less as the wind blows. The next year I moved to Cedar City for my first two years of college, closer to the detonations. There I suffered unexplained seizures.

Falling Out: The Casualties of Blind Obedience, a documentary coming out of film studies at Dixie College in St. George, will document the nuclear testing of the 1950s. St. George is also known as "Little Hollywood" because of the many Westerns filmed in its environment of picturesque red rock hills and deeply carved canyons, its painted-desert pinks, purples, and *creamy whites, with the burnt oranges of Zion National Park nearby and the Grand Canyon on the horizon. I have traveled the world since I left Utah, but I have seen few places so richly colored and layered, a Jurassic paradise revealed in its textures and prehistoric bones, now dusted with radiation.*

My mother had been sad and reclusive for years, but managed before her death to find peace tending her garden and knitting. Nothing had ever been for her—everything was always for others. My uncle liked to tell a story of his first sight of my mother when he was courting my aunt, one of Mother's three sisters, at a community dance: "Who is that beautiful dancer," he asked my aunt. "That's my sister," she replied. He told this story at my mother's funeral. My father, who seldom reserved his feelings in any situation, threw himself over her before they closed the casket. I was standing close by with my brother, and we heard him sobbing quietly. Then he turned to us. "I still want her," he whispered.

My father would later die of bone cancer—second on the list of diseases highly correlated with the bomb.

. . . My dance fell headlong into the night . . . and rose with my father's recitation of Noyes's "Highwayman."

Not till dawn he heard it, his face grew gray to hear
How Bess, the landlord's daughter,
the landlord's black-eyed daughter,
Had watched for her love in the
moonlight, and died in the darkness there.

. . .

I was in California in the late 1960s, and just under the suspicious age of thirty. We marched against the government's course in Vietnam, wore granny gowns, and danced barefoot in the grass. Not until 1985 did I see Japanese Butoh, which originated in the sixties. It so opened a wound in me that I went to Japan to study this dance and returned for more study as a research fellow at Ochanomizu University in 1990. Japan turned toward darkness and the soul in Butoh, evolving into an emotional postmodern theater that contrasted with the more playful and pedestrian experiments in America, even though both had grown from the ferment of the sixties. Butoh is still gaining international momentum, diversifying its aesthetics—ranging from the softness of Setsuko Yamada to the brassy expressionism of Anzu Furukawa and the shape-shifting of Kayo Mikami.

American dancers like Maureen Fleming and Canadians such as Denise Fujiwara are also contributing to this unique dance theater, while in Mexico Diego Piñón performs Butoh Mexicano Ritual Dance, and in Broellin, Germany, Yumiko Yoshioka develops unique Butoh educational resources through EXIT. London dancer Fran Barbie creates dance works that reflect her training in Butoh and modern dance, as well as the Suzuki movement method, and Marie-Gabrielle Rotie profiles her Butoh alongside emerging performers and visual artists who engage Butoh processes. Community building rather than artistic competition is emerging as a major value in the practice of Butoh, especially through the work of Nobuo Harada-sensei in Fukuoka, Japan.

Butoh, like the Tanztheater of German choreographer Pina Bausch, began to revive concerns for conscience and introspection in dance, while Americans concentrated more objectively on movement and form. Butoh and Bausch both had roots in German expressionism and its acceptance of the grotesque, but they were also responding to the graveyards and ruins of World War II. Each in its own way was antiauthoritarian, Bausch in a sassy way, and Butoh by showing deviation from aesthetic rules through hanging, awkward postures for dancing, acknowledging pain and utilizing marginalized, antisocial movement in twisted faces, odd ticks, and intense shaking, sometimes bordering on seizure. Toshiharu Kasai, a psychology professor in Japan who performs under the name Itto Morita, told me that he decided to become a dancer from the time of his first Butoh class, when he began to shake involuntarily. Such movements are the vehicles for trancelike states, comedic and psychosomatic release: even as they carry intense theatrical potential, they can also address trauma. Through somatic exploration and integration, Kasai's work develops both the performative and therapeutic potentials of Butoh on stage and in clinical practice.

Originally an underground movement in Japan, Butoh emerged gradually in the aftermath of war if not entirely in its image. Butoh is not limited to this history, but it would not have developed without it. Atomic bombs had been dropped on entire cities. The unbelievable mushroom spread its sublime power as America shook history in its wake. It was 1945.

Less than a hundred years before, in 1853, American commodore Matthew C. Perry, with a letter from President Millard Fillmore, sailed

Itto Morita, Butoh dancer and therapist. Photo portrait by Katsumi Takahashi in 2001.

into Tokyo Bay and opened Japan's ports to international trade—at cannon point. America's actions were inspired by its desire to trade, to spread the gospel to the yellow pagans, and export American democracy.[19] Overnight, a medieval Japan was catapulted from three hundred years of self-chosen isolation into a rapidly modernizing world. For several hundred years, China and Russia had struggled over vast territories to the north with China occupying Manchuria and Korea, and Russia occupying the Maritime Province. Japan did not enter into the scramble for territory until after 1853. As a part of modernization, it built an army and navy and began to imitate American and European games of forceful international diplomacy. Concurrently, Japanese art and fashion, especially the Ukiyo-e woodblock prints, circled the globe and became very popular in Europe and America. Japanese art exerted a strong influence on the French impressionists and later the European symbolists, paving the way for German expressionism.[20]

The Japanese took to internationalism with determination, and soon the rising Tokyo skyline began to look like that of San Francisco or Chicago. Japan would eventually fight a war against the United States, a country where many Japanese had been educated and a nation the Japanese government had tried to befriend through diplomacy. History would finally record their failed efforts and their conflicting national policies. In retrospect, it is remarkable how many Americans eventually came to admire the Japanese.

As Japan prepared for war with speeches about making Asia safe from Communism, racism, and colonialism, American newspapers reported that "the yellow peril" was not to be trusted. The San Francisco school board, caught up in the hysteria, ordered all Nisei children to attend school in Chinatown. The Japanese government responded bitterly about this "act of discrimination." As in 1924, when Congress passed the Exclusion Act, which barred Japanese people from immigrating to the United States, "Japan felt as if her best friend had, of a sudden and without provocation, slapped her on the cheek," wrote John Toland.[21] The Japanese (better known then in America as "the little yellow bastards") tried to resolve differences through diplomacy, eventually capitulating to every American demand, but were rebuffed time and again by President Theodore Roosevelt's negotiator, Cordell Hull. Sadly, much miscommunication revolved around issues of language translation. Roosevelt shared Hull's suspicion of Japanese motives and secretly warned his commanders in the Philippines to prepare for a Japanese attack.

The Japanese attack on Pearl Harbor, and finally the atrocities committed by Japanese soldiers in World War II, would not be forgotten in the American mind. Japanese-centric accounts do not ignore these crimes, but they show inconsistencies in Japan's aggressive behavior, citing the protective actions of many officers and soldiers toward their enemy. Colonial atrocities of the British in India, the Europeans in Africa, and American settlers toward Native Americans show that every nation can accept responsibility for crimes against others. The lessons of our own brutalities in postwar Asia may give Americans some insight into those of the Japanese a few decades ago.

John Toland's Pulitzer Prize–winning book on World War II, *The Rising Sun*, which is told from the Japanese point of view, illustrates the transient glory and eventual downfall of Japan in the face of Westernization. The Japanese entered a war with an enemy they knew was ten times stronger, but through their fierce fighting and daring they fared far better than they or anyone else expected. The story we know has an atomic/nuclear ending, one that provides impetus for the aesthetics of Butoh. The people of Hiroshima, a romantic city once known as "the Paris of Japan," disintegrated in a flash of melting faces, catastrophic loss, and fiery devastation. One hundred thousand people died the first day and another hundred thousand were doomed. Three days later, Nagasaki, the fabled port city of Madame Butterfly, was hit by another atomic blast. Like San Francisco, Nagasaki was a city of spectacular beauty spread across steep, meandering hills. The Portuguese in 1571 had helped to build it into a port for foreign trade, bringing Christianity and firearms with them. Since then Nagasaki had developed a large Christian population and Japan's most harmonious blend of East and West. In the bombings, two ancient, densely populated cities died instantly, and America had pushed the button while negotiations for surrender were in process. American President Harry Truman considered the bomb just one more weapon in what he called "the arsenal of righteousness."[22] For generations, Japan would face festering problems of radiation, which infected food and water and traveled in the air across a country about the size of California.

Americans failed to see the arrogant and deep-rooted prejudice in their Asian policies. If we had, it is probable that our negotiations with Japan in 1941 could have ended in peace. Then, as Toland puts it, "America would not have been forced to become the moral policemen of Asia for many years." As far back as 1922, Tyler Dennett, an authority on the Far East, wrote: "Each nation, the United States not excepted, has made its contribution to the welter of evil which now comprises the Far East question. We shall all do well to drop for all time the pose of self-righteousness and injured innocence and penitently face the facts."[23]

In the aftermath of overwhelming losses in World War II came America's war heroes and invalids. The United States government, however, still continued to test atomic and nuclear bombs at Frenchman's Flat in Nevada, just over the Utah border. Meanwhile, America continued to be involved in hostilities in Asia. Wars in Korea and Vietnam would multiply America's body bags and invalids. At this writing, in 2004, America is, without the participation of the United Nations, forcefully exporting Western-style democracy to Iraq. Many Iraqis have welcomed their liberation from tyranny while questioning America's means and motives. Western lifestyles and values are not uniformly welcome, as (they were and were not) in Japan after World War II.

Japanese Butoh peaked in the chaotic 1960s, partly as an attempt to rescue the body from the effects of war, as an affirmation of Japanese identity in the face of demoralization and the encroachment of Western values. Yet Butoh dancers did not entirely repudiate the West. Instead, they textured their experimental theater with Western music and costumes and engaged radical (root) conceptualizations of the dancing body, not in the style of Western modern dance, but in the same spirit of investigation. Takaya Eguchi and others who had studied the emerging modern dance in Germany taught Butoh founders Tatsumi Hijikata and Kazuo Ohno. Twenty years Hijikata's senior, Ohno had been an exceptional modern dancer before his Butoh explorations. The dancing body that emerged in the evolution of Butoh was social and natural at once, Japanese at heart and elemental in its earthiness. "I come from the mud," Hijikata said. His dance was confrontational, often comic, and poetically surreal. Ohno's was generous, flamboyant, delicate, and unpredictable. Together they created a postwar dance form so closely tied to basic human emotions and sensations that it bridged cultures.

A Japanese sensibility for slow time, exaggerated theatricality, and everyday postures entered directly into Butoh; other Japanese content entered through the back door. When Japanese dancers in the 1920s and 1930s began to study the New Dance abroad (*Neue Tanz* in Ger-

Atsushi Takenouchi, once a student of Hijikata, creates his own Butoh on the principle of *Jinen* (movement in nature), smears his body with mud, and dances at night on the Broellin castle grounds during the EXIT 2003 festival performance in Broellin, Germany. Photograph by Sondra Fraleigh.

many), they also encountered the East in several guises. The early modern dance they witnessed and participated in was often propelled by an "Oriental" craze. In America this entered emphatically through the Denishawn School and Martha Graham, who had been a student at Denishawn. Japanese dancer Michio Ito, who gained wide recognition in Europe and the United States early in the twentieth century, helped to create Hollywood's image of the "exotic Oriental." Ito also taught at the Denishawn School in the 1920s; his work after World War II focused more clearly on universal human themes, aiding the development of modern dance in Japan. Graham used Indian yoga in formulating her dance technique, and in years to come Japanese stylization also entered her work. Isamu Noguchi's lean set designs, inspired by Japanese Noh theater, channeled the emotional drive of Graham's dance dramas through environments of suave abstraction,

striking a balance between traditional Japanese and modern stylization, East and West.[24] An abstract, tightly emotional, and controlled
"Orientalism" appeared in German dance through Mary Wigman's
ethnological studies and her *Witch Dance* (1926), which sprang from
the features of Japanese and Javanese art.

After World War II, American dance from Cunningham in the
fifties to the formalist and pedestrian postmodern of the sixties developed a physically objective turn. Expression would be the result of
movement, and not the other way around. Dancers were asked to execute phrases, not to express feelings. The subjective human world of
suffering was not the business of American dance, not since Martha
Graham and Anna Sokolow, at least. Cunningham's aleatory breakup
of the historical modern dance of Graham had paved the way for postmodern formalism in America. But rebellious young women such as
Trisha Brown would eventually supersede his influence in the avant-
garde. And the zany style of Twyla Tharp would eventually blend the
playfulness of the American postmodern with classical ballet in exuberant works like *The Upper Room* (1986).

Cunningham's high ground evolved into escalating uses of technology, with film and video dances made for and by the camera, com-
puter-generated bodies, and semiotic deconstruction. He suspended
intentionality. Anything could follow anything; anything could mean
anything or nothing. Any reading was valid. This approach neutral-
izes expression, resulting in highly intellectualized dancing—or meditation. Younger choreographers and dancers devolved technocratic
high grounds in general, rejecting the battlegrounds of Vietnam.

Not until the AIDS epidemic began to kill America's male dancers
did Terpsichore openly grieve, principally through the dance and community action work of Bill T. Jones. The critical response of Arlene
Croce—that Jones was guilty of "victim art" in his identification of art
with death and disease—reiterated America's trouble with death,
grief, and mourning. Jones describes the moral choices he faced:

> At a time when the piercing wail of anxiety and discontent at the loss of
> a true moral voice was at a fever pitch, I felt like a cultural mendicant
> faced with two choices: to go into the cloistered order of individualism
> and art as aesthetic research or to become the warrior engaged in the
> pursuit of art as an instrument for social change. I moved forward with

uncertainty and some joy, equipped only with a gnawing desire to create a belief in the beautiful and the true.[25]

The bitter lessons of war had already turned Japan toward self-reflection. Japanese Butoh in particular was protesting the Westernization of Japan, seeking a form of dance that would resurrect the unashamed body of prewar, pre-Western Japan. At the same time, it admitted the desolation of war in its limping, diseased figures, and in what Butoh teacher and performer Nobuo Harada has called "the melting body." One of Hijikata's early works, *Genbaku to heso* (Atomic explosion and the navel), danced by Hijikata and his wife, Motofuji, was both surreal and comic. Audiences wondered out loud if Butoh dancers might not have escaped from mental hospitals. In a way they had, in owning the effects of war, if seldom literally. War grew from the maladies of their time; Butoh grew in Hijikata's embrace of mud and Wind Darumas, apparitions in Japanese myth that cannot be knocked over. "Start from the place of your handicap," Yoko Ashikawa liked to say in her classes, echoing her years of work with Hijikata.

From the beginning, Hijikata employed a chthonic aesthetic, both phallic and feminine, and later through Ashikawa his dance developed specifically through the potentials of the female body. Butoh reached out, too—through Kazuo Ohno, an old man possessed by the body of a beautiful flamenco dancer, La Argentina, in whose memory he danced. Without apology, the dance of Ohno and Hijikata seemed to bow in at least three directions: acknowledging a scorched Japan amid three thousand years of history, honing new beginnings and freely plying global imagery. Beyond the Japanese box, Butoh finally spanned many culture and gender distinctions, bringing East and West together in its dance aesthetics and cross-dressing. Such aesthetic jumbles and mixed messages are nothing new in Japan, from Ukiyo-e woodblock prints to Kabuki theater. But in Japanese theater, gender confusions occur within traditional forms, and Butoh breached those forms.

...

The original postmodern played out its descendant and minimalist mundane principles in America from its beginnings in Yvonne Rainer's *Trio A* or, stated more somatically, *The Mind Is a Muscle*, as she first named her deceptively simple dance. Brown, Tharp, and others gradually involved high theater in their dances. Expressivity returned to dance training in the guise of "release technique," an approach that emphasizes the optional ways each body can respond to a given impetus in movement. Releasing to the moment and the momentum, dance began to demonstrate a love for organic movement even within a formalist physicality.

The overt return of expression was informed by a development of the skillful dancer, but not dictated by commanding, conforming techniques. Brown's work moved from the pedestrian to the theatrical and began to fly. Choreographers picked up on the new momentum with intuitively derived movement. Contrivance through intellectually imposed methods lost steam. Dancing with abandon returned along with pain-pleasure and the erotic in the work of many artists, notably Molissa Fenley and Bill T. Jones. The "cool" left people cold, for the time being. Heat returned through the European revival of expressionist roots in the work of Bausch, Susanne Linke, and others, reaching back to Wigman and her influential student, Dore Hoyer.

Terrible beauty laced with horror, grit, and an erotic sublime reappeared first in the works of Bausch, then reformed its emotional verve in such groups as Urban Bush Women in America. Somatic attempts to reveal an inexpertly expert and bewildering body through peeling away the social body resounded in the personal identities and autobiographical dancing of Butoh—certainly in the work of Kazuo Ohno. His *My Mother* displayed a tolerant and allowing aesthetic, beginning with a section called "I Shall Not Correct It."

"Not correcting" effects a curious *corporal matching* of one's body, affirming the body as it is, rather than wishing it to be otherwise. It signifies self-acceptance, better yet, the choice to be oneself. When we do not correct ourselves all the time, we can begin to see ourselves more clearly and move better in our dances, which does not mean that for Ohno disruptions are not productive.[26]

Back he spurred like a madman,
shrieking a curse to the sky,
with the white road smoking behind him,
and his rapier brandished high!

How the blood pulsed in my temples, as I begged my father
To find another end for Bess and her outlaw,
Oh why did they have to die?

Blood-red were his spurs i' the golden
noon; wine red was his velvet coat,
When they shot him down on the highway
Down like a dog on the highway.
And he lay in his blood on the highway
with a bunch of lace at his throat.

Descendant Beauty

Speechless, I raised my hands to the moon;
Light rays fell on my frozen palms
As Aphrodite winked,
And draped herself for the dance.

At the Broadmoor International Theater, I sat with floating balloons tied up in my hair, swinging and waiting to descend from the flywell high up near the ceiling. I was not harnessed in; I told myself I had better not look down. I was studying in Colorado Springs with one of the famous pioneers of modern dance from the German-American school, Hanya Holm, once a student of Mary Wigman's. She had cast me to dance a duet with Don Redlich, who had just formed his own company but was still assisting Holm. I was not the best technician, but Hanya told me I had flair and fun, and that technique would come. She cared more about persona and presence, she said. She let me be and allowed me to learn. When I returned to my dance studies at the University of Utah, my teachers asked what had happened. My dancing had improved light-years. "Hanya believed in me," I told them.

After I graduated in 1962, I went to teach dance at the University of Montana. In 1965, Hanya helped me obtain a Fulbright scholarship to study with Mary Wigman in Berlin. Wigman had been her teacher, and the root of German expressionism in dance. I remember making a film of my work for the Fulbright Commission, sailing to Europe on the New Amsterdam, *and studying German for three months at the Goethe Institute in southern Germany (Schwabisch-Hall) before going to Berlin.*

The institute provided me with a clean hotel room and a Portuguese roommate named Mary Magdalene. We got along well with each other and were not bothered (too much) by the cockroaches. For five marks, we could take a salt bath in large wooden tubs on the lower floor of our Solbad Hotel. Mary had an Italian boyfriend who was studying to be a priest (go figure), and I had a Greek boyfriend who danced like Zorba and drove my Volkswagen like a madman through town.

We danced very creative tangos as a foursome at a local tavern. One of the customers named Claus had some idea where my hometown was. When he saw me with my Greek friend, he would laugh, throw his hands up, and shout in disbelief: "There goes Circle Valley and Athens." Now I think of this as a positive form of global warming.

Messy Refuse

In a curious way, I am attracted to Japanese Butoh for its global amalgamations and descendant reasons, that it lets age be, mixes cultures, and is not technically insistent. Kazuo Ohno, the grandfather of Butoh, performed internationally into his nineties, by then dancing in a wheelchair. Ohno moves, he says, through the body of his mother. His costumes are extravagantly female as in *La Argentina*, sometimes lacy and withered, or as simple as a kimono. In his tuxedo dances he might be male or female, Fred Astaire or Lauren Bacall, or any other slick but warm performer. As he nears nudity and all sophistry disappears, we see that he is just an old man, leaning on a crooked stick. His dances and his teaching revolve around Zen-like paradoxes and a descendant belief that "We cannot turn away from the messy refuse of life." Expectations of perfection distract us from the possibility of seeing the beauty around and within us. I illustrate with a "messy refuse" story, American style:

One day I was playing tennis with my friend Sarah Watts. Two men in the next court asked us to leave and take our kids home. The kids were "too noisy" and this "bothered" them.

I told the men something I thought they should already know: that public courts are messy places, and if children at play bothered them, they would have to leave . . . or rent . . . or build . . . etc. . . . . They looked at us in utter amazement—that we wouldn't just pack up our kids and get them "out of their way."

Women have over generations learned how to enjoy their own play with the disorderly play and interruptions of children. Some men believe it is the job of women to keep children neatly out of the way. They miss out on the messy beauty and spontaneity of children—and the flexibility of body-mind that children teach us.

The Reversible Spiral Dance

Phenomenologist Algis Mickunas describes messy beauty in the tensional pulls between "transcending reflections" and what he calls "rescending reflections" (directional pulls in thought and action), and illustrates with examples from religion, mythology, and philosophy. He explains how the Western patriarchal tradition has a tendency toward transcending reflection. He also helps to clarify what he calls "rescendence" as concerned not with a logic of analysis, but a logic of participatory experience: "an immersion and surrender to the 'logic' of life with all of its storms and vicissitudes, a beauty that is equally soothing/inviting and terrifying/dissolving." The Hindus and Buddhists have fascinating depictions of this ambiguous domain, with all of its entrapments and rewards.[27]

I replace "rescendence" with the more common term "descendant" and its ancestral overtones. The descendant dance reflects the very life and beauty that patriarchy would transcend and make over in the image of denial. The descendant dancer comes in many shapes, sizes, and colors; her virtue comes from belonging to herself. Thus she can rejuvenate and share her vitality through "the body that has not been robbed," as they say in Butoh. This body dances into darkness as well as light. The upward reflection of transcendence brings impotence in its extremes—detachment from life and the flesh, anorexia in extreme cases—while the downward descent also has extremes of madness and terror. There is the hideous side of Innana, the queen of heaven and the underworld in Sumerian mythology, but she also effects regeneration and can recover.

The trans-descendant cycle, unlike the unidirectional transcendent climb, admits movements up and down ladders and around in circles; it moves into and out of spirals through somatically sound, beautifully reversible paths. In the spiral, her primary symbol, the Goddess as enchantress, is a skin-shedding serpent moving curvaceously. As gnostic the Goddess is nonjudgmental and all-containing: virgin, career woman, mother, great mother (grandmother), wife, partner, lover, and bag lady.

Parul Shah, a teacher and performer of *Bharatanatyam*, one of India's seven classical dance forms, visited me recently. She spoke to my students about the current feminist work of Chandralekha, her own work, and that of others who extend and subvert the classical dance vocabulary. There is still this fascination in India with the many faces of the Goddess, or double god of Shiva/Shakti, male and female in one.

Daughters of the Ocean (2000), a dance by Anita Ratnam, explores Goddess imagery and recovery of the sacred through a modernist vision of *Bharatanatyam*. As I watched Ratnam's dancers rehearse outdoors on the polished stone floor of her dance patio in Chennai, I observed how the plastic, seductive gestures of *Bharatanatyam*, traditionally a female solo dance, could morph from free-form to structure, and through experiment could respect a wide range of gendered sensibility. I was also aware of a feminine anomie that framed the dancing, a "female gaze," if you will. Ratnam's dance in 2001, performed at several venues in the United States, included the descendant aesthetics of Butoh in a work called *DUST*.

Her Names and Intoxications

If I am in danger of universalizing the feminine, it is because I do not want to lose the darkness. I want its restful warmth when I need to grieve. I place compassion over ambition, and the ability to smile over the need to win. Through my travels in India, I studied the many faces of the goddess Kali, the pulsing of spring, the dark goddess of time and night. She is also Shiva/Shakti, India's greatest spiritual power, and she has many other names. In Saraswati, she has divine gifts of speech and intelligence. Her feminine powers of protection and creation also stand in relation to disintegration and rebirth. Carnage is a perversion of her life-giving powers.[28] She is the mystical vastness of China in the all-containing origin, the Way, the Tao. As Kwan-yin she is devoted to the earth and all living things. Would she not oppose the killing of female infants, then, enforced abortion in China, and pregnancy testing in India for the purpose of aborting female fetuses? Mother Teresa's intimacy with suffering in Calcutta, for example, gives her compassion.

Images of the Great Mother also pervade Western mythology. The Phrygians, who settled in ancient Anatolia (now Turkey) in the second millennium BCE were favored by the Greeks and Romans as slaves for their artistic refinements. Their principal deity was the Great Goddess Kubile, Kubaba, or Matar Kubile, also called Cybele by the Greeks, Kybele by the Lydians, Mater Deum Magna Ideae by the Romans, and worshiped in Lycia, Thrace, Syria, Phoenecia, North Africa, Spain, Gaul, Britain, and Germany. Kubile, traced as Maiden, Mother and Crone, is one and many, and her later names include Hecate, Gaia, Pheraia, Artemis, Baubo, Aphaia, Ortheia (my mother's name), Nemesis, Demeter, Persephone, Selene, Medusa, Eleuthera, Leto, Hera, Aphrodite, Bendis, Hathor, Taeit, and Isis. Kubile is a mountain mother goddess—dancer, healer, and musician. It was believed that the dance Kubile taught the Corybantes could cure mental illness.[29]

The goddess Kubile/Cybele/Gaia was once most certainly worshiped. Her power declined with the rise of the patriarchal order of Zeus when the Ionians, Acheans, and Dorians invaded Mycenia (Greece) from c. 2500 to c. 1000 BCE. The Greek goddesses suffered degradation as symbols of natural powers and became domesticated artifacts. Athena, peaceful protectress, became a motherless military symbol, born from the head of Zeus fully armored. The great mother Aphrodite, associated with fertility, became an abject seductress. The Spartan Dorian invasion attempted to eradicate music, dancing, and poetry on the grounds of its "effeminacy." As the Dorians advanced the worship of Apollo, the male usurped the musical and healing powers of the Goddess. But still late in the archaic age of Zeus and Apollo, women continued to worship the Goddess with music, poetry, and dance. Among these, Sappho of Lesbos in Asia Minor was admired for her love songs: "Love shook my heart, like a wind / falling on oaks on the mountain."[30]

Socrates criticized the Lydian and Mixolydian musical modes for their soft harmonies and intoxications. The Lydians, like their neighbors the Phrygians, also worshiped the Goddess. Plato preferred a harmony that imitated the accents of brave men engaged in "war and enforced business," and found the love of Aphrodite to be insanity and madness.[31]

Tara

The downward reflection is more than an image for me, it is a feeling that comes when I least expect it and a peace painted by my senses. I have experienced such submersion through the vital powers of the Tibetan goddess Tara with her origins in India as she is shared cross-culturally in a participatory dance, *The Twenty-One Praises of Tara,* arranged by Prema Dasara for nonprofessional dancers. This dance, while not a Buddhist traditional form, is nevertheless performed as a sacred dance and blessed by the Dali Lama, who has said that Tara, one of the names of the great mother, belongs to everyone who calls her.

She who is named and called in every conceivable color is vital beauty, glowing intelligence, and ferocious compassion. Tara, star, protectress, and savior, goddess of action, lady of plants and animals, mother of earth, queen of heaven and the underworld, complete and perfect Buddha, was given the choice to become a man, but vowed to reincarnate forever in the body of a woman, to ferry all souls across the sea of suffering. Tara is tolerant and acquainted with grief; she is transformational and leaves room for experiment.[32] I danced *The Twenty-One Praises of Tara* moving through her mandala (sacred maze) with forty-one other dancers on my fifty-sixth birthday, July 2, 1995. The dancers in this performance at Omega were interracial, drawn from several walks of life, and ranged from teenagers to grandmothers. I remember most the sensuous feel of the silken saris, the binding together of feminine beauty, and Prema Dasara's chanting of the praises.

Buddhism offers us the splendid example of Tara, but it also requires that the highest-ranking nun defer to the lowest-ranked monk. Tara is resistive, however, as her insistence on demonstrating enlightenment in female form indicates.[33] Tara is an empowering symbol for feminism as she reconciles with (and subverts the patriarchy of) spiritual traditions based on male supremacy and the suppression of women. As a representation of our bond with nature and an ethics of care, the living Goddess is grace and ultimately free of religious categories. Hers are the rhythms of silence, deliverance, and recuperation. She can sacrifice for others if she chooses to, and with a hand that grows strong in justice she can also be a warrior/protectress; the strength that she exchanges with others comes from her self-sharpening dance and sensible reach.

Through her many names, the Goddess is Eros, the preserver of life, and she knows that Logos moves by means of Eros. Without the impulses and stirrings of Eros, Logos stagnates. Casting generous circles and bending in serpentine lines, the Goddess dances into the earth as toward the heavens. All that she gives is threatened, however. She provides no guarantees, and thus no exacting sacrifice of denial. Experientially, she is not solid and static; she changes, and her mistakes are swallowed in learning. All directions are indicated in her holistic spiral. She is maddening, she dances: she rides horses, she drives trucks and caterpillars like the friend I grew up with who became a card dealer in Las Vegas, then a prostitute, and eventually learned to drive heavy equipment for a living. Eros builds her own house and invites her friends to dinner. She loves because she wants to. Hers are the cults of creation, not sacrifice and salvation. Her belly calls us into being. Rivers course through her veins, and flowers are at home in her hair. She is a shaman who can charm away childhood warts. Metaphysically, she is in the here and now, not the hereafter, and she might smell like apple pie, horses, or gasoline. Most essentially, she comes home to her self and wakes up in beauty.

A Beauty Sufficient in Its Nature

Attractiveness (eros) arises from a dependable self, one that belongs to itself. Sappho's school on the island of Lesbos in the seventh century BCE fostered independence, and young women learned to "belong to themselves first and foremost, not to a male caretaker such as a husband, father, uncle, or brother."[34] As outlaw, the virgin is she who belongs to herself; she dances outside the law of the fathers. Motherhood may be the culmination of such independence—enriched with skills that independence brings—but one does not become a rich or strong woman simply through motherhood. The Goddess is a mother symbol and also a symbol of independence, and those who are not mothers have the divine potential of flourishing in the larger truth of the Goddess—the truly unselfish motherhood of service.

Mickunas studies how divine Eros, the enticement and sign of feminine beauty, is subjugated in purification rituals of philosophy and salvation religion. He sees that there is little place for Eros in the intellectual refractions of postmodern deconstruction—that it is possibly "a last effort by patriarchy to purify the terrible beauty of the maternal domain."[35] *Terrible*, I would add, because of its independence and wholeness. A beauty sufficient in its nature is not needy for vindication or subject to continual correction.

The Girl Who Lives with Cockroaches

When she misbehaves her mother puts pepper on her tongue, and her father beats her. Sometimes the beating prompts escalating waves of anger that build to frenzy. When he is totally beyond control, beating her tiny bottom and back with beastly fire and power, he screams, "I'm going to kill you." But she doesn't shrink. She feels her own power rise as she screams back, "Go ahead, I dare you."

She is the girl who lives with cockroaches.

High on a hill:

> *She dreams she opens a large music case in the shape of a string bass. Inside is a horse—a beautiful chestnut sorrel. It gets out and dashes away from her. Up from below and rounding the curve of the road comes a young couple leading a golden mare that they offer her. But she says, "No, I just want Old Sorrely, he is my father's favorite horse."*
>
> *She has a wild streak, so people say. Children are wild creatures who only gradually domesticate, after all. When she uses "nasty words" she picks up "in the gutter" from other children—swears in imitation of her father, or throws tantrums for things she wants—her mother locks her in the cellar with the cockroaches. Sometimes just the threat of this punishment is enough to control her. Then gradually the punishment loses its power. She learns that fear of the roaches gives teeth to the punishment. She can remain at the top of the stairs where the light flickers around the edges of the door and be quiet and attentive. As she quiets, she can hear her mother crying softly behind the door, and if any roaches make it up the stairs to crawl on her, well, so what.*
>
> *They won't hurt her—she can just flick them off.*

When she follows this train of thought and no longer cries on being put in the cellar, the punishment ceases. She never forgets the power of perspective gained at the top of the cellar staircase, or her mother's comforting arms on the other side of the door.

The memory of the cockroaches returns to her in the silence. She knows they are enduring creatures. They survived atomic bomb tests in the deserts near her hometown.

There are countermodes that subvert the escalations of discipline and mastery. These we find in the rhythms of wholeness, depersonalizing immersions that erase sharp distinction: "The rescending reflection derails the transcending movement of negativity through music, rhythm and dance, thereby eliciting the madness of pulsating powers. . . . Shamanism is perhaps one of the more salient modes of this intimacy with the secrets of the origin."[36] Fear of shamanic (intuitive) powers resulted in the torture and burning of women as heretics and witches in medieval Christianity, one of the most glaring examples of fear of feminine independence and vital powers (beauty).

Descendant reflection may coalesce and unify through its intuitive aspect, resulting in *poiesis*, whereby the feminine is exceptional in the arts, especially in dancing and healing, and in providing visionary advice. Furthermore, if Carl Jung is right, the feminine as anima belongs to everyone, and the proportional mixture of anima and animus in persons creates the pulls and counter-pulls of individuality. The etymology of "matter" is tied to "mater," meaning mother; the overcoming of matter, mind over matter and man over nature, is an overcoming that undermines and destroys the feminine.

Our body is of earth and heaven, and our body-of-birth-and-life is not a Platonic shadow. No. We live our existentially indivisible body-mind. *In the beginning is my body*, and when I dance so do my shadows. My body casts the shadows that dance on every surface, and matter matters. (Matter is not "the unconstructed," an idea that Judith Butler has lent to feminist discourse—and which I take in a different direction.) The coming into being of matter and meaning has been a continuing concern of existential phenomenology, contributing to philosophy that we are beings in process. *Mothers matter*. Matter, our material nature in process from the beginning, holds our history and our future. Mothering matters, and we continue in the existential/magical process of becoming body, remaining possible through our mothers. *Mothers are forever.*

We are all keepers of feminine energies and spirit. We weave, hammer, and write culture, and our science is replete with love and object-subjectivity. When we reject the feminine, we spurn life. We are all feminine, for we have come through this life source and through the alchemy of male and female united in the zygote. Men and women can both realize their feminine wisdom and breathe magic into life. We can calculate the distance of stars, but we also dance their bodies. We pull down the stars and transmute their bodies in our own. The human body, poets and physicists say, is of the same stuff as stars. At their dying, we are born, we become part of a descendant cycling of cosmic substance. *All our computers, stories, and poetry come from this mystery.*

THEY:

Untie technique,
     dance the luscious tumble
          and our fullnessbody stars.

KNOW THAT:

     giving birth severs and joins
     care and loss in a breath, pervading
     death of ego-cysts.

Nothing so simple,
          for spiraling down command
            and control, or
          bumping into something.

(*Lower the head for a moment, close your eyes, and relax the back of your neck.*)

That not giving birth is
          still woman / and torn.

WE ALL:

Inhabit her metaphysics, the
          blue-ish white knowledge,

unbelt the crisp lie
>> that she is just a dot in space
cutting into time
>> the meaning of her days
>>> a gathering, transmuting
>>>> flesh and milk.

s(HE)

Spreads passion into life
>> and natures. Less tolerance
>>> dilutes virginity
containing death-in-the-
>> rounds-and-tasks with peace
>>> or skin-in-line / and wrinkled.

WHEN IT DIDN'T EVEN HURT:

She danced her lower self
and let the answer rise on the
blossoming geranium.

BELIEVED the quaking aspen

>> shimmering in sun and shade.

8 | *Existential Haircut*

When we dance, darkness and
Light move a continuum.
Like falling snow and gleaming coal,
Both can shine the senses,
Burn or freeze into entity.
They flash in the mind's fire,
Flux and change states.

In their free unhurried modes,
They fit and drift,
Fade into riffs,
Grow out of one another.

In their drawing apart, they are balanced by forces of cohesion that hold them together.[1] In the abstract, this connection is aesthetic tension. In the human body, this connection is dance. Tension, rhythm, vibration, and energy ignite "dance"—in Sanskrit, *tan* (tension, sound, and rhythm) and Old High German *danson* (to stretch). The German word *tanz* (dance) also partakes of the sacred language of Sanskrit.

In the flowering and fading of our body consciousness, *tan* livens the soul of our dance, and the dance has a soul when we take time to notice. Through the bodily tension of *tan*, the dance has tone and tonus, and is far-reaching. It can stretch to extension, *uttana*, an extension that can be actively motivated or even passively elongated in yoga postures. In *tantra*, the activation of *tan* becomes fire, meaning

Juanita Suarez in *Legalia* (Legal alien, 2002). *Legalia* explores Suarez's identity as a Chicana choreographer. She enters the gap between her past as the child of migrant workers and her present career as a university professor of dance and women's studies. The two tails of her topcoat symbolize the two tales of her identity. The exuberant androgynous character of the dance and her costume evoke the unisex features of postmodern dance, but the overt expression of *Legalia* places it closer to dance theater than the neutral postmodern. Photograph printed with permission of the National Dance Association/AAHPERD and author/photographer Steven Clarke, from his book *Seeing While Being Seen* (2004).

energy, our learning to handle fire and sexual tension. Like the movement of droplets collecting and dispersing in rainbows, this divine tension animating dance evokes many moving colors and elements. Our rhythmic relationship to nature also has *tan,* as Indira Gosh explains:

> The tension of *tan* is the life within us, part of the vibrant whole of nature. When we dance and sing, we express *tan*—we connect the manifest energy in human form with the impersonal universal whole. This is God, Aum Kar, and Christ-Consciouness within us, and it pervades everything. Sadly, man has lost his relationship to nature and must recover its rhythms.[2]

Nature's tensions shimmer in our dance. In nature, darkness is a rhythmic part of a vibrational whole, not sinister or unholy when "light" is not the master word. Things are as we name and judge them to be, in other words. "We name things and then we can talk about them," Wittgenstein puts it.[3] A fluid, imaginative process, in naming we identify, single out, differentiate, and associate. Eventually we come to language and, to keep the naming vital, to poetry and dance. Identity is based upon interaction and movement, while entity suggests completion.

Darkness has been falsely identified with evil and used against woman in her guise as a dark and evil temptress. My synonym finder lists "black" and "dark," as well as "black-hearted," "blackguard," and "black sheep" as synonymous with "evil." "Witch" is the feminine synonym; "whore" and "wanton" are close by.[4] Such is the prejudicial power of words and naming. Our language is fully packed with words that combine woman with darkness, not to mention sex, the body, and sins of the flesh. Throughout we will reveal darkness as a neglected but crucial existential. We will not deny darkness; in fact, we will celebrate its rich aesthetic tones, but we will deny the tacit association of darkness with evil.

In the language of cosmology and dragons, dance embodies tensional interplay—loops, coils, double loops, laces, tails, and spirals. Affective and physical in the sense of *tan* and the German *Ursprung* (originating leap), dance tensions and extensions leap beyond the ordinary while musing in our most common stretches and relaxations, coiling and unwinding. These very basic tensions, obscure scratch-ings at first, are what phenomenologists study as intentions (in-tensions) relating to the will, *facultas agenti*, the faculty of an agent and the free will it implicates.

Agency, Sexuality, and Natural Powers

Scratching becomes touching, turns thick and moves away. In the meantime, something has been stirring the will into action. Perhaps it is the desire to finish a project or to see through a solution to a problem, to visit a friend, to climb a tree, to make love, return a hurt, hit somebody, to say something, take a better job that pays less. Agency comes through small as well as lofty things. Love, hunger, and anger are all motivators. The overblown exercise of agency in dominion over others, or the need to control others, is a forceful use of agency. But agency might also be exercised in life-enhancing connections, respecting rather than fearing difference without the need to co-opt otherness.

Like dance, human agency makes use of *tan* also. Tensions and relaxations resound in human choices, in creative or destructive actions (like the cosmic dance of Shiva), in energies that can also rest and ruminate in sacred time. Sanskrit, we remember, is a language of symbols based in sound vibrations that resonate through the body—on the tongue, through the breast, in the belly, and behind the eyes—as pictures of the God within. Sanskrit symbols and sounds evolved through bodily rhythms as signs of natural powers and are meant to be inhabited corporeally.

Human beings have natural powers, despite poststructural assertions that power roots in sociopolitical deployment. At the root of poststructural critiques of power, Michel Foucault has a very difficult time dancing around natural power sources when he defends his thesis from "the body having to be effaced" in an effort to "make it visible." (Optics appears again.) He claims that his analysis of the history of sexuality is one in which "the biological and the historical are not consecutive to one another, as in the evolutionism of the first sociologists, but are bound together in an increasingly complex fashion." He does lose track of biology (bios or life), however, even though he conceives his project as a history of bodies, "their vital and material investments." Despite his anti-essentialist portrayal of sex as primarily a historical formation (as we also saw in Butler, and to some extent in

Merleau-Ponty), he is forced to speak of the sexuality that does not appear "in its essential and positive relation to power." He fathoms such an essential but never gets to it; rather, he is interested in how "the idea of 'sex' makes it possible to *evade* what gives 'power' its power."[5]

Michel Foucault (1926–1984) is probably the most discussed philosopher in the postmodern revision of the existential/phenomenological tradition, though he finds ways to circumvent all of these categories. Indeed, circumvention of systems and inversion of ideas marks his philosophy as a work in dissolution. He is a rhetorical tactician and hybrid writer moving past history, sociology, political science, and philosophy, inventing new fields of investigation. He nevertheless depends on his predecessor, Friedrich Nietzsche, in his concerns for will and power, and on Martin Heidegger's critique of consciousness and the subject. Foucault's *History of Sexuality* is conceived along three axes: knowledge, power, and subjectivity—paired respectively with archaeology, genealogy, and ethics.[6]

His principle contribution, according to cultural critic Edward Said, is the undermining of anthropological models of identity and subjecthood governing research in the humanistic and social sciences.[7] Foucault proposes that culture does not emanate from an unchanging ego or the genius of artistry; rather, culture operates like social life itself, as a collective. It is not necessarily the individual gift that allows us to create, in other words, but rather our predilection to follow rules, a view also expressed in Heidegger's postmetaphysics (under the guise of "lack of art," as we pursued toward the end of chapter 6). Foucault replaces the principle of "creativity" with that of "inversion."

There seems to be both strength and weakness in his one-sided view. Like Butler, Foucault wants to expose how the rules of society enforce behavior, but proposes neither an antidote to the tyranny nor a model for empowering individuals. Human agency suffers a small death in his hands. Moreover, his Eurocentric view does not extend to ethnic others. Neither does he take any interest in the empowerment of women, though some feminists, myself included, have learned a great deal from him.

In his "Nietzsche, Genealogy, History" (1971), Foucault contrasts Nietzsche's metaphysical, supersensible ideal with the genealogy of descent, a theme I develop here in claiming the dark. Foucault climbs down from the mountaintop of ascendant philosophies and replaces what Fink-Eitel calls the "bird's perspective" of philosophical discourse through the centuries with the "frog's perspective" of the messiness of life.[8] His project is not the Kantian sublime of mind over nature, but the body with its desires and will. He places these within the auspices of power, knowledge, and society. His archaeological-genealogical method is designed to explore the juncture between discourse and practice. As a strategy, it is far less purely textual than semiotics or deconstruction.[9] Language is not a neutral container for Foucault; context is critical.

His *History of Sexuality* changes from its original intent after the first of three volumes. Indeed, it is change that characterizes Foucault's antisystematic work. His well-researched themes and standpoints emerge from dynamic chaos, as both Fink-Eitel and Said suggest. While recognizing his immense contribution to the study of power, Said criticizes Foucault's shift after the first volume of *History of Sexuality* "from the political to the personal."[10] His shift is ironic—and proves fortuitous—for one so disparaging of the subject. Foucault's disenchantment with the public sphere and creation of a personal ethnology based on the marginalized other foreshadows "the personal as political" in feminism. Said's *Orientalism* also stands in the light of what Foucault unmasks. Said uses Foucault's notion of discourse to identify Orientalism, the discourse by which Europe and then America is able to define the Orient, particularly the Muslim Orient, as the other, and thereby manage it.[11]

Foucault, who showed how "docile bodies" are shaped by seemingly innocent body disciplines, avidly pursued somaesthetic avenues of his own devising through practicing what he preached, gay sadomasochism, and strong drugs, experimenting with his own and other bodies. His philosophy may be read as an intensive self-investigation. As I read Foucault, sexuality and subjectivity are not matters for liberation from convention and the powers that hold it in place; rather, they are complicit in its formation. In *Discipline and Punish* (1975), he studies regulatory power over bodies. In *The Will to Knowledge* (1976), sexuality becomes the most important medium in what Foucault calls "biopower" (a harbinger to Butler's polemics regarding "bodies that matter," as we took up in chapter 4). The final two volumes of *The History of Sexuality* (1984) proceed from the third axis: subjectivity or "the ethical axis." The *Use of Pleasure* is a study of classical Greece during the fourth century BCE, and *The Care of the Self* looks at Hellenist-Roman late antiquity during the first and second centuries after Christ.

In these, the works of his last phase, he finally acknowledges the perspective of the subject, recognizing the self in a space where it can react to pressures of power as he outlines an existential philosophy of the constitution of the self in the "truth" of discourse. The regulatory power of knowledge gives way to personal truth. The agent is revealed, and the collective victim, if not banished, is momentarily released.

Here we can finally mask Foucault
In the self he so avidly dissolved
In collectivity, but now retrieves.
The mask of truth that he wears is fashionable,
As he sees the possibility of fashioning a life—
Despite obstacles.

Foucault's fluid self-inquiry suggests the self as a site for development. But as historical quest, it rests there. This final phase relates to Heidegger's theme of care, which he presents in *Being and Time* and which we investigated earlier in chapter 5. For Foucault as for Heidegger, mastery is at issue, but each arrives at a different place. Foucault's study of history leads him to the foundations of Western culture and the ancient ethics of mastery with its shameful equation of passivity, femininity, and subjugation. (We considered these ancient equations in chapter 4 through Judith Butler in her critique of Plato's view of woman as an "absence.") Classical Greece accords the masculine a "master morality" enjoined by values of self-control. If a man can control his pleasures, he can use them freely, and as a sovereign enjoy aesthetics of existence, turning his life into "a masterpiece."

Pederasty is rationalized since the master, as teacher, can, under the wings of Eros, exchange his knowledge for the sexual favors of young boys and thus remain in control. The means of gaining control is reason, the mainstay of Western philosophy. Reason rules emotion as mind rules the body; the active principle rules the passive, and the male the female. Emotions are passive because they are not within our control; therefore, they are negative, and hysteria is related to female sexuality. Japanese Butoh moved directly into this supposedly negative shadow—in part as a response to the rule of reason, the objectification of the body, and the purging of emotion in Western dance, beginning with Cunningham. It has remained for philosophical feminism, most recently in the work of Martha Nussbaum, to value emotions as indispensable to human life and ethics. In *Upheavals of Thought*, she demonstrates that, far from irrational distractions, emotions like love and grief are intelligent responses that proceed from value judgments concerning situations that are beyond our control but important to our well-being. As such they are part of ethical reasoning.[12]

Foucault's *Care of the Self* determines that in the first and second centuries after Christ sexual morality intensified on all levels. The idea of care of the self evolved into the pressure to control oneself. Pleasures threatened the art of living. Nevertheless, the self-practices of classical and late antiquity were a far cry from the Christian suppression of sexuality. Christianity regarded desire as a sin whereas, by comparison, ancient ethics saw desire as natural, although rules for behavior dictated attainment of mastery and the good life. For the ancients, the self (the male) was something to be developed. With the advent of Christianity, the self was a given to be purified of its "original sin," or "sins of the flesh." (We consider this in chapter 7 as purification of maternal qualities.)

Foucault is of interest to feminism because he combats the social order of normalization that strives to rid the world of the irregular other. (In "Bringing Body to Mind" in chapter 3, we saw how Aristotle conceived of woman as irregular and distorted.) The "othering" of woman is Beauvoir's concern and not Foucault's, but he provides much to think about.

Because of his study of the body's historical investment in sexuality, discipline, mastery, and power, Foucault is an important philosopher for dance with its often-stringent practices, and for somatic psychology and therapy. In *Practicing Philosophy*, Richard Schusterman analyzes Foucault's outlook and makes a disciplinary proposal for a philosophical field of somaesthetics concerned with self-development and "the self as a work of art."[13] Culling relationships of art, self, and somatics, he probes the limits of Foucault's personal somatic practices while advocating alternatives.

I am not convinced that becoming a work of art is the end I want to pursue in somatic practices. I propose a metaphysical space where a willingness to love replaces the will to art in the same way that Butoh dancer Natsu Nakajima states through her work and words: "I am striving not toward art, but toward love." I seek an ethic inherent in somaesthetic practices that listens to the body at the subtle level of care, the principle existential for both Heidegger and Foucault. Care is more than an existential thematic, however. It exists in conscientious action and sometimes in choosing not to act. Perhaps it is time to push philosophical evasions aside and tend to "the vital investments" of the body that concern Foucault but which, through somatic practices, cultivate the body's natural powers for daily renewal and self-healing.

There are useful criteria for choosing one's pleasures and practices. These arise through an ethic of care embodied in the somatic principle of touch: Do no harm is first; listening follows this. As an active listener, I can hear what the body of the other is saying, listen without imposition, hear without judgment. I can have no effective communication, and no shared pleasures, without the ability to listen with empathy. Listening is caring, and caring is the basis for love. The vital investments of the body respond to care, and this gives power its power. When we dance, when we touch the world lightly and handle others with care, when we are lost in the stream of the doing, we draw forth and extend such given powers. The vital material investments of the body are contiguous with its nature and do not respond well to rough violations. They are the natural abilities that give rise to all of our corporeal possibilities, whether self-referential or directed toward others and the environment.

No one teaches us how to open and close our hands as tiny infants, for instance. This is a natural power that becomes stronger and more differentiated with use, just as dancing does. Walking itself cannot be taught, even though parents and well-meaning adults think they can help, but they actually interfere with the infant's natural pacing. This may seem too simple an example, but our powers to move—to get to what we want, or what we need, to make the movements that form the words of our desires—are the basis of a body-mind axis of agency and freedom, the freedom to be and to become in our own best image.

I first began my journey into the emerging disciplines of somaesthetic practices through the Feldenkrais Method of Awareness through Movement (ATM) and hands-on Functional Integration (FI), invented through the explorations and discoveries of Moshe Feldenkrais. In the second week of my training program, the teachers showed us the human skeleton and we began to outline with our hands the contours of the bony structures with various partners. Concentrating on discrete areas, we developed a subtle touch to sense the bones beneath the skin and flesh. I became fascinated with how the hands of others could give me a map of my skeleton that renewed my sense of embodiment, and I also learned about the uniqueness of various hands as they translated the intangibles of intention.

When it came time to outline the pelvis and we were asked to choose partners, I immediately began to scan the room of about eighty people to find someone I could trust, a woman, I hoped. As I looked around the room of people who were still new to me, my eyes caught those of several others, and I understood their trepidation. This was not exactly like lifting an arm or arranging the feet in relation to the knees. Suddenly there was a gentle tap on my shoulder. It was a man. Oh dear, I thought, but then I took a breath and really looked at him. His eyes were timid and shining. He had chosen me because he also wanted someone to trust—and apparently not a man.

I stood in an easy posture as he found the crucial structures of my pelvis, beginning high around the waist with the spreading wings of the iliac crest, then traveling down the back of the ilia to my sacrum. He paused before going to the tailbone to ask my permission. The experience would have seemed incomplete had I not given permission, as also when I allowed him to touch lightly the two perfectly fitting together bones of my pubic structure in relation to the ischial tuberosities (sitting bones).

When I began to touch him, to listen, I could feel underneath his clothing how accessible his whole skeleton was to my touch—too much so. Then I looked at the gaunt features of his face more carefully, and began to understand. This young man in his twenties had all the symptoms of anorexia nervosa. He was seeking, apparently through the Feldenkrais method, to come to terms with his body in a way I could only imagine with my hands. He thanked me for being his partner when we finished, and with the memory of his frailty still in my hands, I pushed back the tears until I could leave the room. I had seen young dancers with this disease, and I had witnessed one death from it, but I had never seen it in a man. I did not see him again after that day. He did not finish the program. Whenever I encounter this problem in dancers and in my clients, I think of how much rides beyond our control—sexuality, for instance—as we lose ourselves in the dance of intercourse when we feel safe. Here an ethics of care turns toward an aesthetics of ambiguity; I realize how much must be surrendered daily of will and fear in order to live pleasurably with uncertainty, and how difficult it is, this grace.

I in the Subject

IF I HAVE NO NATURAL POWERS

> Only those I construct
> And resurrect
> At every moment from
> Nothing but sheer will
> And mental effort (to do what?),
> I mire in total standstill.

The "to do what" of our body-mind is a halting enigma if it does not flow from an unfolding intentionality. We can trust actions to whole, uninterrupted phrases of movement and speech that easily embody the will and at the same time move automatically.

EVERY FIFTH WORD IN SIX EVENTS

> of reason to dogma.
>
> bodily mystery I reason
>
> Sometimes deconstruction
>
> protect I a to next
>
> throw next move,
>
> from expand a of instance.
>
> from to template in instance.
>
> think I otherwise.
>
> me and never get I give abandon to beliefs apart, and
> give up
>
> myself way. fragments originating
> and myself. but irrationals bode

Subjects (conditionals) and contingencies implicate continuities and are something to disrupt or hang from, maybe fall free of. Wholes are like whole sentences. They also have holes and sometimes holiness, but the logical terminus of deconstruction is de(con)struction—skepticism without burden, mysticism without myth. Likewise, the nihilist existentialism of Jean-Paul Sartre—that we are nothing but what we make of ourselves—is another anti-essentialist radical that reduces to mistrust of nature and the conceit of totalizing agency. It has the dignity of commitment, but it dangerously posits the notion that we can control everything if we just try hard enough—definitely a bad idea. Nevertheless, we take from Sartre that it is important to live in "good faith" in the knowledge of our own freedom, and we take from Foucault that sex and power are entwined in a long history. Freedom comes with responsibility, and history should not own us. Maturity knows itself as a chooser, lives with its choices, and thus has a hard time living in blame of friends, partners, parents, and so on.

Fate does not own us, nature does not own us; nor do social pressures, unless we let them. We own ourselves. It is tough to be so free. Where are the pragmatic dependent connections? Our world is social, artificial, natural, familiar, and conditioned by our habits. Then, of course, we all had a childhood. "Freedom is what you do with what's been done to you," says Sartre, and Gloria Steinem reminds us that "It's never too late for a happy childhood."

Performing Freedom: Synergetic Humanism

The anti-essentialist core of Sartre's existential humanism (that fate does not own us) might well be recast along new lines, adopting its concern for subjective responsibility, but modulating it with themes of cooperative interdependence, how we dance together. I speak of a synergetic humanism of coordinated actions and interrelated supports in which human beings are not the measure for everything—or the standard for nature, where darkness and light have no fault line. Rather, are humans now caught up in a dance that is challenging their ability to partner nonhuman nature without being thrown off balance?

When we dance, animals leap through us.
We like the excitement of falling off balance,
of losing control—
and returning
to center.

We breathe in our skin
and believe the silver tree.

THAT: You are reading and I am writing.
Not past writing but in contact
Through the artifact.
THAT: The I who says "I"
Is speaking a moving I.

The subject can say "I"
But where does this "I" come from?
The voicing of "I" announces all that makes
Utterance and movement possible.

Moving our many eyes
Are Others and the Living World.
Without Otherness there are no Eyes,
Or everything is Eye.

"I" is a sound that builds distinctions, and it can build them in many ways, according to intent—to separate an independent opinion, to arrogate authority, to create a pleasing contrast in the midst of a muddle. And "I" can blend and fold, spreading into the mind of others, moving alongside:

That "I" can dance solo
on a diamond-sided

                    Slope
            that speaks for itself alone

Solos are difficult, however,

                    lacking referential supports and tensions
                    that lace duets, trios, and group dances.

Pity an awkward "I" its dances, swells, and
                    wrapping into
                        (w)holiness;

it heals

like
the musky body of sleeping dragons
not marking one
then another
rubbing out redness.

Without the subject, we have no common ground for communication—just isolated/abstruse/object dances—no senders/no receivers/
no arc/no return. When we perform (write, dance, and sing) for others, we implicitly seek a common ground. A performance for others
contains the wish to reach them. Intrinsically, we dance for ourselves,
but a performance finishes something with a self-surpassing wish.

The "I" who understands the conditional
Is the "I" who studies experience.
S(he) studies herself to know others,
And others to subtract herself.

The dance is not dead
Mixed up and lost
              Nor blown to bits and pieces,
                       But group dances do take teamwork.

Freedom and agency are crucial historical concerns of existential humanism, which needs to move past its self-centered lonely heroism.
We carry the history of several humanisms: enlightenment, rational,
universal, and existential, for example. And we call ourselves humans. What we say and do bears this mark. Deconstruction has not
substituted constructive solutions for its "death" of the subject, the
self, and the author. Despite this textual execution, we still use the
same first person pronoun "I" when referring to ourselves. There
seems to be such a thing.

We still have concerns for freedom and power as these intersect,
and our otherness awareness has been multiplied and diversified. We
are wary of universals and ply instead the borders of difference and
identity, sometimes to the exclusion of human connections. For me
the other is not a polar opposite; I grasp the human trace where likeness and difference dance together. Sometimes the difference between

self and other dissolves, especially in our dancing and walking in tandem. The other is as conditional as the self is—not stable but changing in the many textures of relationship.

Arising after World War I and growing through the development of World War II, existential humanism emerges as an anti-utopian, sometimes darkly dystopian philosophy in its criticism of the securities of the easy life and collectivist states. Its uncertainties are radical; they originate in the nineteenth century with Nietzsche and Dostoevsky. The center is broken, cannot hold; old gods are dying. And freedom is not a gift but a "condemnation" for Sartre. Freedom cannot be taken for granted; rather, it is realized in serious matters of choice and agency. Beauvoir is also concerned with themes of death and alienation, anxiety, ethics, and choice. Freedom comes with problems and responsibilities, but for her it also has joy (as we saw earlier) and can "thicken" (her word) into happiness.

Freedom is the root principle of existential humanism, not simply a concept, and it has little to do with the rugged individualism of laissez faire, or the bill of rights of possessive economic pursuits.[14] Freedom and agency are existential conditions of the subject, unpredictables in need of air and bodily activation. They root in bodily powers and synergies—balances, failings, and taking a stand.

Our body is not in space; it is of space, as Merleau-Ponty first articulated. The body is spacious in its structure. We see this in action through the body's architectural "tensegrity"—a term from Buckminster Fuller that defines a self-supporting structure with tension and compression of parts balanced throughout the whole. In the body, this is more than a harmonious relationship of moving parts. It is a functional integrity that provides a freedom of effortless ease in movement. There is agentic power in such freedom. We see it in good dancing, in pleasurable walking and running, in expert diving, and in the amazing grace of ordinary, everyday actions that people perform all the time without even trying—or especially because they are not trying. Healthy children exhibit such buoyancy and postural ease, the head moving freely from the neck and spine in an atlas/axis glide.

Moshe Feldenkrais would have called this "actural" ease since he did not like the static essence of the word "posture." It has pose, post, and posturing in it (though not the post in postmodern or poststructural, we hope). When functional balance breaks down—through poor movement habits, trauma, loss of trust, stress, depression, and so on—the body cannot support itself. We lay ourselves down on everything, and gravity becomes a drag. Results can even be painful—neck and back pain, for example.

But bodily tensegrities can revive, as they often do, and we can feel functional and whole. Function and structure are mutually reinforcing. Or as Ida Rolf puts it: "Behavior is structure." She worked this out through biochemistry and physiology and used deep manual intervention in the elastic soft tissue structure of the body (myofascia) to integrate human structures. But freedom is not an absolute, and Rolf seldom took account of this in her vertical body politics, especially in terms of movement where integrations and disintegrations meet each other coming and going in complex ways.[15] As Feldenkrais began to show, integration does not spell intervention. Freedom is not a battleground for waging wars of mastery and intervention, but a synergy of natural energy and structures (practiced and performed) in life, art, and everyday actions. Our performance of freedom can also politicize and mobilize in sociocultural processes. Freedom can turn anywhere, even toward destructiveness.

Freedom and its power in movement are poised like an egg held in the hand. If the hand tightens around the egg with too much control, it breaks, and if the control is too lax, the egg falls to the floor. Albert Opoku, founder of the Ghanain Dance Ensemble, gave me this definition. In the growth phases of modern dance, Doris Humphrey defined movement as "an arc between two deaths." Static death is at the top of ascendant integration where things freeze into inaction— Apollo locked at his peak. Dynamic death is at the bottom of disintegration. Here is total dissipation—Dionysus at his excessive worst. For Humphrey, movement and dance arise between these two extremes. Her dance sought a spiraling form of freedom through the arc, rejecting classical verticality and ascendancy. Her semiotics and freedom was the holistic, yielding spiral between the two deaths.

Freedom is a sound. It has biophysical and psychological as well as political tones, and somewhere these resonate together. The freedom that knows itself as a chooser is not a victim. It bears contingencies and comes with responsibilities. We create our own lives within our sociocultural and biological inheritance. Biology and culture both play a part; they will resound in our agency, our freedom to choose and act, as well as in our dances.

To Choose My World Freely

> I like dances that are weird and wonderful, that step away from our day-to-day reality. I like dances that show me a new way of seeing. That pull from the commonality of humanity but are not dependent on historical antecedents or successes from the past.
>
> **Brian Francis Taylor,** Texas, 1991

Brian Taylor gave me an existential haircut in my 1991 dance theory class, "Truth in Movement," at Texas Woman's University. I supplied barber scissors on the first day of class and asked my students if someone could make me look like an existentialist. I didn't have a beard, so I thought some special haircut might help. Brian volunteered. I recited all the existential poetry I could think of while Brian cut my hair—or deconstructed my poetry, take your pick. In the next year after our class, Brian died of AIDS. His participation in the course gave particular emphasis to its existential themes. He was ill, as we knew, but he kept a sense of humor. His dances for class assignments seemed to reach outside of his condition while focusing attention inward. He prepared for death through reflection and through his dances; some were staged in performance. Our deaths and dances can both be healing, as Brian reminded me—and so can our lives. I remember that the haircut he gave me was very short around the ears and in back, fluffy on top.

In our consciousness of ourselves as choosers, we become more than our biological or gendered selves. In other words, we become individuals, original works in process. Not merely belonging to a category called woman or man, we become a woman similar to but like no other, and a man unrepeatable in his unique characteristics, even if we see him everywhere. We create our distinct selves as we realize our purposes in action. We make choices in the actions we take, choices for which we take responsibility, and in the consciousness of choosing, our freedom and agency are owned.

This choice to be ourselves also fuels the larger community body. It is not necessarily the choice to be selfish, but stems from the deepest yearnings of our visionary self, the self that seeks to tell its truth. We are empowered in our conscious choosing because we are aware of ourselves as agents. Still, my particular frustration—as a woman—is that I enact my freedom within a world that does not encourage it. I have few models of women who have lived freely, respecting their instincts and deepest motivations, their ancient, inward, and holy body. As a late-twentieth-century survivor, I might carry a healthy dose of anger around my frustrations within a fractured world, but the magic of words and rites bears me on.

HAVING PASSED THROUGH

the age of dreaming and imagining
of separating the imaginable and concrete
reuniting them in the dream-body
unfurling sensuality and protecting it
exploring new worlds
mothering myself and others
seeking self
destructuring self
rescuing childSelf and soulSelf
growing moreSelf
creating and decreating self
bringing near what was far
finding East in my West
and summoning courage,

I now enter the age of choice—
to fulfill the tasks of all the senses—
to choose my world freely and the work yet to be done.[16]

To practice the lessons of the body—one by one—
                as Touch gives rise to feeling
Speech develops hearing and
                fluid relationships
Taste translates sweetness and allows me
                to accept the bitter
Sight brings vision and springs from
                darkness and light

Hearing brings harmony—the interest and
　　　　　　ambivalence of dis-cor-dance that allows me to remain
whole.

Smelling gives me flowers and wine
　　　　　and Dancing sends me
　　　　　along the bright-road path of animation—
　　　　　thrilling, transitory anima.

Dancing allows me to visit all my ages
　　　　　　　to be at home with my breath
　　　　　　　to say less,
To move in timeless mists
　　　　　　　And to never forget my feet
　　　　　　　　　in contact with the earth.

In our century, we will have learned much about independence and
agency through enmeshments of self-destructive codependence, not
to be confused with cooperative interdependence. The lessons of freedom will repeat in addictive relationships and our leaning on drugs
until we can stand literally and figuratively on our own two feet, acquainted with solitude but connected to the earth like the yoga *Mountain asana* as its *tan* grows heavenward through a weight falling downward and a steady radiant core.

　　When it seems the world conspires to keep me dependent—that my
strength is daily won anew—the "I" in my choices draws up the existentialist, the yogini *moving mountain* who has the courage to be
alone, to think her own thoughts and listen to her instincts, who risks
her own dance even when it is out of step with fashion. Sometimes I
vibrate in the surety of the freedom of my existence. I own these times
when I dance, when I make dances, when I meditate, when I teach,
when I write, when I bake bread, and when I integrate my being with
another toward healing. These are the times I hang the sky with stars.

Of the Body Mysterium

Solid mechanics and rationality have maintained a relationship of very
long standing, one against which fluids have never stopped arguing.
LUCE IRIGARAY, "The 'Mechanics' of Fluids"[17]

Existentialism is a humanism, as Sartre held, but I outline these "isms" differently. Like Sartre, I understand that I am free, a chooser, that my life is not determined; I do not need to be a victim in any ultimate sense. I am creating myself, my life is mine to compose. Or more accurately, I improvise my life as I go along. I can also be a still point, when I stop to see the movement around me, and let it go by—but I am in no sense more important than other creatures in my orbits, nor is human will the measure of everything. Nature measures all of us and has many valences. Nature is all-encompassing, excessive sometimes, and cruel—as beyond our control as the weather. Nature also heals.

It lends us the intelligent design of the body, a miracle beyond our doings. Miracles are miracles because they bypass our feeble doings to remind us that, ultimately, we are not the doers. Our human embodiment in its adaptive intelligence surpasses our willful doings, sustaining us at every moment, asleep and awake.

When things go wrong, the body-mind has an innate capacity to heal itself. Its repairs and renewals are so commonplace as to escape notice. Nature, through the body's innately cooperative systems, accomplishes this (for the most part) outside the will. Science can explain the intelligent working of the body's synergetic systems, and medicine can try to effect recovery when something goes awry, but nothing can duplicate the body's functioning as a natural process. Finally, the thing to be restored presents itself beyond explanation or intervention. We want our body back, the body that nature intended. We can will it, we can medicate and meditate, we can even have surgery, but then we wait for nature to do its miraculous part. Something snaps, crosses a synapse, and begins to flow into a restricted or bruised pathway, urging obstructions to give way; then, in our breath and marrow, we begin to recover. Healing is a miracle dance that the body performs for us. We cannot make this happen, but we can send ourselves in that direction, attune to a healing process, and welcome change.

Unlike atheistic humanists, I do not feel alone in an alien world. Though I live in the knowledge of the certainty of my death, I am not as concerned with final ends as I am with life's process—the dance itself. I die and am reborn in the dance of this lifespan. Our deaths and dances should teach us how to live: They can both heal. When I dance, I resonate with mystical existentialists—the "I-thou" of Martin Buber and Gabriel Marcel. I seek with Susan Griffin "what lies under our stillness," and with Luce Irigaray the transpiration of "our overflows." I welcome my emotional body, myself. When I dance, my ego, that sharp sword that separates me from others and sometimes sets me against them, melts. My solids unfreeze and I flow into the larger stream of life—I get down and funky, precocious and alive.

Like the dark Butoh artists who dance the body's memory in existentially awkward and eloquent forms, I tread the mysterious ground of my bodily being connecting me to others and to my molten core. The pathway of my freedom is healing and coactive; it leads from I to Thou to Nature—not distinguishing between I and Thou, Nature and God:

I release the dark and sacred ground,
The constellating potential of my bodily being:
I touch my earth/mother and goddess consciousness.
Night crawls through the dance of my forgetting,
Light beams sting my way.

I move beneath myself into the secret cave,
Untangling male-female, sounding-bones and stilling.
My wounds unwrapped, I drink from the river
Of my sleeping love's tears.
The hurt of his heart drums up my heart,
And my bones make flesh—pink toes, long eyelashes,
Sweet thighs, a spine of diamonds, and breasts of
Sunlight. My somadance awakens him to join.
And when we dance, we dance happily ever after,
For we have "kissed the hag" and found each other.
And that is all the people say.

Untangling Dance[18]

Situated Freedom

The dean of my school had just excused my colleague's bad behavior toward me by saying, "He's just not used to women who are his equal." It suddenly flashed through my mind that as chairperson I had been leading my depart-

*ment successfully for several years, that my colleague was a new chair and
an associate professor: I was a full professor. So I said to my dean, "He's not
my equal," and chanced this vanity for a purpose. Every time I opened my
mouth, the new chair would go crazy and begin attacking me, not just my
positions, but also my person, and my right to speak. It seemed to me that
he had difficulty with women having a voice since he tried to squelch the
voice of the other female chair as well, but not the men in our group. After I
pointed this out to the dean, he agreed with my perceptions and asked what
he might do about it. Nothing, I said; I would not allow myself to be pulled
into my colleague's emotional orbit, and I did not care how uncomfortable
my power made him feel. If he became abusive, I would not. I knew I had
other choices: I could ignore him, or practice the somatic strategy of matching. Rather than trying to master the situation, I would mirror back his
words calmly so that he might be able to hear himself, and if that did not
work, I would leave the room in order to send a message. I also took on the
challenge of listening to my own sensations, matching them, instead of taking his bait. If he wanted a fight, I certainly did not. But I would not be shut
up. No way. It had taken me too long to find the power of my voice.*

We no longer worry whether we as women are the equals of every
man, for we know there are many men who in many ways are not our
equals. Yet in this we are all equal: existentially, the human being is
her-story/his-story in the making. Ontologically we are conditional
selves, whole, yet indeterminate in the actualization of our possibilities. Subjectivity is an ongoing process, as feminism has elucidated,
from Beauvoir's existential ethics to Kristeva's postmodern metaphysics. Biological sex is a given, but there is much conditioning in the
performative femininity and masculinity of learned behaviors. In the
realization of our human possibilities, our daily performance of ourselves, the script is never finished. We are free, Beauvoir writes, despite
our "immense ignorance," but this freedom only realizes itself through
engagement with the world and in view of the freedom of others.[19]
Her ethics defined a situated freedom, much as Carol Gilligan and later
authors expanded the terms of ethics by showing that moral reasoning in women is not based on a linear, lockstep process, but accounts
for the complexities of human relationships in an ethics of care.[20]

In the dance of life, we are free to become what we will through the
choices we make; but this does not mean that we are all equal in our
opportunities for self-realization. As recent feminist criticism is ex-

ploring, there is a feminist hegemony that has ignored the vast cultural and class differences among women, especially the problems and needs of oppressed minorities. When I live in good faith in the light of my freedom, I am obligated to seek the liberty of all. If I am given more by way of education, and have inherited more health and financial means than others, I have a duty to do whatever I can for the welfare of those less fortunate. My self-realization is not an abstract projection into an idealized future. My present and future self, my possible-self, is inextricably tied up in the welfare of the planet and the health of society.

Shadows and Broken Symmetries

Our body casts a shadow. And shadows are neutral until we interpret them. Dancing is one safe way to explore the shadows. It brings us the affective embodiments of darkness and transitory shadows, for in dancing we can conjure every possible and fleeting lived-world. Dancing lives in possible worlds and spatiotemporal moments of performance, gathering up the dwindling day, making it vivid and remaking it in the present. In the time of the dance, present time can take perceptual precedence over fleeting time. Time dances as we dance, stills as we still, and bears our shadow with it.

Darkness is not evil, as it is so often characterized. It has no particular value, good or bad, until some value is placed on it. In the cultural upheavals of the 1960s, African Americans began to reverse the negative put-downs of darkness with a powerful medicine: "Black is beautiful." Darkness is a natural phenomenon with many variations and is beautiful, as racial variety makes clear. Dusk and the murkiness of morning just before dawn is also beautiful. Only in their outer measurements do light and dark appear in high contrast and opposition. The world of movement and variety arises through contrasts, oppositions, incongruities, and tensional factors of many kinds. When particle physicists study the broken symmetries of the molecular dance, they find that differences appear through breaks in symmetry (in space as in time) and are necessary for discernment, change, and movement.

Symmetry has subjective perceptual qualifications, and perfect symmetry creates indiscernability. Asymmetry and the difference it creates are required for perceptual discernment. A play of instability is entangled in our jagged histories, where the bright skeletons also dance. As forms of life, we use and share molecular parts from other forms—from each other through our human birth, from plants, animals, air, and water. Everything shares in the biodance.

Aesthetically, we do perceive and enjoy local symmetry (as less than perfect) when it is not allowed to dominate exclusively, physicist Philip Morrison explains. Difference is part of movement and part of the beauty of discernment. In a perfectly symmetrical world, "nothing would ever happen." But perfect assemblage does not occur, Morrison holds. Instead of stasis we have movement—what he calls "the Act of Becoming"—growth, destruction, change, and transformation. It is probable "that all symmetries are a little bit broken because the real world does show some kind of structure in space and time and direction. We can't put our fingers on it yet, but the universe is not the same in all directions. . . . some feature always breaks every macroscopic symmetry in the end."[21]

We constantly make use of our bodily powers to differentiate movement. We move off-center to pass through center when we walk, for instance. Differentiation grows as we articulate our movement powers in learning skillful actions. Think of the microarticulations in the hands and fingers of the expert pianist, or the quick twists of attention required of the dancer as she or he moves in one direction while looking in another, shifting suddenly to an entirely new, equally complex orientation, another, and another, as time sews the split-second movements elastically together.

What we make of our powers to differentiate on the level of voluntary action poses questions of agency. Choreography has taught me this. A difference can be pressed toward violence, oscillate in pleasing tensions of polarized complements, shift through time, or disappear. When differences fuse or resolve, we can then see their unity. Opposition, likewise, need not signify force. And disagreement need not lead to bitter conflict. Difference is a part of nature, of movement and life. How we value it is a matter of interpretation, and how we use it is a matter of attention. Through oppositional contrasts, disturbances, flows, and resolutions, movement is born. Without differential change there is no movement of the personal body—be it lazy and rolling, as sweetly tense as a sudden intake of winter air, or severely wrought as through critical illness. Without the differences that create change and movement, there is no dance—and no life.

Revaluing Darkness

As man split light and darkness, he gave darkness and mystery to woman—she was not he, and the other can be baffling—and he formed ego through the divide. He became the "I" who separates and names the positions. In the process, he gave morality to goodness and light and assigned evil to darkness. Before this perception of darkness arose through patriarchy, darkness did not symbolize evil. In prehistoric partnership cultures, black, we learn through anthropologist Maria Gimbutas, was the color of fertility.[22] Degradation and torture of women came through the naming of the positions and found its apex in a medieval craze that named "a black art," burning and tormenting independent and intuitive women as heretics and witches. Such are the historical realities of the medieval Christian world, as Riane Eisler studies it:

> "Men of God" declare that the half of humanity from whose bodies life ensues is carnal and sinful, and "witches" are burnt alive at the stake for the crime of healing through "sorcery" (that is, through folk medicine such as herbs rather than through bleeding and other "heroic" remedies prescribed by the new Church-trained and licensed male physicians).[23]

Eisler studies the political and spiritual consequences of the shift from the sacred sex of prehistoric partnership cultures to the sexual politics of warring cultures that shaped human relationships in the image of violence.

The last of the peaceful prehistoric cultures, preceding ancient Greece, Babylon, Palestine, and Rome, can still be witnessed in the erotic and graceful artifacts on the Mediterranean island of Crete, where the story of civilization begins around 6000 BCE. Here reverence for the Goddess continued until the fifteenth century, well beyond the Achaean invasion and the shift from Minoan to Minoan-Mycenaean culture. On Crete, we can see remnants of a past where young men and women danced with bulls by vaulting through the horns and somersaulting over the running bulls rather than fighting them to the death, as in modern blood sports.

While it would be unrealistic to think that prepatriarchal Western cultures were ideal or without hierarchies of any kind, there is no evidence that masculinity was identified with domination and bloody conquest. On the contrary, prehistoric partnership cultures were in essence nonviolent, aesthetically advanced cultures where life-giving powers and the Goddess were worshipped. Dominator cultures shifted from the ideal of bodily pleasure to that of pain, replacing reverence for nature with the worship of Zeus and other thunder-hurling war gods of male ego appeasement. Dehumanization of the male followed the degradation of nature and the domestication of women. Violent sex and rape arose from the confusion of sexual pleasure with sado-masochistic inflictions of pain.[24] Wanting to shed light, we should not demean darkness, the color of life, the beauty of time and night, of dark skin and rich soil. We need to comprehend, however, how darkness has been used to devalue woman. Renee Lorraine, in "A History of Music," details how composers from Richard Wagner and Mozart to Mick Jagger have used musical darkness in chromatic modes and minor keys to signal women as fearful, sexually provocative, and evil. Fearful female characters are typically subdued in opera when chord progressions move from chromatic tension to the stable major keys in triumphant heroic endings.

This musical shift happens in *Tannhauser* when Venus is swallowed up by the earth and morning dawns. Similar resolutions of darkness to light vanquish the queen in *The Magic Flute*, Senta in *The Flying Dutchman*, Isolde in *Tristan and Isolde*, Kundry in *Parsifal*, and signal Carmen's death in *Carmen*. The death of the powerful sexual woman is treated with exciting beautiful music that leads us on an emotional level to want her to die; and when she does, the stage is flooded with light. This progression toward resolution of musical tension is light bearing and associated with the male in opera and rock where the dominant-tonic cadence is "an iconic sign of masculine climax and mastery." Such music leads us, Renee Lorraine says, "to love the music that hurts us." Nonlinear and non-goal-directed music are associated with an attractive and dangerous feminine that needs to be purified in opera and opera ballet, and subtly (or not so subtly) raped into subjection in such rock songs as Jagger's "Stupid Girl" and "Under My Thumb."[25]

Here again is the transcending male reflection and purification of the erotic. The resolution of a heightened *tan* in musical tension and the defeat of the dark feminine happen simultaneously. This is typical: the male has conquered evil (in opera) or satisfied his desires to penetrate and dominate (in rock), and the scene comes to an end. "Under My Thumb" ends with Jagger's quick breaths of relief and "Take it easy baby," as the dominant-tonic resolution holds for several measures.[26] This might just be hard-driving eroticism per se, but not likely so, when the title lets us know who is boss and the music is abusively aggressive.

There are alternative resolutions for musical tension—peaceful rather than heroic—without anyone having to be overcome or harmed. Dominant tonic musical resolutions are not inherently masculine; they are a relaxation of tension and may be employed in a nonsexist manner in music and dance. In Twyla Tharp's exuberant dance *The Upper Room*, bad women do not die on cue. Nobody dies or is feared as body contact and musical tension escalates to the upper registers. Paul Taylor's *Roses* is alive to a play of difference, erotic, smooth, and lyrical. The costumes are gray, white, and black with no judgment implied, just aesthetic difference and the imagination supplying the colors of roses. Men partner women ingeniously. Women also bear weight, but do not heft men aloft. Men dance with men, and women also dance with women in a fanning out of gender roles. *Tan* ebbs and flows in eddies, and the romantic element is not final.

For myself, I want to dance to whatever music moves me, especially the music of women (and men) like Haudenosaunee-Iroquois Joanne Shenandoah, whose voice connects me to my own inner flute and the natural world. I want to dance to music that helps me to feel good about myself, and to move away from musical idealization of pain and heroism.[27]

What They Cannot Have

Men today are adrift, unhinged from the secure knowledge of dominance and mastery. Neither nature nor woman has been tamed—though we see that they are both exploited, harvested for commercial gain, and badly battered.

In my dance and somatics classes, I have heard three battery stories just this semester alone (spring 1994). Sue has been absent from class for the first half of the semester recuperating from a fractured skull, broken bones in her hand, and injuries to her spine. Her boyfriend is stalking her since she informed the police that he beat her. Michele is divorcing an abusive husband, and will raise her child alone. When she herself was a child, she was removed from her parents' home because it was feared that her alcoholic father would kill her in the frequent beatings she received. She was placed in a foster home for protection, where her protector raped her. Alice told me she had been absent from class because her brother had beaten her. Ann is uncovering an eating disorder and an abusive childhood in therapy.

In 2001, I continue to learn of abuses through the body stories my students write in somatics classes. Sadly, I read very few uplifting stories. Rather, I read about eating disorders, abusive boyfriends, and self-abuse, young women who cut themselves compulsively with razors in order to feel alive, and who vomit to stay thin.

Recently we became aware of the destructiveness of sexual abuse of young boys by Catholic priests. Two of my psychologist friends have turned their practices over to victims of childhood abuse because it is so common. Where does all this violence and pain come from? Has it always been with us, but not so apparent before? Has it been hidden by shame? Is abusiveness increasing, or are we becoming increasingly sensitized to sexual abuse? Or still yet, is this all a matter of perception; have we become a society of victims, as some are saying? Gloria Steinem's "What If Freud Were Phyllis" explores the recent revival (unknown to the revivalists) of Freud's "seduction theory," that children have an unconscious wish to seduce adults and victims seek out their own victimization or else they fantasize it.[28] Women who suffered from childhood sexual abuse developed what Freud and others identified as hysteria. Dr. Wilhelm Fleiss, Freud's trusted associate, would operate on the noses of hysterics, removing bone to relieve their trauma.

Literary critic and dramatist Hélène Cixous agrees that Freudian psychoanalysis sanctioned violence against women; her dramatization of the Dora case is a dire indictment of Freud. Catherine Clement, Cixous's collaborator on *La Jeune nee* (The newly born woman), carries through this critique of phallogocentric psychoanalysis. She exposes the historical problems inherent in linking hysteria and witchcraft with the repressed feminine, criticizing her mentor, Jacques Lacan, in his poststructural masculinist beliefs on the hysteric. These works of Steinem, Cixous, and Clement revision the darkness of feminine abjection and repression.

Maxine Sheets-Johnstone revises still further, carefully documenting ties that ignore the personhood of woman in the writings of Freud, Sartre, Lacan, Foucault, and Derrida. In *The Roots of Power,* she traces the gnarled connection between these theorists in their stifling and othering of woman.[29] Sartre's "Look of the Other" underlies the thinking and optics of Foucault and Lacan. The preservation of patriarchy in a psychoanalytic world supposedly friendly to women fixes the body in a bodiless optical gaze—transforming sex into "discourse about sex" in terms of the "seen" or "looked upon" body. Sheets-Johnstone opens with the claim that Foucault's "optics of power" is Sartre's "look" (the gaze of the other) writ large and inflated with importance in terms of sociopolitical practices and institutions. What Foucault's account of sexuality leaves out is the corporeal body in its tactile/kinaesthetic concrete existence. He is even more abstract than Sartre because Sartre's concern touches upon everyday personal encounters. Foucault relies on a visualized body, undefined and undescribed, and thus an optical account of desire and sexuality.

Sheets-Johnstone expands her thesis to problems of power, or a power of optics that objectifies otherness in its wake and denatures the ratio of the senses where vision dominates human interaction and discourse. "Penetration," or in Sartrean terms, "the filling of holes," is eventually effected through a visual body and, according to historical investitures of power, as aggression toward an objectified other: woman and nature.[30] One feels that Sheets-Johnstone is reacting in part to the domestication of the body in language of visual objectification and not to vision itself, certainly not the subjective powers of vision highly developed in aesthetic sensibility, present to the beauty of nature and to others without prejudice.

Sartre was right when he said, "we write for our own time." Along with Beauvoir, he initiated a discourse on otherness and sex, but in the same stroke brushed aside women's sexuality. Today, he might write otherwise. Sartre's view devalues receptivity and darkness. A valuing of the dark might in other hands produce a positive account of love and sex, our intimate dance in close encounters of flesh and body. Sexual desire has been considered dark and often base in transcendent reflections, and woman has represented evil as both temptress and castrating annihilator. Like Aristotelian philosophy and Freudian theory, the Sartrean root of existential psychoanalytic theory also fails to voice a positive view of women's sexuality—the physically internal, receptive, and open center that is not a Platonic absence, a Freudian lack of penile essence that lives in envy, nor an Aristotelian distortion of the normal. Neither is feminine receptivity an obscene black hole, as Sartre describes it: "The obscenity of the feminine sex is of everything which 'gapes open.' It is an appeal to being as all holes are. In herself woman appeals to a strange flesh which is to transform her into a fullness of being by penetration and dissolution." He further describes woman's sex as a "slimy," yielding docility: "a soft yielding action, a moist and feminine sucking like the supreme docility of the possessed, the fidelity of a dog who gives himself even when one does not want him any longer, and in another sense there is underneath this docility a surreptitious appropriation of the possessor by the possessed."[31] In Sartre's phenomenology, the slimy feminine hole, like an unwanted docile dog, surreptitiously appropriates the penis, threatening annihilation of the male's "strange flesh," his penile "filler of holes." As an "appeal to being," woman is ontologically absent, just not there. She is a petition waiting at the door. She does not exist for herself, but only comes into being as "a fullness of being" when she is penetrated. The penis bestows her being, answers her appeal, and lets her through the door to join in the company of other more complete beings whose being is not in question because they carry it with them.

Shedding Her Flesh

Now we face the specter of young women (and also some men) who practice the destructive self-mutilation of starving their bodies. We see this too often in dancers, as many seek to satisfy the terrible beauty of a culture opposed to nature. Here the active principle of personality, yang in Asian aesthetics, locks into overcontrolling actions, and Eros, receptivity or yin, is denied. Anorexia controls matter, "mater" or mother, and is afraid of (purifies) the flesh (called evil), the land.

DISCIPLINE IS GOOD WE SAY

Dance is discipline,
And discipline is freedom
We can't get enough discipline.

We make war on our flesh and will it away
We want to see the bones, the more the better
We "beat time" in every musical measure
We count out loud and eat like birds and butterflies
Conquering the flesh and the land, we separate from our mother
We shed our flesh, and our mind rules.

WITH THE SPEED OF LIGHT

He maps the dark land
And shapes it in the form of his will,
Opens the "turn-out" of her feet, legs,
And hips to 180 degrees—
Hones her body in the bone of his dance.
He stretches her leg into high-extension.
It touches her ear.

Spidery and splayed at the groin, she is wispy and tightly strung as her
curves conform to his geometric. She sees how her toes bleed, and splits
her ex-tensions wider.

She becomes thin for his dance,
                    stops menstruating, and undergoes surgery
                                    to sharpen her profile.
He tilts her head to the right and lifts her chin.
Her back extends, and her eyes look beyond
                    the audience
                            into what
                            (her control, her vanishing)
                    they can never have.

Yin-Yang Reciprocity

Receptivity and darkness can be understood in symbolic terms as yin.
In the nondualist Eastern metaphysics of Tao, yin expresses receptivity and darkness, a qualitative property in constant tensional play and
interchange with the light and active yang. In Taoist texts, yin is
sometimes feminine, but is also simply an interactive aesthetic agent,
part of a yin-yang inseparable unity that both women and men possess, one that may be empty or full according to emphasis. I speak of

yin as an aesthetic agent in the dynamic and original meaning of aesthetics through its etymology in *aisthesis,* the Greek word for sense perception. Yin is never fully yin, and yang is never fully yang because perceptually they are in constant movement of interchange. In Chinese medicine, yin and yang are neither strong nor weak, except as they grow overly dominant or recessive in the personal body. Thus, the heat of yang may be overbearing, or the cooler quality of yin may also become excessive.[32] Balancing the interplay of yin and yang is a matter of health, longevity, and good cuisine in Asia.

Mei-wa Annie Chan conceives the reciprocal power of yin-yang in the dance of Tao:

> Though in its absolute sense the Tao is the indefinable, the inexpressible, in the relative world it becomes every manifestation of the universe—the power which gives rise to the dance of Tao. The problem with western philosophy is that only one family of thinking can be right. Yin-yang, however, is a co-existing, containing concept. You can only understand Tao through adopting and experiencing. Now this adopting is not adopting the Chinese Way, it is adopting the Tao.[33]

Chan says that anyone can adopt the Tao without totally adopting a Chinese way of thinking because Tao encourages coexistence and pertains to other theories. "How can it be 'whole,'" she asks, "if it doesn't?" One understands (adopts) the Tao, not through rationality, but through living and dancing it. Chan writes about the inexpressible void of creative darkness giving birth to the dancing quality of Tao as she translates the ancient Chinese texts of Lao Tzu, Chuang Tzu, and Lieh Tzu:

> In Tao, every word carries in itself its negation. Negation inspires creation, and vital inspiration comes from the Void, an all-dimensional space. Dance is where emptiness finds fulfillment. Tao is inexpressible in words, being no-thing-ness, yet the potential of all things; it can only be referred to by what it is not. It is the non-existent containing the potential of existence; the Void, emptiness, non-appearance, the darkness in which light is as yet to be manifest but out of which light emerges.

Tao is "a spontaneous and unintentional unity," according to Chan. The principal aesthetic of Tao is the cyclic nature of its ceaseless motion and change. "Returning is the motion of the Tao," says Lao Tzu,

Annie Chan, author of *The Tao of Dance* is in the foreground of Sondra Fraleigh's *Meditations*, performed in Tokyo by invitation of Nikaido Gakuen University in 1991. Photograph by Jim Dusen.

and "going far means returning." Within this cyclic pattern are subtle interactions of yin and yang that Chan says not only "inspire movement itself, but also induce transformation in nature and dance."[34] The receptive yin and active yang are interactive qualities of consciousness that emerge from our manner of being-in-the-world. They mingle in varied proportion and rhythms in both men and women.

Undergoing change, these polarized (pivotal) complementary qualities, originally the shady and sunny sides of the mountain, can reverse their momentum and transform into the other. This is the basis for change in the *I Ching*, the Chinese Book of Changes. Receptive and active agents are conceived as complements, neither stable substances nor entities. They are paired qualities of an undulating continuum. They inform each other because they have permeable boundaries and can become the other, just as the two hemispheres of the brain relate across the corpus callosum, and women and men have been able to shift brain activity between the hemispheres through biofeedback.

Yin-yang reciprocity is in fact a way of explaining change and motion. "Yin and yang inspire movement and give rise to the third; and hence to all."[35] The yin-yang symbol is a dance of changes, deconstruction with reconstruction. It gives us an image of integrals that can reverse, fade, grow, differentiate, or integrate.

Yin (blood and moonlight) and yang (breath and sunlight) are equal agents for change, and one cannot be valued over the other. In the *Tao Te Ching* the naming and differential valuing of the positions disappear, since Tao carries its own negation and cannot be named in

Sondra Fraleigh's *Trigrams of the I Ching* (1976). A yin-yang complement with broken symmetry guides the choreographer, and equality of gender is shown in the identical costuming, each one a different combination of earth/heaven colors. The eight trigrams and their movements through the seasons are presented in the dance. "Water flows to what is wet, fire turns to what is dry. Clouds (the breath of heaven) follow the dragon, wind (the breath of earth) follows the tiger. . . . Each follows its kind" (*I Ching*). Photograph by June Burke.

its wholeness. "The name that can be named is not the real name," says Lao Tsu at the beginning of the *Tao Te Ching*. Light and dark, hot and cold, female and male are of equal value relative one to the other and contain a wide range of gradational aesthetic values. Warm partakes of hot and cold, for instance, and dawn crosses over from night to day. Gray is between black and white and comes in many shades itself, and all human affects weave through the bodily lived sensibilities of both sexes. "When ideas are apprehended," says Chuang Tsu, "let us forget the words."[36]

But we cannot yet forget the words that have been turned against woman, teaching her to turn against herself and torture her flesh with fetishes and too stringent disciplines. Words that have been used to devalue her need to be rescued and revalorized. We cannot drop words that are used as weapons; rather, we need to disarm them and also to value them apart from negative connotations, prejudices, and purifications. Women in their yin-yang interplay of receptive and active qualities are no more statically receptive or empty (in a biological or any other sense) than men are perpetually erect and active. The evidence for this is simple observation. Humans live active and receptive capacities entwined and unraveling in unpredictable dances, and the meanings they attach to the motions are interpretations. Receptivity may be passive or alert, an abyss, an absence, a font of compassion, a something, or nothing at all. It has no fixed meaning; rather, it is we who give it significance.

Shared Pleasures

Surely many men and women search for a human nature in accord with earth's nature; but far more continue to exploit the earth and deny the body.

Now we say our bodies
>   are not who we are,
and we have no self;
>   we are postmodern fictions
of history,
>   and have been deconstructed.

Has it not taken us long enough to claim ourselves? And do we not see that woman (would feminism claim there is no such thing in its zeal to surpass gender stereotyping?) is curiously tied to the earth of her biology in a way that man is not? Isn't the crisis of teenage pregnancy and families headed by children-women and abandoned women who cannot catch up with deadbeat dads a good case in point? Notwithstanding their choice in the matter, and they do not control every circumstance, women bear children into the world (we have not deconstructed this yet), and men choose what they will do about it.

Are men freer than women, then?

Existentially, the answer is no.

Human freedom is a matter of consciousness. We are as free in our choices as in our dances: free to give up pain, to let go, or go another way, to feed on love or anger, to slow down, to rest instead of work, to work instead of play, to make work play, and to dance every day—for the taskmaster? for ourselves? for others? for God? Or with God, to continue our quarrels about free will.

When I dance, I am shadowboxing with God.
Stilt dancer *Pamela Wonderlich*, San Francisco, 1998

In many ways women are more biologically free than ever, but we are not all equal in this, and freedom has its traps. There is a need to affirm the bindings of life, the closed doors that require one to stand and wait without force, to sort things out beneath the yang of willfulness, to care for the body, and to trust sparseness and intuitive life. Freedom does not fly through words, open spaces, and open doors. It is a feeling that the body knows—it stirs, thickens, and thins; it opens doors in good time and with goodwill. Freedom is not a force, not of arms, or of legs in extension, or fists fighting. It exists in every choice, however mundane, and is realized in actions taken and not taken. It roots in full body consciousness. It does not control others, its alphabet is grace, and it does not starve the flesh. Freedom finds a yin-yang balance with discipline and unfurrows frown lines. Ecologically, and for healing on all levels, the body in its emotional and spiritual life needs affirmation. There is no freedom and no glamour like the body animated through gladness, skittering over fields and ponds, dancing until dawn.

Some feminists (myself among them) believe that we should celebrate woman's association with nature, that feminine "soft borders" should be cultivated in cooperative rather than competitive modes of being for both men and women. We need to change our stories and our aesthetics by replacing the heroic model with one that respects nature and loves the body instead of glorifying brutal competition and suppressing the softer powers of the maternal feminine. Donna Wilshire, scholar-singer, has attempted this in her hymns to the Triple Goddess: Virgin, Mother, and Crone. She cautions that:

> We have grown up hearing stories that debased this mundane world and our physical bodies, stories that assume competitive hierarchies are built into Nature, stories that foster in us hopes of dominating others before they can dominate us, hopes of someday transcending our bodies and the earth. These same narratives praise male deities and idealize masculine heroes for their detachment, brute force, and accomplishments in battle. . . . This tilted norm—its ideals and stories—have modeled our lives.[37]

Wilshire focuses her work on recovering and singing the nature myths of the Goddess, which lend a richness and versatility to human longings. Extending the work of scholar-futurist Riane Eisler and anthropologist Maria Gimbutas, Wilshire sees that "partnership" as stressed in prehistoric Goddess cultures models a more positive future. The problem is not men as a sex, as these researchers demonstrate, but "a social system in which both men and women are taught to equate true masculinity with violence and dominance."[38] And we need not look far for examples. The bone-crushing violence of American football, our corporate civil religion, is exhibit A.

In myth, nature has been called woman, as Susan Griffin's work demonstrates, and as Joseph Campbell illustrates in his voluminous life's work on mythology across cultures. Myth aside, nature does not belong to one gender alone, any more than it belongs to darkness. "The Dark Continent is neither dark nor unexplorable."[39] When night falls, however comforting or terrifying, we know the day will follow. Night and day are both natural events, just as death is a part of life.

The sun rises in the east
and sets in the west,
and winter will be colder than summer.

It is we who belong to nature—women and men alike—to darkness and light, and to the earth.[40]

When we make the earth our home, we know we choose our
Bodies. We dance to trust our flesh. We choose our mother
To attend us. We know we no longer hope to please.
We allow our sadness. We dance the dark of our depression.
When we dance to dance our bodies, we know our bodies in our dance.
We dance to attend our mother. We know we no longer hope to please.

We allow our pleasure.
We sing when we dance with our pleasure,
We attend our mother's body.
We know when we dance with our pleasure,
Our mother attends our body.
We sing when we dance with our earth.

Darkness is the color of yin at rest in nature, the color of weight and substance. As earth and night, darkness attends the "I" that moves in the depths of the dream-body, the "I" that cannot be forced out. It will speak when we dance our personal truth. In Japan, where the principle deity is the Goddess creatrix Omikami Amaterasu, they like to say, "Nothing can be forced." This has been a hard lesson there, as also here in America, one we continue to learn, but not too well. The yielding yin, symbolizing nature and the earth in Asia, is an important symbol for our time. Devotion to the living earth and the consideration of our bodies as sacred extensions of the earth might provide a corrective for the out-of-balance emphasis on instrumental models for living—possessive individualism and commercial materialism.

The ambitions and aggressions that drive instrumental usage of nature and engender destructive forceful solutions in resolving interpersonal and intersocietal conflicts are not good models for men or women. In the end we are interdependent, and we will heal the earth and our bodies together—or not at all. Ambition should be tempered with receptivity as the active yang of our achievements integrates with the receptive yin of our compassion. We dance the dance of self-realization in relation to the dance of others, and through the integration of our active and receptive powers.

In the yin-yang transformative interaction of feminine-masculine complements there is no possessor and possessed in the dynamic of interacting lovers, as one flesh becomes the other. Making love is about "making" love—literally, creating it. Possessing and being possessed is about ownership, another matter altogether. "Having" (possessing) sex may be a genital act, but "making" love is more, and there are no such things as disembodied genitals—except perhaps in the grammatological games of deconstruction, or the sixties hip musical, *Hair*, when the women are looking for Claude's "thing": I don't have it; I thought you had it; Sue had it last night, but maybe she gave it to Sally; the last time I had it was three days ago (and so on, as I remember it). How can there be a singular mating of genitals, making sex? All genitals belong to somebody, are somebody, and all sexual intercourse (both hetero and homo) is colored by attitude, be it possessive, hateful and violent, apprehensive, simply bored, or an expression of care and plenitude.

Through the interactive yin-yang, the penetrator and the penetrated change places, are fulfilled in each other. Completing and breaking symmetries, they unfold the Tao of the "holoverse," coming to the inside, for they are no longer outside. I go inside to know your darkness, the pleasure of your strengths and vulnerabilities; you go inside to know mine. When we make love, we experience the warm entrance of the dark cave together—no less than the morning light—intersubjectively. Inviting the complements of our flesh, each reaches toward the other's power to love and to heal.

> What was hidden from us
> 　　now becomes eyes
> and then hands
> 　　its pleasure records
> 　　　　our first memory in space.

There is power and mystery in receptivity. Without it nothing would gestate, change, or grow. All would be in whirl-points and nothing could ever come to rest or say thank you. There would be no cadences for our cadenzas, no births and no deaths. Nothing but perpetual motion. There is power in the silence of listening, of empathizing with another in the wake of our own inevitable vulnerability. There is power in not knowing the answers, in flowing with the questions until answers come from deeper sources than we can consciously construe. But we are taught more aggressive means.

Sheets-Johnstone's feminism draws upon our fascination with penetration as power and argues against its intrusiveness. Penetration, she holds, has been the determinant of power in our culture. We like penetrating minds and penetrating thoughts. Often penetration is presented as threatening, even harmful. We penetrate enemy lines in war and in football; the penetrating penis is called a gun. Penetration as a way of being-in-the-world is subtly sustained (thus all the more insidious) in views, both patriarchal and feminist, that continue to valorize the phallic (forceful, masterful, instrumental, extroverted, extended, incisive, piercing, and acquisitive) as the measure of the vitally human. As Sheets-Johnstone critiques the penetrative psychosexual analytic of patriarchy, she makes arguments for redefining cultural values—and power—in recognition of the sexually transformative. She points toward a neglect of a crucial aspect of maleness— its power to couple through penetration (rather than to possess), to pair, to affect relation, a value typically attributed to the female. This positive male power remains largely unacknowledged in the face of penetrative possessiveness. The establishment of cooperative relationship is intrinsic to—in the nature of—maleness. Conquest and domination are not male universals; neither are they necessary in procreation and the nurturing of life. Coupling is.[41]

Love is not war; it is about the power of partnership and creativity, not possession. It requires each partner to "grow a self," as Roberta Gilbert explores in *Extraordinary Relationships,* which discusses her family systems replacement of Freudian theory and psychoanalysis.[42] Love is not a leaning dance, nor a grasping one. Love grows distinctions, but one need not prevail over the other. Love is a dance of dedication, of personal powers equally exchanged. Sex may be politics, but love is soft. Love heals.

Lacan's psychoanalysis consolidated Sartre's ontology of alienation, instantiating penetration as instrumental power. Among its many names, the penis is called a "tool" and a "gun." How did they overlook the fact that the most universal existential of the penis is not its penetrating power, but its transformative character, its not being under control (or why does it take a nap when a man most wants to command it?). The penis, the alleged instrument of rule (why do men measure it?) is indeed unruly. Love and the interacting powers of coupling function through trust, and our not being in control heightens the drama. Orgasm carries the message and fact of the vulnerability of our flesh in the same way that birth can present us with the inexplicable that continuously moves beyond our determination. Until the "I cans" of creativity and spontaneous pleasure replace the "I cans" of controlling performance and performance anxiety—

MIGHT

We slide lower

to

dance

our awkward dance

conjuring

Urban country-dance,
the depth, elegance, and calm swallows
of our sadness.

As beneath gesticulates,

shapes of shadows and paradise,
the sun and moon pools in one hand.

At the "I" of the healing storm is you in your dark joy, singing your own name, gathering scattered bones and shaping your soul dance—untangling love's flow, let go, let go. . . .

Dances to Do

Somadance Untangling

Lie on your back with your arms by your sides and your legs extended for a while. Close your eyes and enter the darkness of your breath and being. To increase the comfort of your back, bend your knees and bring your feet (soles on the floor) underneath the knees, more or less. The feet are then in a standing position, but you are lying down. Experiment to see where you like to stand your feet—closer or farther away from the buttocks—wide, narrow, or a happy in between. Just rest in the here and now with your arms in a comfortable position. If your low back is fine with the legs extended along the floor, let them down again and rest for a while in this yoga floating position. Then bring your feet to standing once more to experience how the lower back can sink closer to the floor and be completely supported. Rest. Pay attention to your breath until the in and out of it eases and lengthens, and let your spine untangle any tensions as it finds more of itself in your consciousness. Allow yourself to give up—to your breath and to the earth.

Get Ready: Remain on the floor and curl over on one of your sides. Keep your knees bent and make a small ball out of yourself, but not a tight one. Explore for a moment to find where your head is comfortable—on or off the bottom arm. You will be roughly in a yoga embryo shape. Settle there with your eyes closed. When you are ready, let your attention begin to travel with your body-self and wrap your arms loosely into a shoulder embrace, hands touching the shoulders on opposite sides. If they do not reach that far, never mind, just let them reach where they do without stress.

Begin: Untangle this position in a free dance, keeping your eyes closed and rolling yourself slowly from side to side, extending and folding the limbs alternately, sometimes rolling onto your front (onto your belly like a baby, perhaps) and returning. Lift your head from the floor when the movement you are doing seems to call for this. Give yourself times to pause and savor the shapes that feel good. Maintain an exploratory sensibility. There is nowhere to go, just the pleasure of moving your body-self close to the ground with your eyes closed. The look of the dance does not matter, just the feel of it, how you feel in the moments of movement that emerge. Open to the qualitative possibilities of your dance as you develop the movement. Does it want to flow or halt, freeze, melt, stretch, pulse, or what? Let it carry you where it will.

Possibilities: The dance might carry you into a sitting position. This can happen quite easily (naturally) from a side rolling motion. Let yourself discover how you like to move without forcing anything to happen, even if this means moving very little. As to size: this might be a minimal or maximal dance, depending on your condition at the time and your desire to move. Minimal movement when given maximal attention can be powerful—each molecule magnified.

Time can become a factor in your consciousness as you move for a short or long duration and stop here and there for punctuation. Intuit how long the dance should be. Curving, reaching, doing, and undoing, sense the place where it feels satisfying to finish.

As a choreographic extension of this improvisatory dance, you may want to carry the process into standing, opening the eyes and paying attention to shapes that emerge. Notice their attendant feeling tones. Connect these shadings of movement with stepping or with running if you want to build speed. Retrace the time/shape of patterns that become intriguing and expressive, repeating the emergent forms to remember them, or experience your dance persona through them. Carry this one step further if you want to. Add music and allow a meaning or story to emerge in your imagination. What do the dynamic forms and balances, the arms and hands of your dance, untangle, freeze, or free in you?

DancePoems

I have conceived the following poems as dances to do. "Flashes of the Moon" is "a void dance," an emergence, or maybe a clearing. It trusts the reader/dancer to the large body of imagination that poetry can evoke. Translate the body of the poem into dance without thinking about it too much: relate more generally to sense, music, image, and place. There is also an imperative in the poem if the dancer wants to follow through with it, shifting away at the end, from instruction to discovery.
. . . take my hand . . . Let go of my hand.

FLASHES OF THE MOON

Take the body of my lover.
No, the cheeks of my nights awake,
And spin a broad, rough
Roof against the sky.

In the high tone,
Your tingling arms
In the process of transformation,
Trail in the shadow.

Take flashes of the moon
And through all, your aim
To avoid every ireful will.
Your throw of speech,
And swelling now
In concentration.

Some dance to be understood.
Some dance the moment.

Not you, yet still to move
The unborn thought,
To make us understand,
Avoid, the obvious.

Peel the gold of your reflection.
No, its carefully constructed box,
And the taut fleshy
Bellies of an asset.

Untoss the pillows of your dream,
And step through the veil of beyond.

In the following poem, "Dancing X," one can attune to the limbic system. Suggestions for developing the dance through limbic resonance are discussed after the poem. I think of X as a dance to be filled: a possible space that opens up another space. As mind, sense, and image separate in the words of the poem then blend in the dance of X, the skeleton can untangle. When we dance, the brain-body circuits unite the natural and the social.

X may evoke a response in dance improvisation, as this may also lead to choreography. Let the poetry draw up your dream-body by resting into it.

DANCING X

Pick your favorite music.

In the manner of your absorption,
Let it be uncultured.

Resonate its anatomy.

Untransplantable tone
Hijacking language,

Turn it off, and lie down.
Drop down into silence.
X yourself. . . .
Fall into limbo (as you are),
And lose yourself, Xing.

How did history come to acquire
This blind spot
And never find a remedy?

X yourself. . . . Then begin
To pay attention to your breath.
X your name,
And leave behind no documents.

For an answer, one could start with those
Cuts and stitches, those cobbled together
Scars that fit so comfortably.

Now begin—from the unguessed place
Of non-sense. Let the dance emerge freely
As it will, and follow its path: through
Silence to sound threading back.

The corpus of history in your bones,
The celebrations of the body
Embedded in the world of you.

What sound did you hear?
Remember if you can,
And if you can't, silence the effort.
Resist explanation.

Mythology and religion
Returning the real of your dance
With plenitude.

Repeat and surrender
The fretful framework
Listen to your heart
Move

In tertiary—of nature
Beauty and you.

Let go of questions, of any assessment.
Lift an arm and stand, if you are not
Already standing. Become a little stooped
And stop any eruptive force.

Breathe, sigh, and sink your body
Into self-remembering,

Transmuting silence in X
Xpanding.

This soma poem lends itself to an exploration of the limbic brain, the emotional brain explained in terms of neuroscience and psychiatry in *A General Theory of Love* by Thomas Lewis, Fari Amini, and Richard Lannon.[43] Here we find that emotional maturity is not synonymous with emotional restraint; rather, it grows through love and nurture. The brain's ancient emotional architecture permeates the dance of life. All mammals have developed a capacity for relationship through the limbic system, an aspect of the evolutionary nature of mammals. The open loop of "limbic resonance" and "limbic revision" allows us to bond with our family, with pets, friends, and lovers. It is also the basis for implicit memory, the hazy dance informing bone and gesture, bodily repetition and habit. The limbic system allows us to tune our nature to the larger scheme of nature. It registers the surge and swell of our hearts when we experience the golden trees of autumn, the unexplainable pang of melancholy-cum-awe in the fall we embody. Perhaps we call it "fall" because of our somatic resonance with things in transition: fading, dying, and falling down.

When you dance X, allow yourself to resonate with the feelings that arise.

Dance X several times and at different times. A choreography may suggest itself, or your dance could remain improvisational.

Try a version in tune with the senses. Remember to involve light and heavy touch, thresholds of light and shadow, as well as kinesthesia—your portal to movement through awareness of tonus and transition in the body—the feeling of turning your neck, for instance, or the slight lift of your toes, a tense claw of fingers and lion twist of the rib cage as one side opens like an accordion and rotates around while the other side folds. These matters of sense and consciousness are newer additions to the more traditional categories of sight, smell, taste, hearing, and touch. As you play with them, you will be bridging the triune brain of instinct (the reptilian), feeling and emotion (the limbic), motor skill, volition, and thinking in movement (the neocortical).

Certainly one can dance X without thinking of the brain in this manner, but it is significant that dance improvisations and choreographies can be conceived to emphasize body-mind systems, aspects of the brain, or levels of consciousness.

Another version of "Dancing X" could attune to the generosity of relationship, enliven the capacity to love, and be comfortable in one's skin. Not every dance needs to slice the air. Some seek resonance with emotional life and memory. X can be danced alone or might be used as impetus for a group improvisation or choreography.

I sometimes dance X with my students. Their dances and responses are quite varied. What their dances have in common is their propensity to release tension and grief and to remain curious. They seem satisfied with the emerging moment and are not self-critical. One dancer told me she was in the early stages of pregnancy, and that the dance encouraged her to experience her condition more fully. In "being rather than doing," she had released nausea. Her dance was close to the floor-earth. As together we reflected on her experience, it struck us ·how little time we give ourselves just to feel whatever we are feeling, to respect the wisdom of our feelings and follow their migrations. Dancing gives us a chance to follow the seedings and flowerings of our senses, to trust their sometimes searing or frayed edges, to respect their chilly features, and to rely on their radiant attachments.

In our conversation I told my student about a remembrance of my father I cannot come to terms with—his holding my mother, my sister, and me at gunpoint—and that sometimes, when I dance into the memory, I see him lay down his weapon and weep. Then in my bones I heal.

Transforming Mastery

I was born in a magical valley in a time beyond time where horses had wings, brooks sang songs to me, and my father recited Alfred Noyes's romantic poetry to my endless delight. My child-self embodied the soul rhythm of his tragic "The Highwayman" from 1880, the fugitive's love for the landlord's daughter, and his blazing ride through the night to save her from the muskets of the king's troops. Every time I heard it, I begged some ending to save her—until now I lay her to rest, in language encircling the earth—on garments of vapor and breath.[44]

NIGHT RIDER

Fierce, she is riding
at dusk in the desert, on
sands that are glowing with pink.

Blood-red, the sun colors her horse
in its pounding, her
robes a swirl in the ink.

How amber her skin on the
blurry horizon, soft as
dew being born.

She is riding on breath in a
pathless land, she is riding
and riding, toward dawn.

The voices of air
and the natural elements
pass her like water in waves.

As over the mystery
she gallops and glides, pausing
to drink and to bathe.

In various shapes
we discern her arriving,
as jackals speak, and they name.

Here, then, the land
without lords, without masters,
just friends of the night and the pain.

9 | The Morality of Joy

My aunt likes to tell a story of how I came to be, how a door saved my mother's life, and how my aunt was the one who finally picked me up and announced, "Look at the baby." My father, who—my friends say—looks like the Marlboro Man, is central to her story:

I was born at home on a ranch nestled in a valley of the Rocky Mountains, attended by a country doctor and midwife. My father, dripping sweat and tears in July's heat, ripped the front door off its hinges with his bare hands. . . . He was like a wild man when the midwife called out that my mother was unable to deliver the afterbirth and needed a hard surface on which to continue her labor. I had been placed in a crib off to the side and was forgotten in the "commotion."

In the Beginning Is My Body

I give the story a more or less romantic twist: I like to say that this is how I became an existentialist. This, and the independence of growing up in the wide-open spaces of the West and in the same town where the outlaw-existentialist Butch Cassidy grew up two generations before me. We were both born in a place where time slows down, where everyone knows your name, and most people are related to you either by blood or by marriage. We were also born in a nation that valorizes individualism and independence as freedom.

As a teenager, I could ride my horse alone into the mountains when spring came, rest in soft meadows and drink from shivery cold brooks fed by melting snows, or gallop like the wind through the spectacular deserts between southern Utah and Nevada. My daughter was born in an antiseptic city hospital. Her birth was announced to my husband over a loudspeaker, but I barely heard it. I had just seen our baby's face emerge from inside me, surrounded by blood and a rainbow aura. For hours, we had worked in harmony, she turning herself around, I dancing with breath and pain on the brink of a new self, emerging. We were both being born—and the experience was neither romantic nor strictly existential. It was magical. Shattering time and space, I had jumped through my own flesh. Scattering into golden dust, I had transformed—pushing white heat through black holes and white holes—life, as I never before had danced it. *My daughter still remembers the sensation of being in the womb. "It was bliss," she says.*

The Land Was Our Body

The land was ourselves, and we needed to care for it as for our bodies. For generations we had depended on the land. For more than a hundred years we had grown there like alfalfa, and our flesh lay in the furrows.

We had learned how to irrigate, how to save the snow, how to coax food from the desert, and with the Navajo had prayed for rain. During my great-grandparents' first hard winter there, Navajos had saved their family from starvation. Our bodies were not expendable. That is, until the federal government set schedules for atomic testing on the Nevada site to coincide with the winds that blew toward southern Utah and away from Los Angeles. Who decides which bodies are more important? And why is it that bodies are always at the behest of some (or someone's) higher purpose? My mother's early death was one of many compensated by the U.S. government through legal suits won by the state of Utah as reparation for radiation poisoning. I remember how the congregation stood motionless at her graveside. A soft wind brushed the sweet-scented pines. They had been planted there in the semiarid desert and needed periodic watering. The tumbleweeds had been cleared at the small cemetery in the foothills. Its patches of green shone like emeralds under the purple mountains. I was not sad on the way back to town; the dusty gray of the velvet road comforted me. My mother's quiet nature and sanity entered my bones.

Ballet Vigil

The sun danced through the window of my parent's bedroom as I wound the gauzy curtains tightly around myself, then spun free of

Sondra Fraleigh. Photo portrait by June Burke, 1974.

them, laughing and falling to the floor. My child's eye saw nothing so beautiful as the way the fluffy cloud of fabric could float and fall when I tossed it. I begged my mother to take the curtains down so I could run and dance with them trailing behind me. This is my first memory of dancing, of never wanting to stop. I remember how the earth curved under my tumbles with the magic curtains, receiving me when I fell breathless into its grassy fragrance, and how the sky drifted through me.

At seven I took ballet lessons from my older friend, Katerina. She taught me all she knew in five lessons, then someone moved into town who taught tap dance. Wow, how I jumped into rhythm: "Buy me some peanuts and Cracker Jack—I don't care if I never get back." I performed "Take Me Out to the Ballgame" with Mac at the recital. He wore a suit and tie, and Aunt Ali, who lived next door, made me a long pink gown with ruffles hemstitched on her new sewing machine. She was really my second cousin, but I called most of the women in town "aunt."

I had already had a career as a hula dancer with Betty Grable movies as my inspiration, *Song of the Islands* made in 1942. My mother, who was very shy, was skeptical about my going onstage with the hula at age four, but Miss Grace (for some reason we all called her "miss" instead of "aunt") could play Hawaiian music by ear on the piano, and she thought I was great. Since she was in charge of the town's entertainment, I danced for all to see, shaking in nothing but a small grass skirt that Aunt Athena had brought home from her trip to Los Angeles. This lasted for three or four years until some of the townswomen wondered if I needed something on top. I still remember the fussing, and that a tiny, scratchy, straw bra was concocted to cover my flat chest. Soon after that I stopped dancing the hula, or whatever I was doing, but I remember that I had learned how to coordinate creative arm and hand gestures with my hips.

How could this child know that she would one day learn a real hula in Hawaii, not the one of airport artists who greet you with a lei of flowers when the plane lands, but the dance of the ancestral great goddess Laka, who blesses the islands.

In first grade, Flossy taught us dancing. I cannot remember her last name, but I do remember that I did not call her "aunt" and that her home was full of adopted Navajo children who went to school with us.

She coached us in squares and rounds, and we began to tour the surrounding territories as her six-year-old Wonderchildren Square Dancers. Even the boys liked it. Flossy had a way with us. My dress was creamy light green with tiny pink flowers and many ruffles. It bounced around my knees when I walked. "Now you all join hands and you circle the ring—Stop where you are, give your honey a swing." As our reward for the touring, we all went to Yellowstone Park on a field trip and got to stay overnight.

The Spiral Was Intoxicating

As an adolescent, I practiced (unbeknownst to me) the techniques that emerged throughout the historic modern dance. I studied the spiral path: falling in curves, rushing and pausing with the wave of my breath, swinging my arms and torso with held suspensions at the top, yielding and rebounding, landing the leap in a rolling fall, twisting my torso to stand up, running in the grass, my scarves blowing in the wind. Until I went to college, I became my own dance teacher and also a cheerleader, dancing and turning cartwheels on the sidelines: "Max, Max, he's our man, if he can't do it Steven can. . . ." Basketball was mania and religion in our town. *Give us a T, E, A, M.*

My older friend Katerina was a senior; she had begun to study ballet in earnest and danced on point in high school assemblies. In the springtime after her graduation, she committed suicide with her boyfriend when he came home on leave from the Korean War. They were found at Purple Haze, the outdoor dance hall in Kingston Canyon where we danced under the moon every weekend. In a note, she asked to be buried with her ballet doll. Only her parents knew the rest of the contents.

She had meticulously planned her own funeral, the speakers, the singer (my father), her gown, and who would dress her hair. Everything was to be perfect, but because of the effects of the carbon monoxide, the casket had to remain closed.

She had attempted to take her life once before. Perhaps real life was not dramatic enough, or perfect enough. Then there was the question of sex. For good girls—and we were—it was taboo in those days, both in word and deed. But we did whisper about it. The girls teased, and the boys had the responsibility of not responding while remaining interested. Some lovers crossed the line. At this point it was the girl's fault. She paid with a ruined reputation and for a while a broken life. The fear of censure was a powerful deterrent.

Katerina's death composes my memory of those times, imprinting in sfumato pictures of soft sepias, like the Parker family's fading photos of Butch Cassidy (aka George Leroy Parker). My inner adolescent harbors the romance and tragedy of her ending; my adult conjures the melodrama of its transgressive poetry—why she had to die.

I spent my childhood in love with Aunt Ada. Every morning I would run through our orchard of apple trees to Aunt Ada's house and unlatch the big gate overgrown with vines. She was famous for her garden, her flowers, and her love of children. When I was older, I realized that she suffered from depression and lived largely within her created haven. She was the best person I ever knew, and she seldom went to church. She was not really my aunt, but I called her aunt; in fact I never heard anyone call her anything else—except her own children.

Aunt Ada's husband was as sour as she was pleasant. There was a large deer head, a buck with widespread antlers, on their wall. This was a permanent fixture and an endless curiosity for me. I was tempted to touch it, but never could bring myself to. Once I was sure it helped cure a wart Aunt Ada charmed off my finger. At least it watched over the whole ritual. *She pricked the wart with a needle,* instructed me to hide the needle in mud, and keep secret the hiding place. *The wart was gone* in three days.

On the wall adjacent to the deer head in later years there hung two large photographs, one of Aunt Ada's son in his uniform from the Korean War, and one of his girlfriend, Katerina, the beautiful ballerina in her junior prom gown. The gardenias she wore to the prom wreathed her dancer-shoulder, a permanent reminder of the son lost to suicide and the daughter gained in death.

Katerina died with her lover in the spring. Sometimes I wonder what she might be doing now if she were alive, how she might be dancing—then suddenly, slipping through time and space, I feel her coaching in my feet.

Falling Bravely

I often dream I am falling through space. For some reason I have had to leap from a tall building or a high cliff. Or I revisit my youthful dar-

ing, diving from a large rock on the mountainside into the river winding through the town where I grew up. I am going down too deep to
make it to the surface, and I feel I will shatter or suffocate. Sometimes
I wake up in a sweat, but on better occasions my subconscious solves
the problem for me: the landing is cushioned, I am caught in the arms
of a silver tree, the water becomes my dance partner and lifts me, or I
find I can fly. What joy! I find a way to survive—like the diving dancers
in Bill T. Jones's *D-Man in the Waters* (1989).

The drive and joy of *D-Man* do not come lightly. It races and raves to
the music of Felix Mendelssohn's Octet, E Flat Major (Opus 20). The
speed of the strings as they pluck and carry the swift melodies lends
the dance its pace and tension. The dance rides on the running pace of
the music, showering the stage with rapturous movement. It flares
right from the beginning as dancers run headlong onstage, one after
another, stopping to stand at the front of a line dance, fanning their
lower arms in short, vibrating gestures between their own faces and
that of the next dancer in an evolving communal game. The dance re-
generates itself through the power of play. It also reminds us of our
watery relationship with nature: for the ancient Greeks, *aletheia*, the
river of forgetfulness and unforgetfulness, arising through the wholeness of the heart.[1]

Army-green clothes contribute a casual appearance to the quirky
line dances that curve around and change directions capering
through space. Swimming gestures begin to develop in the arms; daring belly-flop-slides drop to the floor, and diving preparations mount
into the air. The air moments build to take away our breath as dancers
ascend through the help of partnering. Sometimes they remain suspended at the height of a lift, are dropped and caught, or carried aloft
offstage.

The dancers toss themselves and catch each other with abandon.
They show an intimate acquaintance with contact improvisation, but
as professionals they develop a technical language of touch and contact, extending it beyond the comfort of seasonal dance-ins. Their
dance is supported through the rigors of technical means and mechanics, but that is not what captures us. The skillful, expressive
dancers move us toward our possible-selves, and we are filled to the
brim with the risky dancing.

At the ending of *D-Man in the Waters*, the diving preparations extend the arms of the dancers overhead as they jump skyward out of their darting runs. They lean back on the air; their bodies slice the expanse as their chests lift into full-bodied extensions and their feet leave the ground. They imprint the space and soar.

Some phrases return as the dance speeds to its finish in solos and contact duets. A "hugging duet," with dancers facing and running in a lumbering crouch across the stage, is particularly original. One dancer must run backward and one forward in the odd integration of bodies. Their legs need to be wide to navigate the running stagger. This awkward relationship becomes more graceful through a dynamic exchange of energy, as the dancers work it out through various androgynous pairings and in pointillist timing.

The end is pulled tenaciously together in time, blasting the dancers through a barrier of hands held by partners linked like an interlocking fence in the center. Dancers run directly toward the audience and the boundary, as one after another they break through. This conjures the thrilling impact at the break-moment of childhood rough play when firmly gripped pairs of hands are breached. But this game is a dance, and everyone wins; as hands break apart, they allow a joyful jumping passage right through the middle. A boundary gives way when the tight barrier opens, thrusting dancers and audience alike beyond physical and psychic limitations. Through the dance we can remember our strength and live it joyfully.

The process intensifies as the speed and range of the dance elicits vocal sounds from the dancers, and they burst into screams. Then in a split second as the lights are blacking out, dancers gather suddenly in a close group. The last thing we see in a flash before the blackout is a dancer being tossed high in the air by all the others. He seems not to come down—the lights cut to black after the toss. We see him thrown in the air through the magical momentum of the group—their arms and faces stretch upward, and it is over in an instant.

The first time I saw Jones perform, in 1973, he was a student at the State University of New York at Binghamton, studying dance and theater with Percival Borde. Jones had been a student in our dance department at the State University of New York at Brockport where I had just joined the faculty. He was returning for an informal performance, a contact improvisation with another one of our students, Lois Welk. Jones was tall and black. Welk was short and white. Despite their difference in size and gender, they moved with complete abandon and togetherness, like animals at serious play. They threw each other all over the stage—into the air, rolling on the floor, falling, landing without fear, lifting, trusting each other to find the right balance spontaneously, diving into each other's arms, springing over backs, and optimizing the outcome. I thought their blithe dance might be called contact courage—not all improvisation is that powerful.

Jones and Welk, along with Arnie Zane, formed the American Dance Asylum in 1971. After that 1973 performance, I saw Jones dance many times. Now I notice in particular his distinctive grit. His dancing is sculpted with delicate, detailed movement, and his impetuosity extends to an inclusive recognition of the audience. Jones reaches out and touches us spiritually. His dance cares without being too careful.

"The matrix of our moral sensibilities is based in the arts," playwright Tom Stoppard observes.[2] The arts play a central role in our search for a more peaceful future, as Jones continues to investigate. The conscience, aesthetics, and morality of his works lie in the dancing itself, not in dramatic plot or militant edges, though we can certainly find these. His choreography has great heart and an enduring curiosity that keeps it a step ahead of critical categories. His dances do not simply state their moral sense; they are ethical tests that create critical stirs.

The making of *Still/Here* with its subject of death and AIDS prompted the outcry of "victim art" by critic Arlene Croce, who refused to see the work. This became the subject of a documentary by Bill Moyers and David Grubin that premiered on PBS in January 1997. Unlike the objective American postmodern choreographers who follow in the wake of Merce Cunningham's movement events and his fascination with the visual, Jones ventures into social commentary. He also displays an ethics of care in this: How do we face death? How do we grieve? How do we live? What is courage—and joy—in the body?

Ancestors, Wait!

In Swedish dancer Irene Hultman's improvisation to Gustav Mahler's *Adagio*, her single program note says, "For my mother" (October 22, 1998). I revisit the ethos of her dance below:

OPERA

She whispers
In her brown stretch pants
Bunched at the ankles,
And her comfortable black shoes.

A white blouse hugs her body,
Its tailored lines flared at the wrist
Unexpectedly slit to the elbow.

She paints the air,
Mahler's *Adagio* paints the ear,
As one, they glisten there.

The dancer dances
To find her honest self
And become more whole.
Except to be happy
Knowing
How many dances have ended.

Unite these figures in joy
Stretch and curl tight the female
Body, descending weight
Drop shadows through the floor.

The dancer is not hungry
Nor is she full.
Luscious sounds
Drift through her sudden clouds,
Land raining postures.

Moving when we least expect it,
She waits in the flood of the music.
Not in its eye, but at its
Source.

Like Hultman's improvised dance, Santo Giglio's choreography for four women, *Last Voyage* (1995), is also performed to Mahler's *Adagio* and dedicated to his mother:

THROUGH SILK

Blown

> By the dancers passing,
> Gathered-in and folding over.
> Like newly fallen snow,
> Soon she will be gone
> But not forever.

> Four dancers face the summer sun
> Fully themselves, edged brightly
> In stillness and torque,
> Not by chance,
> The looking back and touching.

> Ancestors, Wait!
> We are conceived
> In your fading colors, and shaken.

> Treading instead the sandy shallows
> All slips into disappearance.

Kazuo Ohno also dances for his mother: Here I remember Ohno's spontaneous performance of his Butoh dance *My Mother* at his studio in Yokohama in 1986. Still teaching and performing at eighty years old, he improvised this dance after an evening workshop in August and served tea and plums. It is hot in the dance studio, and we are still sweating:

IN SILENCE

Ohno steps onto the small wooden box,

> Then settles down,
> Diminishing his body
> And concentrating.

Dance he must in patches and poetry

> To reach anyone,
> To serenade us as we are.

The studio relaxes as he moves

> Spontaneously on the box,

His age in his fingers

> Tenderly placed
> In time's space.

No music of things as they were,
As we are there
In the silence of the moment

> In the dance.

Nothing changes, only the place.
He tunes his ears to listen,

> To hear his heart and ours
> Yet to be made.

Exceeding the music of silence

> His performance flies in tiny
> Circles and buzzing,

Calling with his gestures

> Flat and bare in the light
> From the unadorned ceiling
> Across the things as they
> Are arranged in the room.

> Life's a tune wisping where we are
> The tea and the plums on the table,

> *Adagio,* the age of breath.

"When you dance, go back into your mother's womb," Ohno says, "and feel how your embryo self reaches."

Epilogue: The Fugitive in Her

In good time, she heard her grandfather: "I was working in the fields with Butch's father when I was a small boy. Butch rode up through the sagebrush. Cassidy's real name, you remember, was George Leroy Parker. He wanted to give his father money, but old Mr. Parker wouldn't take it. Butch was hurt. His father had no words for him, so he turned back.

"I will never forget how Butch looked as he rode off all dressed in black on his black horse, sitting astride a black saddle polished to a fare-thee-well and studded with silver, his black hat cocked at a tilt.

"Butch's father watched him ride away, and then looked back at me. 'Son,' he said, 'there goes a man who kills.'"

There were other myths about Butch told in our town. That "he never killed," contrary to his father's belief, that he stole from the rich and gave to the poor, was Utah's Robin Hood, a law unto himself, generous to widows, and that he was slippery because he dared to go into places most men would not. He rode deep into the night without fatigue and, wedded to his horse, could jump amazing distances, disappearing into dark lakes and ghostly canyons. The unprofessional posse of farmers and ranchers, those in the back shooting those in the front, did not stand a chance in the chase.

Not only was Butch a lonely existentialist, he was a devil of a deconstructor, covering his tracks, marks, mar, and wound. With swift digs to the horse's flanks, he scaled the smoky pink cliffs, squeezing through a hole-in-the-wall that took Pinkerton detective Charles Siringo years to find.

Butch's baby sister, Lula Parker Betenson, saw him at their home in Circleville, Utah, years after he was reported dead in 1908 in San Vicente, Bolivia—or so the story goes. The shoot-out in which Butch and Sundance supposedly died was not documented until the late 1980s—the year that Lula died. Her son Mark, a distant cousin of mine, is, as everyone says, "the spittin' image of Butch." Paul Newman invited Lula to New York when he was making *Butch Cassidy and the Sundance Kid,* and our town waited with bated breath for more stories upon her return. Butch's brother, Ebenezer Maximillian Parker, remained silent on the subject of Butch. I remember Eb as a reclusive bachelor, and finally an old man loitering about town with a crumpled Stetson pulled over one eye. In a storytelling town, silence can be deafening. From the time I was a child and through my teens, I heard about Butch and his daring exploits, and I swam at "Parker Dam," a pooling spot in the winding Sevier River across from the log cabin where Butch was born. I swam there in the sun and the rain, and learned how to back dive from "The Rock" on the mountainside. To this day, I have trouble with chlorinated swimming pools. I identify with Butch—with nature, freedom, and Western romance.

Where there are laws there will be outlaws, and in the known lives the elusive.

... And when we come to the end of mystery,
As to the end of history and romance,
Then will we be a new people?
But will we still have poetry, and will we dance?

NOTES

Introduction · Beauty's Ways

1. Martin Heidegger, *Being and Time*, trans. John Macquarrie and Edward Robinson (New York: Harper & Row, 1962), 63, 62.

2. Ibid., 51. Husserl referred to "things in themselves" very basically as the root of phenomenology.

3. Peter Gold, *Navaho and Tibetan Sacred Wisdom: The Circle of the Spirit* (Rochester, NY: Inner Traditions, 1994).

4. See especially Merleau-Ponty's essays "On the Phenomenology of Language," in *Signs*, trans. Richard C. McCleary (Evanston, IL: Northwestern University Press, 1964), part 2, chap. 2, 84–97. See also how he develops themes of depth and thickness in "Eye and Mind," his essay on art in *The Primacy of Perception and Other Essays*, ed. James M. Edie, trans. Charles Dallery (Evanston, IL: Northwestern University Press, 1964), part 2, chap. 5, 159–90. Merleau-Ponty believes Descartes's error was in setting space beyond depth and thickness. Merleau-Ponty conceives space as bound to existence through such lived qualities as orientation, spreading, polarity, and envelopment. Dancers give flesh (thickness) to these very terms, as to space-time phenomena in all their specificity.

5. Marija Gimbutas, *The Language of the Goddess: Unearthing the Hidden Symbols of Western Civilization* (San Francisco: Harper & Row, 1989), xix.

6. Rik Pinxten, Ingrid Van Doren, and Frank Harvey, *Anthropology of Space: Explorations into the Natural Philosophy and Semantics of the Navajo* (Philadelphia: University of Pennsylvania Press, 1983), 168.

7. See FieldPoem, in Bonnie Stone Sunstein and Elizabeth Chiseri-Strater, *Fieldworking: Reading and Writing Research*, 2nd ed. (Boston: Bedford/St. Martin's, 2002), xvi. Sunstein and Chiseri-Strater's work, "Writing Self and Writing Culture," defines a research process of "stepping in" and "stepping out" that aids my synthesis of theory, story, and poetry. It is possible to use postcolonial fieldwork techniques to support various kinds of research, as Sunstein and Chiseri-Strater's work shows.

8. Bruce Aune, *Metaphysics* (Minneapolis: University of Minnesota Press, 1985), 11.

9. John J. Ratey, *A User's Guide to the Brain: Perception, Attention, and the Four Theaters of the Brain* (New York: Vintage Books, 2002); Maxine Sheets-Johnstone, *The Primacy of Perception* (Amsterdam: John Benjamins, 1999).

10. Ratey, *A User's Guide to the Brain*, 32, 148, 360–61.

11. See the work of developmental psychologists such as Ulric Neisser, Daniel Stern, and Eleanor Gibson in *The Perceived Self*, ed. Ulric Neisser (Cambridge: Cambridge University Press, 1993). My article in this book explores the ecological self in terms of dance. See "Good Intentions and Dancing Moments: Agency, Freedom, and Self-Knowledge in Dance," 102–11.

1. Embodying Metaphysics

1. Judith Butler, *Gender Trouble: Feminism and the Subversion of Identity* (New York: Routledge, 1999), 179.

2. *New York Times*, March 30, 1997.

3. Algis Mickunas, "The Terrible Beauty and Her Reflective Force," in *Ideals of Feminine Beauty: Philosophical, Social and Cultural Dimensions* (Westport, CT: Greenwood Press, 1994), 11.

4. "The soul, because it is intelligence, is tripartite, it is one and also many and the proportion that fuses them." Huntington Cairns, introduction to *Collected Dialogues of Plato*, ed. Edith Hamilton and Huntington Cairns (Princeton, NJ: Princeton University Press, 1961), xx–xxi. Quote in text is from Plato, Law 12, no. 959, 1503.

5. *Hermetica: The Ancient Greek and Latin Writings Which Contain Religious or Philosophic Teachings Ascribed to Hermes Trismegistus*, ed. and trans. Walter Scott (Boston: Shambala, 1993), 14; quotation from 239–55.

6. This view has a foundation in pre-Socratic cosmology and the movements of the stars and planets in the Pythagorean doctrine of "the music of the spheres," which Plato also writes about. In bringing the body close to the rhythms of the planets, we can calm the troubled motions in ourselves. *Timaeus*, no. 47, in Hamilton and Cairns, *Collected Dialogues of Plato*, 1174–75. For a fuller discussion of Plato's microcosmic view of dance, see Sondra Fraleigh, *Dance and the Lived Body: A Descriptive Aesthetic* (Pittsburgh: University of Pittsburgh Press, 1987), 79–80.

7. Aristotle's aesthetics is examined by Katherine E. Gilbert and Helmut Kuhn, *A History of Aesthetics* (Westport, CT: Greenwood Press, 1972), 62–64.

8. Andreus Huyssen, "Mapping the Postmodern," in *Feminism/Postmodernism*, ed. Linda J. Nicholson (New York: Routledge, 1990), 234–77; Sondra Fraleigh, "Gaining and Losing," and part 2, "A Tension of Oppositions," *in Dance and the Lived Body*, 123–29, and part 2, 77–158; see Jean-Francois Lyotard, "Answering the Question: What Is Postmodernism?" in *The Postmodern Condition: A Report on Knowledge* (Manchester: Manchester University Press, 1984); and Lyotard, "What Is Postmodernism," in *The Continental Philosophy Reader*, ed. Richard Kearney and Mara Rainwater (London: Routledge, 1996), 415–37.

9. Witness the big flap in 1995 between critic Arlene Croce and choreographer Bill T. Jones concerning his dance on AIDS. Croce refused to attend the perfor-

mance, presupposing Jones to be guilty of victim art, which plays on the sympathies of the public, rather than rendering skillful work that stands on its own merits. (How could she know if she didn't go?) Many back-to-the-earth rituals of modern dancers who dance for peace combine dance and politics. *All People Earth Natives,* performed at a site on Lake Ontario in 1995, is an example. This ritual was coordinated and choreographed by Christina Sears.

10. The integration of ballet into university dance major programs, where teaching methodologies center on the learner, retreats from rigid positions of authority in ballet. These methods deconstruct the master model through somatic strategies that account for differences in body types and individual rates of learning. Melanie Bales, who teaches ballet at The Ohio State University, provides a prominent example.

11. Boeber is completing her doctoral work, *Perceived Influences of Feldenkrais Somatic Practices on Motor Learning and Control, and Creativity in Dance,* at the Laban School for Movement and Dance in London, and Wolfgruber is a professor in the Department of Dance at the State University of New York at Brockport.

12. Excerpts from Nietzsche's *Joyful Wisdom* are included in *A Casebook on Existentialism,* ed. William V. Spanos (New York: Crowell, 1966), 256–60; quote on 125.

13. See Julia Kristeva and Luce Irigaray in Kearney and Rainwater, *The Continental Philosophy Reader,* 378–401, 411–12.

14. See Fraleigh, *Dance and the Lived Body,* for development of themes of embodiment in relation to dance.

15. Judith Butler notes the extent to which phenomenological theories by Sartre, Merleau-Ponty, and Beauvoir tend to use the term "embodiment." She feels it inscribes the dualism they wish to avoid. Since "it is drawn from theological contexts," this term preserves a dualism that results from figuring the body as "a mode of incarnation." Butler makes a great leap from "embodiment" to "incarnation," a related word that has very different connotations. Her own writing has made liberal use of the term "embodiment." See *Gender Trouble,* 152n15.

16. See my discussion on the origin of the word "dance" in Sanskrit *tan* (tension) at the beginning of chapter 8. The letters *t* and *d* are close to *n* in Sanskrit.

17. Julia Kristeva, "Women's Time," in Kearney and Rainwater, *The Continental Philosophy Reader,* 378–401.

18. For the development of feminist standpoint theory, see Sandra Harding, *Whose Science? Whose Knowledge? Thinking from Women's Lives* (Ithaca, NY: Cornell University Press, 1991). Donna Haraway, *Simians, Cyborgs, and Women: The Reinvention of Nature* (New York: Routledge, 1991), proposes an alternative theory of "situated knowledge," partial and local. Phenomenology had already articulated a philosophy that resonated with individual experience. Simone de Beauvoir would draw upon these concepts in her study of woman's situation as "the other" in *The Second Sex,* trans. and ed. H. M. Parshley (New York: Knopf, 1957); originally published as *Le deuxieme sexe* (Paris: Gallimard, 1949).

19. Simone de Beauvoir, *The Ethics of Ambiguity,* trans. Bernard Frecthman (1948; reprint, New York: Carol Publishing Group Edition, 1994), 18.

20. Christina Hoff Sommers, *Who Stole Feminism? How Women Have Betrayed Women* (New York: Touchstone Books, 1994).

21. Kristeva, "Women's Time," 397–99.

22. My research in Japan, India, and Germany and my international colleagues and students have taught me to appreciate how movement similarities and differences translate from culture to culture, metaphysically. The Tao of China, for instance, is a metaphysical concept with corporeal applications not limited to China, as the smooth and global transfers of weight in tai chi can be practiced by anyone without adopting the Taoist religion. I take this up in the last section of this book through Annie Chan's "The Tao of Dance." I will also describe how yoga (unity) and *tan* (tension and rhythm) in India constitute a corporeal metaphysics. Yoga embodies metaphysical practices of embodiment that have evolved over thousands of years, adapted in various ways for the West in this century. But, more important for this text, *tan* is a Sanskrit source word for dance, and applies to a metaphysical approach.

23. See "Heidegger (1889–1976)," in *The Continental Philosophy Reader*, ed. Richard Kearney and Mara Rainwater (London: Routledge, 1996), 23. In some passages, Heidegger seems to give weight to the word "being," in what Jacques Derrida critiques as "the quest for the proper word and unique name." See Jacques Derrida, "Différance," *Speech and Phenomena, and Other Essays on Husserl's Theory of Signs* (Evanston, IL: Northwestern University Press, 1973). As I read Heidegger, "being" does not stand over "time." "Being" and "time" are both modifying (and therefore deconstructive) elements, but one needs to read contextually to understand this.

24. Hannah Arendt, *Between Past and Future: Eight Exercises in Political Thought* (New York: Viking, 1961).

25. Shigenori Nagatomo, *Attunement through the Body* (New York: State University of New York Press, 1992). Chikako Ozawa-De Silva, "Beyond the Body/Mind? Japanese Contemporary Thinkers on Alternative Sociologies of the Body," *Body & Society* 8, no. 2 (2002): 21–28.

26. Tatsume Hijikata, "Inner Material/Material," from the Tatsumi Hijikata Dance Experience *no kai* (recital pamphlet), 1960, published in *The Drama Review, Hijikata Tatsumi: The Words of Butoh*, ed. Kurihara Nanako, trans. Jacqueline S. Ruyak and Kurihara Nanako (Spring 2000): 36–42. The works on the Dance Experience recital in July 1960 included *Hanatachi* (flowers), *Shushi* (seeds). *Divinu sho* (divine), a solo for Kazuo Ohno, and *Shorijo* (disposal place).

27. Nagatomo, *Attunement through the Body*, xvii–xviii. Nagatomo further states that in going beyond this limitation, Ichikawa develops the idea of "the body as structure," the body subject as related to the objective body.

28. Sanda Akihiko, "Fragments of Glass: A Conversation between Hijikata, Tatsumi and Suzuki Tadashi," *The Drama Review*, 68–69.

29. "Body-Object, Body-Subject," in Fraleigh, *Dance and the Lived Body*, 13–15. In this section I explain spirit, soul, and body as aspects of the same reality.

30. Ichikawa, quoted in Ozawa-De Silva, "Beyond the Body/Mind?" 27.

31. Kayo Mikami, "Deconstruction of the Human Body," unpublished paper.

32. Ozawa-De Silva, "Beyond the Body/Mind?" 28, examines Ichikawa's exploration of *mi* and *ki* and the relationship between them. Anna Yeatman, "A Feminist Theory of Social Differentiation," in *Feminism/Postmodernism*, ed. Linda J. Nicholson (New York: Routledge, 1990), 287.

33. Daruma is also an abbreviation for Bodhidharma, a mythical Middle Eastern priest who carried Zen practice and teachings to China about 500 CE.

34. Tatsumi Hijikata, "Kaze Daruma," trans. Jacqueline S. Ruyak and Kurihara Nanako, *The Drama Review* (Spring 2000): 71–79, quotation on 73–74. "Wind Daruma" was originally printed as *"Kaze darume"* in *Gendaishi techo* (May 1985). Hijikata's "Kaze Daruma" is a lecture originally titled *"Suijakutai no saishu"* (Collection of emaciated body), given the night before the Butoh festival in February 1985. He spoke for a general audience.

35. Ozawa-De Silva, "Beyond the Body/Mind?" 35.

2. First Sounds

1. Sondra Fraleigh with Powell Shepard, *A Day at the Wigman School* (1965), film.

2. Lisa Appignanesi, *Simone de Beauvoir* (London: Penguin Books, 1988), 74.

3. During preparations for the First German Arts Exhibition in Munich, Goebbels wrote in his diary: "Ufa is making a dance film. I have prohibited the philosophical dance of Wigman, Palucca and others from taking center stage. Dance must be buoyant and must show beautiful women's bodies. That has nothing to do with philosophy." Goebbels is quoted by Susan Manning in *Ecstasy and the Demon: Feminism and Nationalism in the Dances of Mary Wigman* (Berkeley and Los Angeles: University of California Press, 1993), 202.

4. Ibid., 45.

5. Marion Kant discussed Wigman's connections to Fascism at the conference, "Grounded in Europe: Tanztheater and Its Legacy," sponsored by the Center for Performance Research in Wales. The conference was held at Roehampton University, December 1, 2001. Kant has since then published *Hitler's Dancers: German Modern Dance and the Third Reich* with Lillian Karima, trans. Jonathan Steinberg (New York: Berghahn Books, 2003). Kant believes through her research that Wigman and Laban vied for leadership of dance under the Fascist regime, thereby providing support to the Nazi cause. How much they knew about the inner workings of the party at the time and its mission of genocide is not clear in my mind because of the twisted reality created by Nazi racism. I believe it would be naive to think that Wigman and Laban escaped knowledge of the racist imperative altogether. Jewish hatred in Germany has a long history, going back at least to the Baroque period with Sancta Clara, a monk who preached hatred for the Jews throughout Germany. Sancta Clara was the subject of Heidegger's first essay as a student, and one of his early heroes, unfortunately. Heidegger had a steep learning curve throughout his career on the subject of his own racism, eventually falling in love with Hannah Arendt, one of his Jewish students. The Germans were quite brainwashed by the

time Hitler rose to power, and this conditioning allowed him to appeal to their deeply ingrained prejudices. Still, as I discuss toward the end of chapter 3, Wigman sought permission from the Third Reich for Jews to attend her school.

6. See Sally Banes's further critique of the once fashionable "male gaze" as reductionist in "Talking Women: Dance Herstories," *Dance Research Journal* 3 (Fall 1999): 117–21. Sondra Fraleigh, "A Vulnerable Glance: Seeing Dance through Phenomenology," *Dance Research Journal* 23 (1991): 11–16.

7. In our dance composition classes she urged us to explore a wide range of sensibility, from lyrical to narrative, not dismissing the abstract. The visual surface mattered, but not as much as the spatial and motivational dynamic. She had a dramatic grip on movement, and could shake us up, but she also had a motherly kindness that flooded the classroom. She never embarrassed anyone to exert her power, contrary to my dance studies in the United States where I saw students kicked out of class for yawning or momentary lapses of attention.

8. Peter Brooks, *The Melodramatic Imagination: Balzac, Henry James, Melodrama and the Mode of Excess* (New Haven, CT: Yale University Press, 1976), 41.

9. Richard Murphy, *Theorizing the Avant-Garde* (Cambridge: Cambridge University Press, 1998), 144.

10. Mary Wigman, *The Language of Dance*, trans. Walter Sorell (Middletown, CT: Wesleyan University Press, 1966), 42; originally published as *Die Sprache des Tanzes* (Stuttgart: Ernst Battenberg Verlag, 1963).

11. Ibid., 40–41.

12. Beldam is another word for witch, earlier dame, mother, and grandmother. See *The Oxford Universal Dictionary* (London: Oxford University Press, 1955), s.v. "beldam." One of the many means of killing women who practiced healing with herbs—the so-called witches of the Middle Ages—was to pull the intestines out through the mouth. Denunciations and persecutions beginning in the fourteenth century reached epidemic proportions in the latter half of the fifteenth century. The treatise *Malleus maleficarum* (1487) was an encyclopedia for detection of demonology and handling of witchcraft. Barbara Tuchman, *A Distant Mirror: The Calamitous Fourteenth Century* (New York: Ballantine Books, 1979), writes of the rise of witch hunts and persecution of heretics: "In 1366 the Council of Chartres ordered anathema to be pronounced against sorcerers every Sunday in every parish church. . . . Though old and indigenous, demonology was never more than an aberration, but in so far as it offered an alternative answer, it was seen by the Church as dangerous" (318). Even if it was no more than recovering a straying lover or curing a peasant's sick cow, help was being offered outside the approved church channels of prayers and saints. The lore of witchcraft developed from the minds of the prosecutors and the hallucinations of the accused. "Together they laid the ground for the rage against witchcraft that was to explode upon the next century" (318–19).

13. *Niwa* (The garden), a two-act dance theater work lasting about one hundred minutes, was first presented in Tokyo in 1982. I saw its North American premiere in Montreal at the Festival of New Dance, September 18, 1985.

14. For the German expressionist roots of Butoh, see Sondra Fraleigh, *Dancing into Darkness: Butoh, Zen, and Japan* (Pittsburgh: University of Pittsburgh Press, 1999), 35–42.

15. The beginning of *Niwa* travels from the upstage left third of the space, a powerful *jo* place for slow beginnings in Japan's classical Noh theater. It stops in the center, or *ha*, the climactic spot that opens a new beginning. This will lead toward ever contracting and expanding cycles, culminating in a dramatic release called *kyu*. This cyclic aesthetic of *jo-ha-kyu* at the heart of classical Japanese theater is also at the heart of much Butoh, especially *Niwa*, as noted by Susan Klein, *Ankoku Butoh: The Premodern and Postmodern Influences of the Dance of Utter Darkness* (Ithaca, NY: Cornell University Press, 1993), 55–86.

16. What is Emptiness? (A Zen Koan or riddle). "Emptiness" is an English translation of the Japanese Zen word *mu*.

3. Thickening Ambiguity

1. Simone de Beauvoir, *The Ethics of Ambiguity*, trans. Bernard Frecthman (1948; reprint, New York: Carol Publishing, 1994), 135.

2. Dorion Sagan, *Biospheres: Metamorphosis of Planet Earth* (New York: McGraw-Hill, 1990), 3–4.

3. David Bohm, *Wholeness and the Implicate Order* (New York: Routledge & Kegan Paul, 1980).

4. Annemarie Schimmel, "The Ritual of Rebirth," in *Parabola* 4 (May 1979): 89–90; quote on 89.

5. Judith Butler, *Bodies That Matter: On the Discursive Limits of Sex* (New York: Routledge, 1993), 32.

6. Eleanor Gibson, "Ontogenesis of the Perceived Self," in *The Perceived Self: Ecological and Interpersonal Sources of Self-Knowledge*, ed. Ulric Neisser (Boston: Cambridge University Press, 1993), 25. See also the work of J. J. Gibson, *The Senses Considered as Perceptual Systems* (Boston: Houghton Mifflin, 1966); Daniel Stern, *The Interpersonal World of the Infant* (New York: Basic Books, 1973); and George Butterworth, *Infancy and Epistemology* (New York: The Harvester Press, 1982).

7. Martin Heidegger, *Being and Time*, trans. John Macquarrie and Edward Robinson (New York: Harper & Row, 1962). See "Falling and Thrownness" and "The Question of the Primordial Totality of Dasein's Structural Whole," 223–25.

8. Women are "monsters . . . deviated from the generic human type." Aristotle, *De generatione animalium*, in *The Works of Aristotle*, trans. J. A. Smith and W. D. Ross (London: Oxford, 1912), 1.4.2, 767B5–15. Women are merely "mutilated males" (2.3, 737a); men are "more divine" (2.1, 732a).

9. Susanne Langer, *Mind: An Essay on Human Feeling*, vol. 1 (Baltimore: Johns Hopkins University Press, 1967).

10. Deane Juhan, *Job's Body: A Handbook for Bodywork* (New York: Station Hill Press, 1987).

11. Mabel Elsworth Todd, *The Thinking Body* (Brooklyn: Dance Horizons, 1959).

12. Candace Pert, with foreword by Deepak Chopra, *Molecules of Emotion: The Science Behind Mind-Body Medicine* (New York: Touchstone Books, 1997).

13. Nobuo Harada, author's correspondence with his student Tamah Naka-mura, e-mail June 2002.

14. Mihaly Csikszentmihalyi, *The Evolving Self* (New York: Harper Collins, 1993), 160–62, and *Flow: The Psychology of Optimal Experience* (New York: Harper & Row, 1990).

15. Jean-Paul Sartre, *Being and Nothingness*, 3rd ed., trans. Hazel Barnes (New York: Citadel, 1965), 300.

16. Pert, *Molecules of Emotion*.

17. Maxine Sheets-Johnstone, "What Is It Like to Be a Brain," in *The Primacy of Movement* (Amsterdam: John Benjamins, 1999), 451–82.

18. Beverly Stokes, *Amazing Babies: Moving in the First Year*, VHS (Toronto, Canada: Amazing Babies Videos, 1995).

19. Martha Graham, quoted by Merle Armitage, *Martha Graham* (New York: Dance Horizons, 1966), 101.

20. Beauvoir, *Ethics of Ambiguity*, 41.

21. Bruce Wilshire, *Wild Hunger: The Primal Roots of Modern Addiction* (Lanham, MD: Rowman & Littlefield, 1998), 12.

22. Hélène Cixous, "Sorties: Out and Out: Attacks/Ways Out/Forays," in Hélène Cixous and Catherine Clement, *The Newly Born Woman*, trans. Betsy Wing (Minneapolis: University of Minnesota Press, 1986), 92.

23. Susan Manning, *Ecstasy and the Demon: Feminism and Nationalism in the Dances of Mary Wigman* (Berkeley and Los Angeles: University of California Press, 1993), 204–5.

24. Ibid., 171.

25. Yvonne Hardt, "Relational Movement Patterns: The Diversity of Movement Choirs and Their Social Potential in the Weimar Republic," Society of Dance History Scholars Proceedings, Twenty-Sixth Annual Conference, University of Limerick, Limerick, Ireland, June 26–29, 2003, 45–50.

4. Anti-Essentialist Trio

1. Allison Jaggar, *Feminist Politics and Human Nature* (Totowa, NJ: Rowman & Allanheld, 1983), 108.

2. See Judith Butler, *Bodies That Matter: On the Discursive Limits of "Sex"* (New York: Routledge, 1993), and Susan Bordo, *Unbearable Weight: Feminism, Western Culture, and the Body* (Berkeley and Los Angeles: University of California Press, 1993), especially "Postmodern Subjects, Postmodern Bodies," in part 3.

3. Maxine Sheets-Johnstone, *The Roots of Power: Animate Form and Gendered Bodies* (Chicago: Open Court Publishing, 1994).

4. Anna Yeatman, "A Feminist Theory of Social Differentiation," in *Feminism/Postmodernism*, ed. Linda J. Nicholson (New York: Routledge, 1990), 287.

5. Camille Paglia, *Sexual Personae: Art and Decadence from Nefertiti to Emily Dickinson* (New York: Vintage Books, 1991), 37–38.

6. Helen Fisher, *The First Sex—The Natural Talents of Women and How They Are Changing the World* (New York: Ballantine Books, 1999), 31.

7. See Riane Eisler, *The Chalice and the Blade: Our History, Our Future* (San Francisco: Harper San Francisco, 1987). Marija Gimbutas, *The Goddesses and Gods of Old Europe: 7000–3500 B.C.* (Berkeley and Los Angeles: The University of California Press, 1982), and *The Language of the Goddess: Images and Symbols of Old Europe* (New York: Van der Marck, 1987).

8. Eisler quotes Engels's "The Origin of the Family, Private Property, and the State," in her *The Chalice and the Blade,* 45–47.

9. Simone de Beauvoir, *The Second Sex,* ed. and trans. H. M. Parshley (New York: Knopf, 1957), 7. Maurice Merleau-Ponty, *The Phenomenology of Perception,* trans. Colin Smith (London: Routledge & Kegan Paul, 1962).

10. Ibid., 122.

11. As quoted by Toril Moi in *Simone de Beauvoir: The Making of an Intellectual Woman* (Oxford: Blackwell, 1994), 148.

12. See Susan Bordo, "Feminism, Postmodernism, and Gender-Skepticism," in *Feminism/Postmodernism,* ed. Linda J. Nicholson (New York: Routledge, 1990), 133–56.

13. Judith Butler, "Performative Acts and Gender Constitution: An Essay in Phenomenology and Feminist Theory," *Theater Journal* 40 (December 1988): 519–31.

14. Butler, *Bodies That Matter,* 30.

15. Ibid., 54.

16. Bill T. Jones, in his speech, "Falling and Catching: Dancing through the Other Door," discussed his survival workshops with severely ill persons and his dance aesthetics at the George Eastman House, Rochester, NY, June 5, 2000. Jones related "brave falling" and "trustworthy catching" to Doris Humphrey's theory in this lecture.

17. This is discussed by Margery Collins and Christine Pierce, "Holes and Slime: Sexism in Sartre's Psychoanalysis," *Signs* 1, no. 2 (1975): 487–503. See also Maxine Sheets-Johnstone, "Penetration and Being 'in the Form of a Hole,'" in *The Roots of Power,* 163–89. For Sartre's original comment, see Sartre's *Being and Nothingness,* trans. Hazel Barnes (New York: Philosophical Library, 1956), 614.

18. Judith Butler, "Phantasmatic Identification and the Assumption of Sex," in *Bodies That Matter,* 93–119.

19. Beauvoir, *The Second Sex,* 37.

20. Merleau-Ponty, *Phenomenology of Perception,* 154–73; Butler, "Performative Acts and Gender Constitution," 519–31; Elizabeth Grosz, *Volatile Bodies: Toward a Corporeal Feminism* (Bloomington: Indiana University Press, 1994), 34.

21. David Abram, *The Spell of the Sensuous* (New York: Random House, 1996), 31–72.

22. Beauvoir, *The Second Sex,* explains that woman should be defined through her existential possibilities, not through her biology (34).

23. Merleau-Ponty. *Phenomenology of Perception,* 170–71.

24. Luce Irigaray, *This Sex Which Is Not One*, trans. Catherine Porter (Ithaca, NY: Cornell University Press, 1985), 213.

25. Merleau-Ponty, *Phenomenology of Perception*, 170, 154.

26. Ibid., 198, 364–65.

27. Ibid., 345.

28. Ibid., 365.

29. Butler, *Bodies That Matter*, 10–16.

30. Judith Butler, *Gender Trouble: Feminism and the Subversion of Identity* (New York: Routledge, 1990), 110.

31. Donna Haraway, "A Manifesto for Cyborgs: Science, Technology, and Socialist Feminism in the 1980s," in *Feminism/Postmodernism*, ed. Linda J. Nicholson (New York: Routledge, 1990), 204–5. See also her study of feminism and technoscience, *Modest Witness@Second Millennium: FemaleMan Meets OncoMouse* (New York: Routledge, 1997).

32. Oppositional tendencies and productive rivalry are explained by Deane Juhan, *Job's Body: A Handbook for Bodywork* (Barrytown, NY: Station Hill Press, 1987), 104–5.

33. Lynn Margulis and Dorion Sagan, *Mystery Dance: On the Evolution of Human Sexuality* (New York: Summit Books, 1991), 190–91.

34. S. Kessler and W. McKenna, *Gender: An Ethnomethodological Approach* (Chicago: University of Chicago Press, 1978).

35. Bronwyn Davies, *Frogs and Snails and Feminist Tales: Preschool Children and Gender* (North Sydney: Allen & Unwin, 1989), 8–9.

36. Margulis and Sagan, *Mystery Dance*, 12.

37. See Arthur I. Miller, "Visualization Lost and Regained: The Genesis of the Quantum Theory in the Period 1913–27," in *On Aesthetics in Science*, ed. Judith Wechsler (Cambridge, MA: MIT Press, 1978), 72–102.

38. For feminist standpoint theory, see Sandra Harding, *Whose Science? Whose Knowledge? Thinking from Women's Lives* (Ithaca, NY: Cornell University Press, 1991). Feminists have not been able to agree on a standpoint theory that would adequately address the complexity of women's lives across class and culture. Donna Haraway, *Simians, Cyborgs, and Women: The Reinvention of Nature* (New York: Routledge, 1991), takes a postmodern approach in proposing an alternative theory of "situated knowledge," partial knowledge, and local solution. Underlying these theories is the assertion of phenomenology that consciousness is already perspective: "Consciousness is always consciousness of something," as first stated by Edmund Husserl.

39. Sondra Fraleigh, *Dancing into Darkness: Butoh, Zen, and Japan* (Pittsburgh: University of Pittsburgh Press, 1999). See especially the introduction, also the gender bending of Kazuo Ohno in "Amazing Grace."

40. Merleau-Ponty, *Phenomenology of Perception*, 154.

41. See explanations of existential contingency in Margulis and Sagan, *Mystery Dance*. See also Howard E. Gruber, "Darwin's 'Tree of Nature' and Other Images of Wide Scope," in Wechsler, *On Aesthetics in Science*, 121–40. Recently, the phenomenology of Alphonso Lingis, *The Imperative* (Bloomington: Indiana University

Press, 1998), revises Kant's views on nature to show that there is an order in the natural world that shapes our thought and behavior.

42. Iris Young, *Throwing Like a Girl and Other Essays in Feminist Philosophy and Social Theory* (Bloomington: Indiana University Press, 1990).

43. Sally Banes, *Dancing Women: Female Bodies on Stage* (London: Routledge, 1998), 38; Lynn Garafola, "The Travesty Dancer in Nineteenth-Century Ballet," *Dance Research Journal* (double issue) 17/2 and 18/1 (1985–86): 35–40; Ivor Guest, *The Ballet of the Second Empire* (Middletown, CT: Wesleyan University Press, 1974), 14–20.

44. Banes, *Dancing Women*, 41.

45. Ibid., 42–44. This dance invoked not only "the Golden Age of France, but also that of the Russian aristocracy, beginning with the reign, 100 years earlier, of Catherine the Great, Russia's own Louis XIV." That this dance became a classic in reactionary times in Russia is curious. In many ways, Banes says, ballet was isolated from these struggles. Creating an illusion of order, *The Sleeping Beauty* reinforced royalist values that were constantly under threat (43).

46. Jan Van Dyke, "Gender and Professional Dance in America" (paper presented at Congress on Research in Dance, New World School of the Arts, Florida, 1995).

47. Matthew Biro, *Anselm Keifer and the Philosophy of Martin Heidegger* (Cambridge: University of Cambridge Press, 1998), 154–55.

48. Tharp's comments are from her program notes at the 2000 performance of the Australian Ballet in Melbourne.

49. Glass renounced Western music in favor of researching and applying Eastern techniques. This culminated in his four-and-a-half-hour opera, *Einstein on the Beach*, and in later works such as *Satyagraha*, *Aknaten*, and in his scores for the films *Koyaanisqatsi*, *Powaqqatsi*, and *A Brief History of Time*.

50. Ramsay Burt, *The Male Dancer: Bodies, Spectacle, Sexualities* (London: Routledge, 1995).

51. Laura Lanphier, e-mail communication, March 12, 2003.

52. *Department of Dance News Bulletin* 2003–2004, Florida State University, School of Visual Arts and Dance.

53. Heidegger also uses this early word *phusis* to explain the life "venture" to which we are given over, "the Being of beings that is revealed in metaphysics." Heidegger, "What Are Poets For?" in *Poetry, Language, Thought*, trans. Albert Hofstadter (New York: Harper & Row, 1971), 101–2.

5. A Dance of Time Beings

1. Maurice Merleau-Ponty, *The Phenomenology of Perception*, trans. Colin Smith (London: Routledge & Kegan Paul, 1962), 168. Page numbers are hereafter cited in the text.

2. Martin Heidegger, *Being and Time*, trans. John Macquarrie and Edward Robinson (New York: Harper & Row, 1962), 387–88; hereafter cited by page number in the text.

3. Paulo Freire, *Pedagogy of the Oppressed* (New York: Continuum, 2003).

4. Matching is a somatic strategy that phenomenologist and somatics educator Elizabeth Behnke explains as a somatic matching technique: "In its most schematic form, the matching technique may be said to consist of three parts: (1) awareness of something in one's own body; (2) an inner act of matching or aligning oneself with this; and (3) allowing something to change. In actual practice these can flow together." See Behnke, "Matching," in *Bone Breath & Gesture: Practices of Embodiment*, ed. Don Hanlon Johnson (Berkeley, CA: North Atlantic Books, 1955), 317–37.

5. Martin Heidegger, "The Thing," in *Poetry, Language, Thought*, trans. Albert Hofstadter (New York: Harper & Row, 1971), 179–80.

6. See Luce Irigaray, "I only see through the touching of the light," in *Ethique de la différence sexuelle* (Paris: Minuit, 1984), 155; Maxine Sheets-Johnstone examined the power of optics and its male orientation in *The Roots of Power* (Chicago: Open Court, 1994); Elizabeth Grosz is also concerned with optics and power in *Volatile Bodies: Toward a Corporeal Feminism* (Bloomington: Indiana University Press, 1994), 156.

7. Val Plumwood, *Feminism and the Mastery of Nature* (London: Routledge, 1993).

8. I first experienced this improvisation technique that I now call the "Doubling Dance" in the studio of Yoko Ashikawa in Tokyo, June 1990. I have taught several of my own variations on this theme to American students. It is the Butoh technique they seem to enjoy most.

9. The question as Heidegger puts it is: "What makes it ontologically possible for entities to be encountered within-the-world and Objectified as so encountered? This can be answered by recourse to the transcendence of the world—a transcendence with an ecstatico-horizonal foundation" (*Being and Time*, 417–18).

10. Philip Morrison, "On Broken Symmetries," in *On Aesthetics in Science*, ed. Judith Wechsler (Cambridge, MA: The MIT Press), 65.

11. Antonia Damasio, *The Feeling of What Happens: Body and Emotion in the Making of Consciousness* (New York: Harcourt Brace, 1999); see chap. 3, "Core Consciousness," 82–107.

6. Letting the Difference Happen

1. Fred Dallmayr, *The Other Heidegger* (Ithaca, NY: Cornell University Press, 1993), 188.

2. Martin Heidegger, *Contributions to Philosophy (From Enowning)*, trans. Parvis Emad and Kenneth Maly (Bloomington: Indiana University Press, 1999); hereafter cited by page number in the text.

3. Translator's foreword to ibid., xx–xxi.

4. Claude Lefort, *The Political Forms of Modern Society: Bureaucracy, Democracy, Totalitarianism*, ed. John B. Thompson, trans. Alan Sheridan et al. (Cambridge, MA: The MIT Press, 1986); *Writing the Political Test*, trans. and ed. David Ames Curtis (Durham, NC: Duke University Press, 2000).

5. Dallmayr, *The Other Heidegger,* 170–79.

6. See Sally Banes, "Happily Ever After? The Postmodern Fairy Tale and the New Dance," in *Writing Dancing in the Age of Postmodernism* (Hanover, NH: Wesleyan University Press, 1994), 280–90.

7. Don Hanlon Johnson, *Body, Spirit and Democracy* (Berkeley, CA: North Atlantic Books, 1994), 16.

8. Upon her death at age ninety-five, Thiele left me her books, personal photographs, and paintings—some begun at the Bauhaus where painting, sculpture, and architecture coalesced with dance. I am just completing an article about Thiele's stories of dance and war—"A Life in Dance and War: *Nie Wieder Krieg."*

9. Dallmayr, *The Other Heidegger,* 96.

10. Jacques Derrida, "Différance," in *Speech and Phenomena, and Other Essays on Husserl's Theory of Signs* (Evanston, IL: Northwestern University Press, 1973), reprinted in *The Continental Philosophy Reader,* ed. Richard Kearney and Mara Rainwater (London: Routledge, 1996), 463.

11. Ibid., 463.

7. Messy Beauty and Butoh Invalids

1. *Shorter Oxford English Dictionary,* 3rd ed. (Oxford: Clarendon Press, 1964), 488, s.v. "descendental."

2. "Descendance" is also spelled "descendence." The *Shorter Oxford English Dictionary,* ibid., lists "descendance, -ence. Now used rarely." It lists "descendancy –ency" as a variant and shows in the same paragraph "descent" (488).

3. Algis Mickunas, "The Terrible Beauty and Her Reflective Force," *Ideals of Feminine Beauty: Philosophical Social and Cultural Dimensions* (Westport, CT: Greenwood Press, 1994), 13.

4. Richard Tarnas, *The Passion of the Western Mind* (New York: Ballantine Books, 1991), 442.

5. Prima ballerina Susanne Farrell finally talked freely about her romantic attachment to ballet master George Balanchine in a videotaped special on her life. He had molded her dancing and her career, had been the conduit for her dreams and her talent. It was 1962, she was seventeen and thin. He was fifty-eight and Balanchine. They walked hand in hand along the Seine. As she rose to stardom and their romance blossomed, others talked, and her fears grew. She had to be ready when he wanted to see her, but he came around when it was convenient. She would not be the first, just one in a long line of. . . . Because Balanchine was married, Farrell's mother pressured her to give in to George and live with him. After all, Mr. B was not just anybody. "It never occurred to me that anyone would resist him," Farrell says. Eventually, she started to gain some distance as she matured: "I was worried that if I didn't leave something was going to happen; suicide entered my mind," she remembers. See *Suzanne Farrell—Elusive Muse,* VHS, directed by Deborah Dickson and Anne Belle (New York: Winstar Home Entertainment, 1990).

6. In 1997, at the National Association of Schools of Dance in Houston, Texas,

members were treated to lectures by dieticians and dance medicine experts who cited the problematic statistics on anorexia and bulimia among ballet dancers. The dietician carefully outlined a plan for keeping dancers 15 percent below normal body weight without compromising health. Why would it be assumed that dancers needed to weigh-in under the norms? For the ballet aesthetic, she said. Some of us pointed out that there are forms of dance where differences in body type and weight are desirable. This seemed like a new idea to her. She had been employed by experts in dance accreditation to address a national convention of dance, and she did not know that we have been revolutionizing the dancing body for the last hundred years. Perhaps it was not her fault that her singular understanding of dance was ballet, but the organizers of the convention (the experts in dance) should have known better.

7. Riane Eisler, *Sacred Pleasure: Sex, Myth, and the Politics of the Body* (San Francisco: Harper, 1996).

8. Charlene Spretnak, *Lost Goddesses of Early Greece: A Collection of Pre-Hellenic Mythology* (Berkeley, CA: Moon Books, 1978), 103–10. "Begging for pity" quote from H. G. Evelyn-White, *Hesiod, the Homeric Hymns and Homerica* (Cambridge, MA: Harvard University Press, 1941), 288–91.

9. Mara Lynn Keller, "The Eleusinian Mysteries: Ancient Nature Religion of Demeter and Persephone," in *Reweaving the World: The Emergence of Ecofeminism*, ed. Irene Diamond and Gloria Feman Orenstein (San Francisco: Sierra Club Books, 1990), 41–51; Spretnak, *Lost Goddesses of Early Greece*.

10. Roger Copeland, "Merce Cunningham and the Politics of Perception," in *What Is Dance?* ed. Roger Copeland and Marshall Cohen (Oxford: Oxford University Press, 1983), 322.

11. Arlene Croce quoted by Copeland in ibid., 322.

12. Ibid., 311–12; my emphasis.

13. *Life into Art: Isadora Duncan and Her World*, ed. Doree Duncan, Carol Pratl, and Cynthia Splatt, foreword by Agnes de Mille (New York: W. W. Norton, 1993), 13.

14. Simone Forti, *Handbook in Motion* (Halifax: Press of Nova Scotia College of Art and Design, 1974), 34.

15. Gerda Alexander, "Eutony: The Wholistic Discovery of the Total Person," in *Bone, Breath and Gesture: Practices of Embodiment*, ed. Don Hanlon Johnson (Berkeley: North Atlantic Books, 1995), 273–93.

16. See also my definition of "yielding descent" in Fraleigh, *Dance and the Lived Body: A Descriptive Aesthetic* (Pittsburgh: University of Pittsburgh Press, 1987), 148–53.

17. Ann Daly, *Done into Dance: Isadora Duncan in America* (Bloomington: Indiana University Press, 1995), 89.

18. The government will further pollute America's West and gravely endanger Chicago as the hub through which tons of nuclear waste will need to be transported daily over a period of twenty-four years, not to mention the many other cities and towns en route. *CBS News Report with Dan Rather,* October 26, 2003.

19. John Toland, *The Rising Sun: The Decline and Fall of the Japanese Empire, 1936–1945* (New York: Penguin Books, 1970), 54.

20. Siegfried Wichmann, *Japonisme: The Japanese Influence on Western Art in the Nineteenth and Twentieth Centuries*, trans. Mary Whittall and James Ramsay (New York: Harmony Books, 1981).

21. Toland, *The Rising Sun*, 55.

22. Ibid., 766. When Truman was asked by Toland in 1958 if his decision had come after considerable soul-searching, he said, "Hell, no, I made it like"—he snapped his fingers—"that" (766).

23. Ibid., xxxiv.

24. For Noguchi's work with Graham and his absorption of Noh theater, see Dore Ashton, "Toward a Theater of Two Worlds," in *Noguchi: East and West* (Berkeley and Los Angeles: University of California Press, 1992), 45–61.

25. Quoted by Ann Daly in "From Living Treasures, Coins of Artistic Wisdom," *The New York Times*, August 26, 2001.

26. When Ohno teaches, he becomes disruptive in small ways. I took workshops with him in Yokohama in 1990, where he would sometimes tell us to do the opposite of what we were doing, not because we were wrong, but to unsettle us—or wake us up. As in Zen, one's energy flow in meditation can also be awakened by a short, rebounding slap on the shoulders, akin to the finite whacks of massage. Westerners mistakenly believe this is sadistic and punishing. One asks for this by raising a hand during meditation. The rebounding slap keeps one from falling asleep and wakes up an energy flow. This is administered only if one's shoulders are well covered, and when asked for (in my experience).

27. Mickunas, "The Terrible Beauty and Her Reflective Force," 12, 40.

28. Perverted forms of the Goddess are scarcely more than fiends to be satisfied with bloody sacrifices. "Even Kali and Durga, though in some aspects very exalted symbols of spiritual transformation, have been so misunderstood that human sacrifices to Durga continued into the 1830s, while Kali's temple in Calcutta is still a slaughterhouse," Martin Willson states in *In Praise of Tara: Songs to the Saviouress, Source Texts from India and Tibet on Buddhism's Great Goddess* (London: Wisdom Publications, 1986), 16.

29. Renee Lorraine, "A History of Music," in *Feminism and Tradition in Aesthetics*, ed. Peggy Zeglin and Carolyn Korsmeyer (University Park, PA: The Pennsylvania State University Press, 1995), 161, 162.

30. Ibid., 164.

31. Ibid., 164.

32. Willson, *In Praise of Tara*, 11–25. "Tara the Tantric Deity has to be drawn precisely according to the traditional prescriptions that come to us through Tibet. Tara the Bodhisattva and Tara the Mother Goddess is not—there is room for experiment, as one can see from Indian Buddhist art" (25).

33. For a study of spirituality and feminism with an emphasis on cross-cultural perspectives, see Carol Lee Flinders, *At the Root of This Longing: Reconciling a Spiritual Hunger with a Feminist Thirst and Enduring Grace* (San Francisco: Harper,

1998); and China Galland, *Longing for Darkness: Tara and the Black Madonna: A Ten Year Journey* (New York: Penguin Books, 1991).

34. Donna Wilshire, *Virgin, Mother, Crone: Myths and Mysteries of the Triple Goddess* (Rochester, VT: Inner Traditions, 1994), 119.

35. Ibid., 119.

36. Mickunas, "The Terrible Beauty and Her Reflective Force," 7.

8. Existential Haircut

1. C. K. Ogden studies oppositions in relation to the body in *Opposition: A Linguistic and Psychological Analysis* (Bloomington: Indiana University Press, 1967), 90–92. Ogden critiques philosophy's explorations of the terms of opposition, from the cosmologists and Aristotle through Kant, Hegel, the logisticians, and the evolutionists. Oppositions are of various kinds (not necessarily antagonists). All have directional factors bearing a relationship to the human body and are founded in sensation. Cyril Stanley Smith, "Structural Hierarchy in Science, Art, and History," in *On Aesthetics in Science*, ed. Judith Wechsler (Cambridge, MA: The MIT Press), provides this perspective of oppositions and tensions: "Without both tension and compression and the balance between them nothing could exist, for it would either expand to infinity or shrink to nothing" (25).

2. Sondra Fraleigh, "Interview with Indira Gosh: *Yoga, Tan and Tantra*," May 7, 1997, unpublished interview transcript.

3. Ludwig Wittgenstein, *Philosophical Investigations*, 3rd ed., trans. G. E. M. Anscombe (New York: Macmillan, 1958), 13.

4. J. I. Rodale, *The Synonym Finder* (Emmaus, PA: Rodale Press, 1978), 370.

5. Michel Foucault, *The History of Sexuality*, vol. 1, trans. Robert Hurley (New York: Pantheon Books, 1978), 152–55; my emphasis in quote.

6. Hinrich Fink-Eitel, *Foucault*, trans. Edward Dixon (Philadelphia: Pennbridge Books, 1992), 8.

7. Edward W. Said, *Reflections on Exile and Other Essays* (Cambridge, MA: Harvard University Press, 2000), 196.

8. See Fink-Eitel, *Foucault*, 44.

9. This comparison of Foucault's method to the "purely textual" interpretive strategies of semiotics and deconstruction is made in *The Johns Hopkins Guide to Literary Theory and Criticism*, ed. Michael Groden and Martin Kreiswirth (Baltimore: The Johns Hopkins University Press, 1994), 279.

10. Ibid., 194.

11. Edward W. Said, *Orientalism* (New York: Vintage Books, 1979), 3–4. Said distances, however, from Foucault's heavy reliance on anonymous collectivity, navigating between the collective and "the determining imprint of individual writers" in establishing the discourse of Orientalism (23).

12. Martha C. Nussbaum, *Upheavals of Thought: The Intelligence of Emotions* (New York: Cambridge University Press, 2001).

13. Richard Schusterman, *Practicing Philosophy: Pragmatism and the Philosophical Life* (New York: Routledge, 1997), chap. 1; "Somaesthetics: A Disciplinary Pro-

posal," *The Journal of Aesthetics and Art Criticism* 57 (Summer 1999): 299–313; "The Self as a Work of Art," *The Nation*, June 30, 1997, 25–28.

14. William V. Spanos, *Existentialism* (New York: Thomas Y. Crowell, 1966), 6.

15. Ida P. Rolf, *Rolfing: The Integration of Human Structures* (New York: Harper & Row, 1977), 11. See also Don Hanlon Johnson, "Vertical Enlightenment: Ida Rolf," in *Body, Spirit and Democracy* (Berkeley: North Atlantic Books, 1994), 75–96. Rolfers such as Laurie Latner eventually evolved less invasive approaches to structural integration than Rolf herself. Latner, who has taught at the Rolf Institute, uses a softer method that she calls "Inner Rolfing."

16. This is a brief meditation on stages of maturation envisioned in terms of the changing tasks and values of woman by Clarissa Pinkola Estes, *Women Who Run with the Wolves* (New York: Ballantine Books, 1992), 447–48. As a Jungian psychologist and storyteller, Estes describes seven-year archetypal changes of woman's consciousness.

17. Luce Irigaray, "The 'Mechanics' of Fluids," in *This Sex Which Is Not One*, trans. Catherine Porter (Ithaca, NY: Cornell University Press, 1985), 113. Irigaray maintains that "Considerations of pure mathematics have precluded the analysis of fluids except in terms of laminated planes, solenoid movements (of a current privileging the relation to an axis), spring-points, well-points, whirlwind-points, which have only an approximate relation to reality. . . . Certainly these 'theoretical' fluids have enabled the technical—also mathematic—form of analysis to progress, while losing a certain relationship to the reality of bodies in the process" (109).

18. *Untangling Skeleton Woman* (1995), a dance by Sondra Fraleigh based on an Inuit story told by Mary Uukalat and retold by Estes in *Women Who Run with the Wolves*. Performed by SUNY Brockport dancers, *Danscore Concert* (Spring 1995).

19. Simone de Beauvoir, *The Ethics of Ambiguity*, trans. Bernard Frechtman (1948; reprint, New York: Carol Publishing, 1995), 78, 159.

20. Carol Gilligan, *In a Different Voice* (Cambridge, MA: Harvard University Press, 1982). See her writing on the values of intimacy, relationship and care, sensitivity to the needs of others, and personal rather than positional moral reasoning in women in her chapter 1.

21. Philip Morrison, "On Broken Symmetries," in *On Aesthetics in Science*, ed. Judith Wechsler (Cambridge, MA: The MIT Press), 55–70.

22. Marija Gimbutas, *The Language of the Goddess: Unearthing the Hidden Symbols of Western Civilization* (San Francisco: Harper & Row, 1989), xix.

23. Riane Eisler, *Sacred Pleasure* (San Francisco: Harper, 1996), 154. See also Margaret Murray, *God of the Witches* (London: Oxford University Press, 1970); Heinrich Kramer and James Sprenger, *Malleus Malificarum* (New York: Dover, 1971).

24. See Eisler, "The Last Traces of the Sacred Marriage," in *Sacred Pleasure*, 143–57.

25. Renee Lorraine, "A History of Music," in *Feminism and Traditional Aesthetics*," ed. Peggy Zeglin Brand and Carolyn Korsmeyer (University Park, PA: The Pennsylvania State University Press, 1995), 160–85.

26. Ibid., 178.

27. Although I know the romantic/classical cannon (as well as Gregorian chant) is peppered with sexism, I am not going to stop listening to historical music, and for the same reason that Lorraine states. I like the music—apart from its suppressive narrative elements—but I also want to be alert to the efforts of dancers to overcome misogyny in dance in its relationship to music.

28. Gloria Steinem, "What If Freud Were Phyllis," in *Moving Beyond Words* (New York: Simon & Schuster, 1994), 19–90.

29. Maxine Sheets-Johnstone, *The Roots of Power: Animate Form and Gendered Bodies* (Chicago: Open Court Publishing, 1994).

30. Sheets-Johnstone, "Penetration and Being in the Form of a Hole," in ibid., 163–89.

31. Jean-Paul Sartre, *Being and Nothingness*, trans. Hazel Barnes (New York: Philosophical Library, 1956), 614, 609. He continues with, "Conversely woman senses her condition as an appeal precisely because she is "in the form of a hole." This is the true origin of Adler's complex (the complex of *inferiority*). "Beyond any doubt her sex is a mouth and a voracious mouth which devours the penis—a fact which can easily lead to the idea of castration. The amorous act is the castration of the man; but this is above all because sex is a hole." Margery Collins and Christine Pierce discuss this issue at length in "Holes and Slime: Sexism in Sartre's Psychoanalysis," *Signs* 1, no. 2 (1975): 487–503.

32. In *The Yellow Emperor's Classic of Internal Medicine* (second century BCE), we learn that blood and nourishment are yin and circulate internally; they are protected by yang. Energy and resistance are yang and emanate externally; they are nourished by yin. The four foundations of health are blood (*hsueh*), energy (*chee*), nourishment (*ying*), and resistance (*wei*). Physiologically functional manifestations of yin and yang, they are interactive and mutually dependent, and their condition and relative balance determine the state of one's health and the strength of one's resistance to disease and degeneration. In the alchemy of the four foundations, blood is the primary ingredient and regulator of health. See Daniel Reid, "The Four Foundations," in *The Complete Book of Chinese Health and Healing* (Boston: Shambhala, 1994), 40–41.

33. Mei-wa Annie Chan, "The Tao of Dance" (Master's of Arts thesis, Department of Dance, School of Arts and Performance, State University of New York, College at Brockport, 1994), 36.

34. Ibid., 42, 16, 27. Chan translates and quotes Lao Tsu in the *Tao Te Ching*, 6, 26.

35. Ibid., 28. It is significant that Carl Jung's psychology uses Taoist symbolism, conceiving of yin-yang in terms of female/male interpolations of anima-animus. He thus departs from Freudian views of feminine lack. The anima-animus tensions he describes manifest in both male and female, but in differing proportions. The *I Ching*, which Jung valued greatly, does have sexist interpretations of yin-yang differentiation at the literal and poetic level, although either principle can undermine itself or become fuller, and tenuous affective balances sometimes call

forth change as one slides into (becomes) the other. I am not going to stop reading the *I Ching* because part of the long history of its development was in the service of emperors. Its creative structure and wisdom spark when I liberally substitute "she" for "he" (the strong and wise man), and return to the original (spiritual) interplay of complementary qualities of Tao. These were the spiritual complements that inspired Jung and many Western readers of the *I Ching.*

36. Chan, "The Tao of Dance," translates and cites Lao Tsu and Chuang Tsu (21).

37. Donna Wilshire, *Virgin Mother Crone: Myths and Mysteries of the Triple Goddess* (Rochester, VT: Inner Traditions, 1994), 2.

38. Riane Eisler, *The Chalice and the Blade* (San Francisco: Harper & Row, 1987), xviii; Maria Gimbutas, *The Civilization of the Goddess: The World of Old Europe* (San Francisco: Harper, 1991), and *The Language of the Goddess: Unearthing the Hidden Symbols of Western Civilization* (San Francisco: Harper & Row, 1989).

39. Hélène Cixous, "Sorties," in *The Newly Born Woman,* with Catherine Clément, trans. Betsy Wing (Minneapolis: University of Minnesota Press, 1975), 68.

40. The typical attribution of gender in mythology, mother earth and father sky, is sometimes reversed, as in the Egyptian sky goddess Nut and earth god Geb.

41. Sheets-Johnstone, "Penetration and Being," 188.

42. Roberta M. Gilbert, *Extraordinary Relationships: A New Way of Thinking about Human Interactions* (Minneapolis: Chronimed Publishing, 1992).

43. Thomas Lewis, Fari Amini, and Richard Lannon, *A General Theory of Love* (New York: Random House, 2000).

44. "According to Ogotemmeli, an elder of the Dogon tribe of Mali, spoken language was originally a swirling garment of vapor and breath worn by the encompassing earth itself. Later this undulating garment was stolen by the jackal, an animal whose movements, ever since, have disclosed the prophetic speech of the world to seers and diviners." See David Abram, *The Spell of the Sensuous* (New York: Random House, 1996), 87.

9. The Morality of Joy

1. *Lethe,* the river of forgetfulness—*a-lethe,* unforgetfulness, terms from Greek philosophy.

2. Tom Stoppard interview, *McNeill-Lehrer News Hour,* PBS, March 10, 1999.

INDEX